THE
DARKEST
GLARE

Jerry Schneiderman, 2004

Praise for **THE DARKEST GLARE**

"The engrossingly bizarre tale of a murder plot within Los Angeles real estate circles… An entertaining true-crime period piece built around a chillingly odd sociopathic villain."

—*Kirkus Reviews*

"…horrifying and hilarious."   —*Publishers Weekly*

"Jacobs' chops are on brilliant display in The Darkest Glare, a delightfully off-kilter true-crime tale. The prose is intimate, darkly funny, and crisp. This isn't an old song in a new key, but an entirely new song about crime, fear, and a weird kind of redemption that could only happen in the general vicinity of Hollywood."

—**Ron Franscell**, bestselling author of *The Darkest Night*

"This is not just another Hollywood Whodunit. In the end we find it is really about one man's search and struggle to find his own personal truths and redemption. Well written and highly recommended."

—**Steve Hodel**, bestselling author of *Black Dahlia Avenger*

Praise for Chip Jacobs

"A riveting and enjoyable look at how local myths are constructed, and a vivid depiction of a time and a place that felt full of possibilities."

—*Booklist*

"A completely original and genre-defying work—both historical novel and metaphysical noir. The author has caught the brass ring and given it to us as pure gold."

—**Tristine Rainer**, author *Apprenticed to Venus, My Years with Anaïs Nin*

"[A] remarkably entertaining and informative chronicle of the birth and—so far—inexorable evolution of smog…This book is just amazing, a gripping story well told."

—*Booklist* (starred review and one of the top environmental books of the year)

"Style delivers substance in true Hollywood fashion, with character-driven plots draped in glamour and sensation... the history of smog has never been so sexy."

—*Los Angeles Times*

"Jacobs…is an exceptional storyteller, and his lively look at the extraordinary career of Gordon Zahler…is a peculiar page-turner."

—*Publishers Weekly*

"This amazing book is all heart…Chip Jacobs blends the skills of an investigative journalist, the glitz of Hollywood, and the smooth storytelling of fiction to weave a profile of his larger-than-life uncle that will leave you crying, laughing and gasping in wonder!"

—**Denise Hamilton**, bestselling author of *The Jasmine Trade*

THE
DARKEST
GLARE

A True Story of Murder, Blackmail,
and Real Estate Greed in 1979 Los Angeles

CHIP JACOBS

RARE BIRD

LOS ANGELES, CALIF.

THIS IS A GENUINE RARE BIRD BOOK

Rare Bird Books
453 South Spring Street, Suite 302
Los Angeles, CA 90013
rarebirdlit.com

FIRST TRADE PAPERBACK EDITION

Set in Dante
Printed in the United States

The Darkest Glare was previously released in significantly different form
as *The Ascension of Jerry,* March 2012.

10 9 8 7 6 5 4 3 2 1

Publisher's Cataloging-in-Publication data

Names: Jacobs, Chip, author.
Title: The darkest glare: a true story of murder , blackmail , and real estate greed
in 1979 Los Angeles / Chip Jacobs.
Description: First Hardcover Edition. | A Genuine Rare Bird Book | New York,
NY; Los Angeles, CA: Rare Bird Books, 2021.
Identifiers: ISBN: 9781644281918
Subjects: LCSH Kasparov, Richard. | Schneiderman, Jerry. | Crime—California—
Los Angeles—History—20th century. | Real estate business—California—Los
Angeles. | Real estate business—California—Los Angeles County. | Los Angeles
(Calif.)—History—20th century. | Los Angeles Region (Calif.)—History—20th
century. | Los Angeles (Calif.)—Social conditions—20th century. | BISAC TRUE
CRIME / General | HISTORY / United States / State & Local /
West (AK, CA, CO, HI, ID, MT, NV, UT, WY)

Classification: LCC HV6795.L6 .J33 2021 | DDC 364.9794/94—dc23

"The evil that men do lives after them;
the good is oft interred with their bones."
—William Shakespeare

PROLOGUE
THE CUL-DE-SAC

THE MAN IN THE rusty Volkswagen had a message, a message he was bursting to share as he rolled up alongside me at the stoplight that I would forever detest. The instant his minibus's spindly tires came to rest, he stretched himself across his gearshift, cranked down the passenger-side window, then pantomimed for me to follow suit.

Crap, I thought, let's get this over with—the hasty lecture about how teenage drivers like myself needed to be more careful. And he wouldn't be wrong. Two blocks back, I made him swerve, in the briefest of asphalt drama, when I tried merging my parent's station wagon into the lane that his weather-battered box of bolts was puttering in, sub-speed limit.

Of course, I was distracted. Isn't that shorthand for most seventeen-year-old boys?

"Sorry, sir," I'd tell Mr. VW with bogus wholesomeness. "I'll check my mirrors better next time."

The grouch had already tooted his reedy horn to register his displeasure, so I guessed this was his coda. But when I slid my window down and swiveled my head, intending to nod with sheepish contrition, the guessing was moot. I got a taste of the unforeseen: a pair of seething, bloodshot eyes that sent my core body temperature reeling.

"*Hey, motherfucker!*" he yelled over his clattering muffler. "I'm gonna get you."

Get me?

Spittle pelted out of his window with every other syllable, and he pumped a fist for emphasis. The stranger gunning for me over a traffic peccadillo was adhering to a codebook whose fine print wouldn't let "this" go with a disapproving eyebrow.

"Yeah, you, motherfucker," he said, changing things up. "*You.*"

I suddenly disliked that pronoun, even as I was too petrified to watch him repeat it. So, I gazed straight through my windshield, piecing together what I'd seen. A stork-ish figure whose hippy-long, chestnut hair splayed over a tattered US Army jacket. Veins bulging around the whiskers of a bearded neck. A fixed glower engraved into his cheeks. If Martin Scorsese needed to cast an everyman one small offense from detonation, he'd found his next Travis Bickle in this hothead.

Seconds dragged out like minutes at the red light trapping me next to him. While I'd checkered my early driving record pretty good, dinging and denting that troop-carrier-size Pontiac Grand Safari, there was no analog for this. We were on Woodman Avenue, a windy road through suburban Altadena, the small, Bohemian city north of my hometown, Pasadena, and I had no idea what to do.

"I'm gonna get you!" the thirty-something regurgitated in a voice still molten with dander. "*You.*"

Once the light changed, I tapped the gas pedal, praying he would rumble past. Movement in the rear scuttled that delusion. By popping his clutch, he'd jerked his white, orange-trimmed cube behind me in tactical advantage for whatever punishment he was devising. Then the subsequent light flashed red, like it, too, was in on the conspiracy. Idling there, I avoided my mirrors. Viewing that scowl once was enough to make you want to unsee it.

Sitting to my right that misty, spring afternoon in 1979 was my best friend, Dave Ferris, who had never known the car as anything other than a faux-wood-sided chariot for our expanding liberties. In it, we'd traveled to smoky rock concerts at the Fabulous Forum and to keg-fueled house parties blissfully free of chaperones; to the hilltop, all-girls Catholic school where we trolled for dates until the fleet-footed nuns rousted us off the grounds.

On the rain-slickened road, none of that juvenile carousing meant squat now. Neither did the anecdote we were snickering about when all this exploded: how the dentures of our Napoleon-sized history professor recently fell out of his mouth mid-lecture, prompting our class to erupt in hysterics. Apologies, Mr. Hamilton.

I flicked off our preferred radio station, KROQ, leaving us in ringing silence except for the VW exhaust pipe crackling like it had mechanical emphysema. Dave and I stared at each other in disbelief, spectators to our undoing. We were isolated with little other traffic around, and definitely no sheriff patrol cars that we glibly called "Omar" (as in Omar Sharif). Notions about raiding the pantry at my house for an after-school snack were gone. I never felt grimmer about my lifespan.

When the stoplight changed this time, I stomped the accelerator connected to the Pontiac's burly, V-8 engine, thinking we'd zoom away. Unfortunately, it only zoomed us to the next red light. The VW now vibrated inches off my chrome bumper, too close for its obsessive master to spot the neon Led Zeppelin sticker. I needed separation. As soon as this light winked green, I steered slowly into the right lane, trying to act chastened. Maybe if he flipped me the bird, confident that he'd taught me a lesson, he'd tear away.

Yeah, right. He motored up parallel to us a second time to whet his lips and re-screw that frown into his reddened face.

At that moment, even this sheltered, high school junior realized I had to do something drastic or risk being a body bag filmed for the top of the six o'clock TV news. As soon as the stoplight changed, I glided a block—before veering off with a sharp, ninety-degree turn onto the first street we passed.

Psycho killer, qu'est-ce que c'est.

You've been ditched: That's what!

I checked my rear-view mirror, anxious for relief, before feeling another cold stab to the belly. Not only was our pursuer still behind us, his van was obstructing our escape on the bottom of a block. A block that was actually a cul-de-sac devoid of anyone but us.

This "motherfucker" kid had no way out.

The world was a cantankerous, random place then, just as it seems to be today as our iPhones ping alerts about the latest mass shooting, the latest suicide bomber, the latest person pushed beyond their structural limits. There was no Google or Priuses yet, no melting glaciers, Russian hacking, or global pandemics. There were phone booths and tricked-out Camaros, computers as big as steamer crates and eye-watering smog that was supposed to be long gone.

At our school, Flintridge Preparatory, just above the Jet Propulsion Laboratory, we learned about how history waterfalls in cycles, where prosperity crumbles into recession and fascism bristles into nationalism. Yet no grown-up ever explained to us late-stage Baby Boomers why average Americans were lashing out in uncoined road rage and cult violence; why people were hanging state leaders in effigy and applying for gun permits in droves.

To me, as a teenage sociologist, it was generational venting: every twenty years or so, the demoralized were bound to snarl that the system they thought had liberated them from tyranny was a candy-coated mirage more interested in selling them Buicks than binding societal wounds. Everything was going south in the red, white, and blue. Disillusionment after Vietnam and Watergate had fermented into embitterment and insecurity about the eighties. Twice this decade, Arab nations embargoed the oil that powered the economy while a dour Jimmy Carter cajoled us to turn down our thermostats in his Mr. Rogers sweater.

Here in Southern California, the only folks still portraying the zeitgeist as mellow, or worse, charmingly kooky, worked for the chamber of commerce. Yes, the coastline still shimmered in golden hues and tourists bought maps to celebrities' homes. Behind those images was the blistering reality of a tottering "paradise" of rising crime and waning opportunity. Local factories were yanking up tentpoles in the first whiffs of globalization. In once tranquil neighborhoods, homeowners were double-locking their doors to bar predators—"The Freeway Killer," "The Hillside Strangler," "The Dating Game Killer"— stacking up the corpses.

It's easy to see this dark spirit mirrored in today's refraction. An orange comb-over, reality-TV star pledging to "Make America Great Again" is a poor-man's Ronald Reagan, who adored comparing America's potential to a "shining city on the hill." Today's sucker-punched middle class was yesteryear's causalities of "stagflation." Wall Street bailouts during the Great Recession recall the $1.5-billion federal loan to Chrysler Corporation that many jeered as corporate welfare. Citizens mistrustful of public institutions should revisit the national mood after a military helicopter crashed in Iranian sands trying to rescue our hostages.

The American dream: overpromised, under-delivered.

The surreal events of March 1979 confirmed to this book's protagonist a quirk of Los Angeles topography: even a high-desert area contains ravenous creatures you'd associate with marshland hazards. They just happened to walk upright. As a young space planner from a cloistered childhood, he never could've imagined that his city of scattered high-rises, Hollywood sets, and aerospace giants would be capable of dispatching do-anything killers after him. Never could've envisioned that he would be on the run before he'd really lived.

Climbing out of his old VW to confront us, the stork man was taller than I surmised, easily 6'3". It seemed to take him only five gangly strides to reach the Pontiac, where Dave and I became statues as he sidled up to the driver's side window. Any moment, I expected his hand would wave a pistol, knife, or club.

Then the oddest thing happened: My mind drifted above my expected doom.

When I should've been fashioning a defense, I found myself perplexed about what existential misery—divorce, illness, unemployment, post-Vietnam voices in his head—he needed to exorcise by splattering blood over the caramel-leather upholstery. Some part of me had to decode his suffering before he mangled us over it.

Now came our comeuppance. The stork man thrust his head so deep into the car's interior that I had to tilt awkwardly toward Dave, while simultaneously trying not to shit myself, to keep from touching his scraggly beard. You could tell an ancient rage smoldered around his temples. Panic coiled around mine.

"Don't ever—ever—do that to me again!" he said with a snort. "You hear me?" His breath reeked of nicotine as well as something harder to define, something diseased.

"Yes, sir," I stammered."

He peered deep into my twitchy eyes, calculating the pros and cons of what he'd like to inflict upon us. His right fist swayed near my chin, which had yet to meet its first razor blade. What was in his other hand, the one concealed outside the car?

Our father, who art in…

Abruptly, he seemed to realize what he was doing, that he'd unleashed his inner demons where they didn't belong. He retracted his hand, then his long neck, stomping back to a vehicle synonymous with the peace-and-love movement. Dave and I exhaled, our shirts damp.

"Never again!" he shouted over his *pffff-pffff*-ing muffler as he floored it.

Something tells me that we weren't the last ones he'd stalk over the trivial in the home of the free.

Chip Jacobs
Pasadena, California, 2020

CHAPTER ONE
A DECK FOR ALL SEASONS

THEY HUDDLED AT THE base of the stairs. Panting steam. Packing bad intentions.

Above their heads, a patch of soft light glowed through the sliding-glass window outside the master bedroom of the two-story home where two people lay in bed. People oblivious to approaching invaders while rain from another heavy storm pounded down. People who assumed they had all the time in the world to get high and then naked.

The ringleader—here to supervise the task that his minions had bungled with almost comical frequency—whispered how the midnight operation was to unfold. Their movements needed to be cat-quick and meticulous, not so much as a cuticle left behind. The soggy evening with the neighborhood toasty under mid-century roofs was an advantage they dare not squander.

Everything rode on the bullet scheduled to fly from the barrel of a vintage rifle originally mass-produced to kill Nazis. So much hinged on a single projectile needed to free up the spoils in the kickoff of a lucrative enterprise that Los Angeles had never seen before. If the designated shooter misfired, and his chief's brackish vengeance went un-expunged, beware. The next bullet might have the assassin's name emblazoned on it.

Whoever said the San Fernando Valley was dishwater dull?

The trio crept up the flight, past a potted fern, toward the deck overlooking a backyard pool sloshing chlorine whitecaps in the deluge.

They arranged themselves into position next, just as they'd rehearsed, squatting on the opposite edges of the window to evaluate the scene inside the fishbowl-lit room. What a glorious sight it was! The fellow they'd been hunting for months was mere feet away, reclined sideways on his queen-size bed, listening to a cute woman in a male pajama-top reading.

The killers who'd driven in from points east were different breeds united by a common purpose. The triggerman was a diminutive, helmet-haired character salivating to use the big gun he'd acquired in a crafty haggle. His wingman was a thin, lyrically named crook without his cohorts' felony notches. Both were atop heroin dragons when tonight's launch button was pressed, but they'd made emergency landings to attempt sobering up in a snap. Coffee. A frigid shower. The last thing they intended to do was quibble over timing with a boss whose buzzard-y face was the final visage a handful of unfortunate sorts ever saw.

Anyone fuzzy about what "Pat" was capable of doing should interview their ex-associate, the one who'd developed misgivings after accepting this contract and fled town. Welching on his promise had visited terror on his family and nearly resulted in his own skull being rearranged with a .357-Magnum on a San Francisco sidewalk. Someone else who'd infuriated Pat was unable to vocalize any warnings. He'd gone from sipping cocktails on a fall afternoon to being set ablaze in the scrubland outside LA. Pat's management philosophy about his underlings completing their assignments was absolute. He'd tolerate no job-suggestion boxes. Only compliance.

Now he crouched over his marksman's shoulder, eyes glazed, mouth ajar, waiting for the muzzle flash that he'd been fantasizing to rubberneck.

Ding!

What better timing for another in a series of *what-now* hiccups to frustrate them again like klutzes in a clown show? He'd been seconds from flashing the signal. The new message: how fickle opportunity can be.

The target, a college boy, real estate entrepreneur who once employed him in a manipulative partnership, must've heeded the beep of a Darwinian radar; must've attuned to an inner frequency that he and his woman might not be as alone as they figured. The rustling of feet; a squeaky plank; heebie-jeebies that foreign eyes were watching them: whatever his sixth sense detected was worth investigating.

The man they'd come to obliterate lifted his drowsy head off his snuggly comforter, twisting it the opposite direction of the blonde with him. Next, he did something nobody here had anticipated in their elaborate preparations: he stared directly at *them*, behind the window representing the single barrier between him and his supposed last gasps of air.

Hey, was someone out there?

From his recesses, Pat cringed and cursed, fit to be tied, questioning if he should've toted along a lucky rabbit's foot. How gruesome things would get for prey and predators alike, he knew, if that window's glare didn't thwart his quarry from seeing the truth.

From realizing what lurked beneath his dripping eaves.

CHAPTER TWO
THE SPACE MEN OF MIRACLE MILE

THIRTEEN MONTHS BEFORE THAT disquieting bunch assembled on the sun deck, Gerald "Jerry" Schneiderman pulled up a chair inside a tacky Mexican restaurant, preparing himself to hear out a man excited about a little greed. Richard Kasparov—his coiffed, older partner—was already in presentation mode by the time Jerry strolled in from Pico Boulevard with a sales chart poking from his breast pocket and a schedule cleared for the afternoon.

Jerry, unable to recall the last time that he arrived at a meeting after his chronically late associate, blurted the obvious.

"Wow, Richard. This must be a big deal."

"Be nice," Richard said with a Cheshire cat grin. "You're going to be thanking me later."

For the next ninety minutes, Richard attempted with an impassioned appeal to show how they could enrich themselves by further expanding their footprint. They were already risk-takers compared with their more seasoned competitors, who staked their tentpoles diagraming interior layouts on schematics given to general contractors to "build out." By giving their space-design clientele the ability to hire *their* suite building and furniture-services subsidiaries, they had created a "one-stop shop" that maximized efficiencies in what was often a dizzying decision-making process.

Executive offices and secretarial pods, conference rooms and smart hallways, wallcoverings and light fixtures, electrical outlets and reception areas: there was little that Richard and Jerry couldn't streamline.

Richard's genius notion now? To export those skills into remodeling luxury homes. It was quixotic. It was daring. And it was so Richard, who craved to socialize with and schmooze the LA money crowd.

"Think about it," he said mid-pitch. "We've been in real estate forever. We know the trades. We have the back-office staff. And it could introduce us to a new set of people, maybe even investors. Stop me whenever I reach a negative."

"As if I could," Jerry said, crunching a tortilla chip.

"You've got to say yes. Look where we are."

Both men laughed with a whimsical tinge. Don Ricardo's was wedged in the basement of the checkerboard-mirrored office building across from the Hillcrest Country Club, where they'd hatched Space Matters, their double-entendre-named firm, eighteen months earlier. They'd scarfed down many a burrito here under the cramped stucco ceiling since then before relocating to a larger office after demand for their business swelled.

Something, though, was different, something obvious. Jerry had rarely seen Richard's face so animated, even in their hectic, early days when they were punch-drunk from pulling all-nighters on bad coffee and other stimulants.

"Peruse this, dude," he said, "while I hit the head. It'll get your heart pumping."

He slid over a freehanded chart depicting projected sales curling up like a ski jump. As Richard strode off, several attractive female lunch patrons shot him flirtatious glances without his libido broadcasting interest.

"Never changes," Jerry muttered under his breath.

And it never would.

At thirty-eight, Richard could have fallen out of a *GQ* magazine spread featuring beautiful California males. He was a lean 6'1" with a clipped beard-moustache combination and a thick mane of feathered brown hair. His million-dollar smile and extroverted air worked synergistically with a blocky forehead and full lips. Clothes also adored him. Whether in tailored suits at a high-stakes meeting, or in a secondhand Army jacket flipping burgers at a backyard BBQ, Richard evoked a sizzle that made ladies swoon and some men envious. In his bachelor days, he probably spent more time cavorting just at Pip's and the Friars Club than his partner had spent in bars his entire life.

Jerry had envisaged this odd-couple team precisely because he lacked Richard's gregariousness, lacked the flair that made people want to root for him. He was a skinny 5'10", 160 pounds, with medium-brown hair that twirled into a natural frizz. His unlined, youthful face caused more than a few executives to mistake him for a college student or intern. Sleepy, green-brown eyes and faint smile lines gave him a kind of mousey allure. To appear older than his twenty-six years, he outfitted himself in suits that weren't just off-the-rack.

"Why hamstring ourselves just to the commercial market?" Richard continued, scooting up his ratty, Naugahyde chair. "I have a group of rich people interested in us doing their houses."

"You do?"

"I don't see much downside, only blue sky that might not come again."

Jerry quizzed Richard about the specifics of his proposal. His response, a pastiche of exuberance, salesmanship, and detail, represented an entrepreneur who aspired for more. Jerry didn't know that Richard would suggest they broaden into the residential market, but he always expected something like this was inevitable. After all, they were both strivers. When he urged Richard to leave the space-design conglomerate where they met to charter their own company, visions of money, challenge, and legacy danced in his own head.

Richard's pitch continued for another twenty minutes before Jerry lofted a palm.

"You sold me," he said with a grin. "Let's do it."

"Really? You're not just acquiescing?"

"Really."

"Here's to a new adventure, then. And pouncing on what others haven't."

A clink of their margarita glasses formalized it. They'd christen their home-remodeling offshoot "CM-2," as in "Construction Management, Too."

Jerry's *frijoles* had gone cold while Richard hyped their futures.

From the Mexican restaurant, Jerry steered his white Mercedes-Benz convertible north onto La Cienega Boulevard, hanging a right onto one of the city's mainstay thoroughfares. Wilshire Boulevard was still lined by signature architecture—vintage towers crowned with mounted clocks, the Art Deco Bullocks department store, the Mediterranean-meets-grandeur of the Ambassador Hotel—as well as more contemporary, mirrored high-rises on its ends.

A few miles east of the La Brea Tar Pits, where fake prehistoric animals sat in murky-black pools, Jerry pulled off Wilshire into the company parking lot. Then he scurried inside. The office that swallowed him fifty to sixty hours a week was a funky, Spanish-style mansion on the edge of one of LA's oldest blue-blood communities. He and Richard wanted a headquarters with curb appeal as unique as the designs they were crafting, and the old manor with a red-tile roof and pimply, white stucco exterior called out to them. Vaulted ceilings and French doors accented the interior, with wrought-iron railings across the upper floor and the haunting bust of a woman in front. The staff and Richard worked on the second level of the five-thousand-five-hundred-square-foot building, Jerry was the only soul on the ground floor.

At $232,000, the place was a steal. And theirs.

On the day they took the plunge into home-remodeling, Space Matters' existing success tickled Jerry's senses. He watched Bert, one of several Filipino employees there, examining an architectural schematic, and overheard his French-born decorator, Lillian, speaking frenetically to a supplier. The sound of collective bustle—the crinkle of unfurling blueprints, the thud of the front door closing as someone rushed out to an appointment, the jingling phones—had become a second heartbeat. So, after he caught up on messages, Jerry galloped up the stairs, shifting from desk to desk to ensure that his people had their projects under control. When he was done, he returned to his paper-blizzarded office to resume drawing himself.

The next time he lifted his head from his sketches to check his watch he was dumbfounded to see that the hour hand was in a full sprint. At 7:45 p.m. he was the last one left in the building. Before fishing his car keys out, he took another stroll upstairs, sniffing a few fabric samples stacked on a desk. It was heady. They were on pace to finish the year with $200,000 in net profits, about two-thirds of that in design work—a handsome dividend for an upstart firm.

All those grueling hours, all his belief had turned his savings into generational achievement. Jerry, well before thirty, was earning triple what his father had ever made. And he had accomplished it as the youngest person at his own firm, all without a lick of management experience.

He daydreamed about all this on a commute home that whisked him across Hollywood's Vine Street, by the stacked-disk Capitol Records building, then onto the 101 Freeway near Universal Studios. When he got to one of LA's newer super-highways, the 118 Freeway, to take him west, he turned on the radio he usually listened to for company. But Jerry wasn't a classic-rock connoisseur. He favored AM news stations like KFI, which repeated its top story. It was all too familiar. The body of a twenty-year-old woman had been discovered in the trunk of an orange Datsun off Angeles Crest Highway, a twisting road in the San Gabriel Mountains not far from where Jerry was raised. Police speculated it was the handiwork of the serial killer nicknamed the "Hillside Strangler."

Pretty soon, Jerry was at his exit, climbing the road toward his house under the mustardy foothills of Northridge on the western scrim of the San Fernando Valley. When he opened the door, his peppy wife, Tammy, was there with their one-month-old son cooing in her arms.

"Congratulate me," he said with wry fatigue. "Richard talked me into a new business."

"And was your shirt collar like this all day?" Tammy said, trying to tamp it down.

Sometimes as he lay in bed trying to quiet his frenetic mind, Jerry bounced his legs on the mattress as a reality check. This splendid life he was cobbling was no hoax. It had arrived.

•••

RICHARD ALWAYS EXCELLED IN two areas: spitballing ideas and displaying showmanship at the onset of something fresh, be it romance, friendships, or a new job. It was the granular detail and unglamorous devotion to see endeavors through where he often sabotaged himself. CM-2 was his opportunity to prove to everyone, himself included, that he had learned from his mistakes as gray flecks crept into his scalp.

So, when an old colleague—at a firm he once tried convincing to merge with theirs—expressed reservations about CM-2 straying from Space Matters' bailiwick, Richard decided to listen carefully, even though it deprived him of the affirmation he was craving to hear from a respected associate.

"C'mon," this man named David said. "What do you guys know about the technical side of home renovations? It's a lot more intense than room measurements. It's about the people."

"What do you mean?" Richard asked.

"That you have to be careful managing some of these guys with tool belts and circular saws. They're different. Someone once compared it to animal training. And you never know what animals are thinking up on those beams. What I'm saying is this could backfire."

Richard, too prideful to abandon what he just sweet-talked Jerry into, realized they had overlooked an important element. Simply put, they were unequipped to run so much hard-hat work simultaneously while tending to their forte, space planning and design. He conferred with Jerry, and they agreed they needed someone with battle-tested field experience to oversee the day-to-day activities not just for CM-2, but their commercial projects as well. Neither of them had ever logged a shift slicing carpet padding with utility knives or hanging sixty-pound solid core doors that felt like one hundred. Neither understood the nuances of hiring union-protected tradesmen or ordering drywall by the pallet.

In no time they drew up the criteria for a construction supervisor. He needed to be a multitasker capable of juggling numerous job sites, troubleshooting errors, and interpreting blueprints—someone committed to making money without letting it become a circus. They quizzed their industry contacts to see if they knew anyone who fit their bill. The response was underwhelming. Richard, unbeknownst to Jerry, afterward took the initiative by widening the net. He bought ad space in the *Los Angeles Times* and other papers seeking a "superintendent familiar with high-rise interiors."

A man who noticed the solicitation phoned Richard expressing interest. His chief reference was his last boss at the local branch of New York-based Smythe & Hargill, which at the time owned and managed millions of square feet of real estate across the country. Richard phoned the company's top LA executive to inquire further about Howard Garrett. Victor Platte's response was heartening. He called Howard dependable, proficient, and well-qualified. And who was Richard to argue with the estimable Smythe & Hargill, whose local portfolio sparkled with the historic Roosevelt and Jewelry Mart buildings downtown, west LA's Wilshire-Comstock Apartments, and Manhattan's Empire State Building? (It wasn't until 1992 that the multibillion-dollar company's reputation was dinged when the woman who managed its hotels, a flamboyant, tyrannical doyenne who famously scoffed at peasants who paid their taxes, went to prison for *tax* fraud.)

In Howard's thirty years employed in the industry, Platte told Richard, he had supervised dozens of projects for them. Name a major building in town and chances are Howard either worked in it or knew someone who did. In recent years, he was an independent contractor and freelance foreman choosy about where he practiced his craft.

Richard, elated at what somebody with Howard's credentials could mean, invited him to a sit-down interview at Space Matters' mansion. Howard Landis Garrett Jr. was polite, quiet, coarse around the edges—and positive that he was their guy. Next to some of the hairier projects he had ridden herd over for Smythe & Hargill and another employer, realtor Alma Smith, this would be a breeze. Ever repair a disabled fire alarm system in a subterranean garage? Pour a massive foundation with a shoestring staff? Frame hundreds of square feet over a weekend with a trick back? Well, he had.

Forty-seven-year-old Howard looked the part. He had a narrow face marked by leathery jowls, penetrating blue-green eyes, and stringy, dirty-blond hair he swept over a faint bald spot. Though he was a wiry six foot one, his belly pouched out, suggesting a weekend beer drinker. One acquaintance compared him to a fair-skinned Charles Bronson; to Jerry, he could've been a wind-burned cowboy from a 1950s TV western. What you saw with him was what you got: a grizzled, seen-it-all journeyman who referred to the suits in charge as "chief" and idiots as "clowns." He could light a menthol cigarette with one hand while toting a nail gun in the other. There was an intrinsic toughness about him, as if he'd been a Marine. He lived in a Pasadena condo after downsizing from a ranch-style house close to Santa Anita Park in Arcadia.

Though old Howard was not going to win any personality contests, he nevertheless could smile; when he laughed, it rattled with the bronchial crackle of a nicotine enthusiast. Besides his experience, Richard was plenty impressed with Howard's entrepreneurial spirit. Not only did he stockpile his own carpentry gear, he still maintained two small design businesses. Howard, in fact, said that he had once brimmed with so many clients himself that he leased an office.

Commercial, residential, industrial: he assured Richard he could do it all.

They jumped to salary negotiations. Richard offered him a $22,000-a-year salary. Sounded dandy to him, Howard said. Richard, though, wanted him on his payroll for more than worksite street cred. That's because Howard owned a golden ticket in his long-held California general contractor's license, something that his potential employers needed to comply with state regulations for residential work. Without such a certification, Richard or Jerry themselves would have to enroll in school and pass an exam. That effort alone could gobble up a year. Who knew where capricious California real estate would be by then? Yep, Howard seemed ideal.

His only stumbling block was a commitment that would take him away from LA for a couple of weeks. As much as he hated bringing it up, it was a standing obligation. In March, he would need time off to be in San Bernardino, the sparsely populated, rugged county east of here. He said he was a witness in a court case starting then, and the district attorney was relying on his testimony to put a crook away. Prosecutors were unsympathetic when Howard recently informed them that his mandatory appearance inland might interrupt his formative time at a new job. They threatened to subpoena him, which blue-collar Howard said he was unable to abide. He apologized for the inconvenience that his absence might create.

Richard, picturing a money machine within his grasp, said no sweat. Even stellar candidates tote complex histories. Jerry was miffed that his partner solicited a specific candidate without consulting him first, but he valued Richard's industriousness. Then he gave his blessing. They had found their foreman after a single interview!

From the moment Howard scrawled his name on the dotted line, Space Matters would never be the same. What was a two-man team metamorphosed into a three-headed hydra? Lines of responsibilities were divvied up. Jerry would continue designing for prized clients while tending to in-house administration. Rainmaking Richard would add home remodels to his other standing duties. Newbie Howard would coordinate the flannel-and-boots laborers they hired *ad hoc*, accustomed to picking dust out of his teeth.

Brains, flash, and grit: it was the makings of a dynamite team of space builders open to anything.

•••

ITS BEGINNING WAS EVERYTHING Richard promised and more. Under Howard's watch, suite building commenced at the Pacific Stock Exchange downtown, a few skyscrapers to the west, and at the house owned by Michael "Mikey" Krakow, a smarmy Valley tax lawyer whom Jerry knew from way back. Unexpected opportunities cropped up too. An elderly OB-GYN pleased with the remodel that the company finished at his West LA medical office inquired if Richard and Howard, whom he got to know during the construction, would nurture his own get-rich aspirations. Dr. Joseph Marmet was hoping to develop a 160-home subdivision in western San Bernardino County, sensing in Jerry's associates the expertise that he sorely lacked. Asked if they were interested, both said absolutely.

Working on so many types of properties simultaneously required heaps of coordination, and that kept Richard and Howard offsite much of the day. It also engendered surprises, such as the latent friendship the pair developed despite personalities as dissimilar as their appearances. After they became better acquainted, they swilled after-work drinks at Richard's tastefully decorated Van Nuys home. When they discovered that they and their spouses would be in Palm Springs during Father's Day weekend in mid-June, it presented another chance for socializing. The four dined at Pal Joey's, a popular hangout favored by white-shoes celebrities. Richard's wife would never forget the atmosphere.

Jerry, who heard only nuggets about the Richard-Howard buddy-loop as the nerdy one in the group, generally confined himself to the office. Swept up in the grind of managing Space Matters, he barely even knew about Dr. Marmet's flirtations to recruit his associates into his subdivision development. An inbox bulging by the day acted like a chain around his leg, if a welcome one at that. Commercial clients in belt-cinching mode as the US sputtered into recession saw the beauty of a company able to be their one-stop shop. Richard's salesmanship reeled in the contracts with well-heeled homeowners, just as he promised. Howard, thankfully, was as good as advertised: adept at his job without needing much oversight. Whatever the staff impression of him as a taciturn redneck who left earwax on the office phone and swore like a football coach, the man saw his projects through to completion. Combine it all and the checks were coming in as fast as Jerry could count them.

Jerry needed to acknowledge that his partner's instincts on expansion were well calibrated. People you'd never expect to see working hand in glove—him, the shy workaholic from nondescript North Hollywood; Richard, the West LA charmer as the public face of the company; and calloused-hands Howard originally from ham-and-egger Alhambra—appeared to have coalesced as one.

CHAPTER THREE
SHORTCUTS TO BENJAMINS

B Y THE TIME HE flung off his bedsheets most mornings, Jerry was hurrying. Hurrying to plant himself behind his desk, as if he never departed the night before. Rushing to unloose his imagination on schematics, in an office abounding with T squares and fabric samples, while ensuring his staff kept apace. Today, coffee and a goodbye peck to Tammy and his son, Jude, he lead-footed it out of Northridge toward a different landing. Thirty-seven minutes later, still yawning, he pulled his car into the world's largest parking garage beneath the recently finished Century Plaza Towers.

At approximately six hundred feet tall, the black and gray edifices didn't so much punctuate the West LA skyline with their formidable triangular shapes as dominate it. The aluminum-clad high-rises—designed by the architect behind Manhattan's World Trade Center—threw shadowy blades across the Ahmanson Theatre and other swanky area landmarks in its square.

Up the elevator Jerry rode, reaching the nineteenth floor where workmen were constructing a legal suite that he designed to suffuse Old World charm, from parquet floors to burnished-wood paneling. Then he stood idle to soak it all in. There was an Erector Set rhythm to the job that was engrossing to watch, a magic coupling of power tools and adept hands. But Jerry could only gape for so long. When the racket died down, he needed to quit watching the show and help orchestrate it.

Before long, the cabinet guy, carpet man, and other craftsmen ambled up with questions and updates about the multimillion-dollar renovation underway. Many of them a good twenty years his senior, they took instructions from the "skinny kid" in the blue suit, for his was the last word in this modular, sawing-framing commotion. Every answer the tradesmen needed Jerry supplied either from memory or from the dog-eared schematic he unfurled across a sawhorse. He could ill afford to get anything wrong.

Of all the active suite remodels in the Space Matters hopper, the job here was paramount. Paul Fegen, the eccentric real estate magnate who hired the company, already confided to Jerry that he was leaning toward using his modular design here as the prototype for other floors in the towers that he controlled. Hence, Jerry needed to be sharp, and worked to quash his mild if persistent acrophobia. With his boyish face and deferential manner, it was challenging enough to inspire confidence that he could quarterback a top-shelf makeover with the middle-aged, construction vets in paint-splattered boots. Dashing to the restroom to throw up would've sowed doubts hard to reverse.

A while back, he and Richard were on the forty-third floor of one of the Century Plaza Towers as guests for a "topping party." Just the building's skeletal framing and concrete shafts were installed. With no windows, and at an altitude offering unobstructed views of the Pacific Ocean, wind whistled through the space. On that day, Jerry tethered himself in the center, focusing on his conversation with a leasing agent, not his fear of heights, while Richard schmoozed the daughter of insurance magnate Barry Kaye.

Jerry's queasiness calmed after returning to the office whose location underscored that his success was no precocious fluke. The mansion halfway between the jagged skyline of downtown LA and the tony shops of Beverly Hills rose at the southwest corner of Wilshire and Fremont Place. The locale put it on the southern tip of Hancock Park, an exclusive neighborhood peppered with palm trees, sweeping driveways, and dynastic estates that made you think California

Kennedys. Some of the state's most august families—the *Los Angeles Times*-owning Chandlers, heirs to oil tycoon Edward Doheny—had lived on these blocks for generations. So had the city's mayors in the official Getty House residence. Just beyond Space Matters' door was more gilded ambience in a pair of enormous, white Tudor columns along Fremont. On any given day, employees spied famous names passing through them toward their own expansive residences, the archbishop of Los Angeles, Rolling Stones front man Mick Jagger, and heavyweight champion Muhammad Ali among them.

The company was surrounded by nostalgia as well as celebrity. To the east, toward downtown, was the luxurious, flesh-colored Ambassador Hotel, where Hollywood's biggest stars once hobnobbed at the Cocoanut Grove nightclub and Robert F. Kennedy was assassinated by a Palestinian-born stable boy in June 1968. To the west a couple of blocks was the Miracle Mile, a historic corridor of audacious architecture, iridescent green theaters, and wing-shaped apartments dating from the Roaring Twenties. When Jerry wasn't slobbering over the design styles there, he often fantasized about cultivating business inside of them.

That time wasn't now. Definitely not. Inside his office that afternoon, about two months after they widened into luxury home renovations, Jerry gazed out the window at his company's parking lot, feeling pressure like never before paddle his blood stream. Space Matters was now knee-deep in real estate projects whose total value was in the tens of millions of dollars. Moreover, he and Richard had an office full of people depending on *them* for their livelihoods. Under their roof were four draftsmen, one of them arguably the best in town, and three decorators, including a chatty, prancing designer and a European woman whose husband allegedly worked for the Las Vegas mob. There was Howard, secretaries, a gofer, a bookkeeper, plus bills from lawyers, insurers, a messenger service. Occasionally, Jerry required the assistance of a brawny Moroccan with an interesting past, and he didn't work for free.

Sketch and build, Jerry chanted to himself when his heart raced. *Sketch and build.*

Little voices reminded him, just the same, that it was better to be periodically frazzled with half-moons under his eyes than sitting around mentally willing the phones to ring. And there was rarely silence at Fremont Place with a roster of A-list clients like the Bank of America building in Beverly Hills, the Prudential & Equitable Life Insurance tower midcity, and a web of high-rises nationwide leased by Fegen's empire. Jerry was determined to satisfy them all with well-honed designs regardless of taxing deadlines or tricky demands.

No matter how stressed out his workload made him, he still adored doing what he was when he never adored that much work-wise before. Every night when he left for Northridge, his mind toted home a thousand tactical details, like an insomniac baseball manager plotting for the day's next game. And he was already paving the groundwork for Space Matters Phase II by stockpiling blueprints for every substantial building in Los Angeles, hundreds in all. The rationale: get a leg up on rivals in future bidding wars.

When it came to his own sketches, left-handed Jerry prided himself on playing assassin with a pencil. Traditional space planners (interior architects in some taxonomies) practiced a herd mentality in which they converted blank office space into cookie-cutter arrangements. Waiting rooms here, C suites always there. Jerry, by synthesizing client needs, natural light, pedestrian-traffic flow, and each building's particular contour, was less about common aesthetics and more about brutal efficiency. Hallways in his blueprints sometimes lined building perimeters to optimize square footage. Bulky file cabinets that no one had figured out where to cram hung from the ceiling. *The ceiling!* The geometry of it flowed as naturally to him as the art of presentation came to Richard.

For a while, the two pitched everyone within ear range. They did it for jobs that made sense for the firm's capabilities, and even a handful for which they probably should've refrained. They attended leasing parties organized by developers and agents seeking space-planning bids. They haggled invitations to compete against former employers. They worked with Synanon, a wealthy mainstream drug rehab that needed space plans for primal-scream sessions—before its messianic leader, Charles Dederich, turned it into a cult of personality that delighted in pummeling its critics. They paired with another shop to design the Sunset Boulevard offices of the Center of Family Therapy, a commune-like setting that advocated catharsis through nudity and pot smoking. They drew up schematics for bigger clients like Great Expectations, a dating service on Sepulveda Boulevard in the Valley, and knocked them out for a smaller psychology-psychiatry office on Wilshire.

This is what hungry companies did in the late-seventies LA of social experimentation. They fed the need, caring little if it were for a chiropractor, pop psychology gimmick, or conglomerate. In the fifties and early sixties, interior architecture was sort of an afterthought priority often farmed out to interior decorators. The pattern began to shift once architectural firms, which had looked down their noses at people who mapped out their floors essentially as draftsmen who couldn't hack the technical side of their profession, realized how lucrative space planning could be. A building is created once. Its inner layout is forever evolving, and thus forever making someone money.

Given the demand for his companies' services, Jerry expected their hot streak would blaze hotter in the months ahead. The company accountant, after zeroing in on some worrisome math in the books, cautioned not so fast. Jerry loosened his tie. According to the bookkeeper, CM-2, their new home-remodeling spinoff, was burning through money at a clip that already dragged it into minor arrears. Bills now exceeded customers' payments.

Jerry alerted Richard to this gap, but he showed little alarm. He preached patience. Every small business, he noted, lived with deficits at some juncture even as their revenues blossomed; experts tabbed it "the prosperity curve." Bridge financing and a big picture perspective would eventually put CM-2 on the right side of that graph.

Besides, he uncovered a shortcut.

"Leave it to me," Richard said. "I have something in the works."

Soon after that conversation, he waved Howard into his office while Jerry, probably uncoincidentally, was out. Richard, following some pleasantries, minced no words. He admitted that he and Jerry had dug themselves a little hole with their home-remodeling spinoff. Yet it was an eminently patchable hole if Howard would be so accommodating. What, Richard asked him, would he think about permitting them to tap his active credit lines, which Howard had established for his previous freelance work, as stopgap financing? Within a few months, Richard forecast, CM-2's cash flow would stabilize, and they would continue kicking ass as if there had never been a deficit.

Howard sighed, gyrating uncomfortably in his chair while he mulled a response. Helpful as he'd like to be, he said he was hesitant about agreeing to another favor. He already put up his contractor's license, which the state could suspend any time if it discovered anything hinky. Before issuing a decision, he needed to understand why the partners couldn't repair their own missteps?

Golden-tongued Richard anticipated that question. Approaching a bank for a measly $3,000 a month, he said, could elicit doubts about their managerial competence. Transferring funds from Space Matters could also lead into murky waters because "comingling" accounts invited tax headaches, maybe an IRS audit. Until they seeded their own credit line for CM-2, as they intended to do, they needed easy money to finance labor, paint, lumber, drywall, caulking, nails, drop cloths, and related items.

"So, what do you say, Howard?"

Not much. He sat there quietly, deciphering the proposal he heard. He had been around the industry long enough to translate linguistic flamenco dances like this. The truth: *he* would be keeping this spinoff afloat if he signaled his assent. Richard could sugarcoat the predicament all he wanted when in reality it was a mini crisis. By recognizing what Richard refused to spell out, it conferred on him bargaining power, which he tilted decisively in his favor. In exchange for opening up his hard-won credit, against his better judgment, he demanded hefty concessions. He wanted a one-third equity interest in CM-2, which effectively granted him partner status. Condition Number Two: his base salary would have to jump from $22,000 a year to thirty-five thousand. It was a take-it-or leave it offer.

"Deal!" Richard answered.

Why would Richard acquiesce to such a lopsided concession? Simple. Because he regarded it more as a flexible arrangement sealed with a handshake, not a binding contract blurred with fine print about painful consequences for default.

•••

SCHIZOPHRENIC: SOUTHERN CALIFORNIA'S REAL estate economy, circa 1979, had multiple personalities, at least through Jerry's lens as someone straddling its sectors. On one hand, the region boasted a dense residential market flush with soaring home values after voters approved Proposition 13, the watershed, property-tax-slashing initiative spearheaded by a jack-of-all-trades Angeleno. His name: Howard Jarvis. Suddenly, tens of millions of dollars earmarked for government coffers returned to homeowners' pockets. For remodeling outfits nimble enough to exploit it, there was a fortune to be made. Another boom was underway in indoor malls in Arcadia, Santa Monica, and other attractive suburbs. These consumer Astrodomes, where department stores sold underwear next to corndogs kiosks, heralded an era of retail as entertainment.

But inside the commercial office market that represented Space Matters' meat and potatoes, it was no Babylon. It was cash-flow survival. There was more demand than supply, and appetite for risk plunged. Companies that ordinarily would've hired Jerry and Richard or their competitors to contour a new headquarters just renewed existing leases.

Brighter times were forecast with fifty new buildings citywide and a billion-dollar downtown redevelopment in the pipeline. Unfortunately, the valve on that pipeline wouldn't turn until the early 1980s.

For now, LA's trophy development would remain the mid-seventies' Bonaventure, a futuristic, thirty-three-story hotel with a revolving penthouse restaurant already prominent in Hollywood film shoots. The façade of the cylindrical, rocket-ship-esque structure on downtown's Figueroa Street was as emblematic of its habitat as any high-rise. Wrapped in silvery glass, it reflected everything around it like a giant vanity mirror without revealing anything going on inside its membranes.

These cold realities were grist for Richard to remind Jerry that mettle and improvisation, like Howard's agreement to open up his credit lines, would carry them through the lean times. To do his own part, Richard announced that he'd be increasingly out of the office prowling for luxury homes to remodel. When he later heard about a dilapidated Victorian in Hancock Park, it appeared he bagged big game. The job to overhaul the castle-esque property was worth a whopping $80,000.

Better yet, the antiquated property on June Street required a floor-to-ceiling refurbishing. The owners recently fired a couple of bumbling, pricy remodelers who were more poseurs than professionals. Since it was his lead, Richard was scheduled to meet with the woman of the house to review the scope of the job and take measurements. He didn't. He stood her up on this introductory appointment, forcing Jerry and his top draftsmen, Bert, to drop everything to cover for him. It was getting to be a trend.

"How many meetings can one man blow off?" Jerry asked on the ride back.

When Richard finally surfaced at the Victorian after being MIA, he illustrated he wasn't just a slick salesman, wowing the property owners with novel ideas on where to shift a bathroom, how to open up the kitchen. Like that, he'd restored the clients' faith in him, though Jerry wished he were burrowed down with him at Fremont Place.

He definitely could've used a sidekick after receiving a surprise call from an administrator at a hospital shoehorned up against the Harbor Freeway downtown. An ambulance, it seemed, had wheeled in a man in a diabetic coma, a man with a Space Matters business card in his wallet. Howard must've passed out drinking in the bar of the Roosevelt Building, where he once worked.

Doctors had brought him back to consciousness with medication, and now he was drifting in and out of sleep. Little of what the administrator relayed computed until Jerry drove to the hospital. There, he was briefed about the hormonal turmoil inside his foreman's anatomy. Howard was a Type-1, or insulin-dependent, diabetic, a relentless condition triggered when a person's immune system destroys insulin-producing bodies manufactured in the pancreas. Without that essential hormone, glucose that cells need for nourishment from carbohydrates cannot be absorbed, as if they were hermetically locked out. Denied entry, excessive glucose (or blood sugar) accumulates in the bloodstream. Left unchecked, it can skyrocket, spilling into the kidneys, where it acidifies, or cause sufferers to pass out. Even die.

Twice a day, Howard injected himself with insulin that he kept chilled in a thermos. He must've forgotten to increase his dose as he was getting schnockered on hard alcohol teeming with carbs. Jerry was astonished. Howard, who looked like he could stare down a badass threatening him with paint thinner and a match, was more brittle than his rawhide facade suggested.

Jerry was in a chair next to Howard's bed when Howard fluttered his eyes open like some tousle-haired carcass come back to life. Noticing his visitor, Howard fish-flopped himself toward Jerry in a hospital gown speckled with blood. His mouth curled into a grateful smile revealing yellow, cigarette-stained teeth.

"Oh, Jerry. Thanks for coming. You have no idea how much this means."

"Don't mention it. I'm surprised the hospital called to say you'd been admitted. I had no idea."

"Me, either. I'm drinking, minding my own business, and next thing I know I'm here with all these tubes and crap connected to me."

Jerry nodded as compassionately as he could, trying to ignore his fear of germs as he listened to Howard recount his daily grind against diabetes. Twenty minutes later, he gripped the armrest of his chair, eager to leave this uncomfortable spot. More out of politeness than duty, he inquired if there was anything he could do. Howard's response gave him momentary tachycardia.

"How about a hug, man?"

There was nothing Jerry could say, and he dared not demur. He hoisted himself up and embraced Howard, surprised to find that Howard's arms were stronger than they appeared under the loose Hawaiian shirts that'd become his signature outfit. His armpits were gamey with un-showered body odor too.

"If this headache will go away and I can get my blood sugar back to normal, I'll be on the job by tomorrow," Howard said post-hug.

"Take your time," Jerry answered. "Don't worry if you miss a couple days. We're okay for the time being. The jobs aren't going anyplace."

"Not my style. I'll be back tomorrow, assuming they'll Goddamn release me."

Jerry doubted that was possible, but what did he know about the human metabolism? Howard made it moot anyway by turning up as promised, gaunt and puffing a Kool cigarette.

•••

As the weeks rolled by, Howard's coma proved less alarming than Richard's tendency to be absent when internal brush fires smoldered. Twenty years before cell phones, when pagers constituted space-age communication, you'd have an easier time tracking Sasquatch in the Great Northwest than finding Space Matters's other partner in Greater

Los Angeles. A pager is only as good as those who heed its vibrations. Jerry tried extinguishing what he could. Though Howard's credit lines were financing residential construction materials, invoices still higher than they should've been begged for his attention, along with more blueprints than he could count. Dealing with creeps at dinner meetings was another area where he went it awkwardly alone. At a boozy client meal, an executive informed him of *quid pro quo*: if Space Matters aimed to lock down contracts at the high-rise that'd become the massive First Interstate skyscraper downtown, somebody from the firm was going to "have to suck a little cock." Jerry, unsure if it this line was bluster or negotiation, gave no reply.

By the next morning, he asked himself again why Richard was being so absentee. The better question might've been who Richard was.

Viewing him as a dichotomy was a decent jumping-off point.

"Don't listen to what I say," he'd tell clients that he bowled over with charm. "Watch what I *do*."

Everyone at Space Matters appreciated that magic, as well as a cultured air unlike anyone there. On cue, Richard could speak like a continental traveler, despite his fear of flying, about the nuances of post-modern architecture or the playful fruitiness of a Merlot. In downtime, he always shared the strongest weed, recommended the best albums, and knew his gourmet cuisine.

On the back slope of this coolness was fire, the fire of someone whose temperament was about as predictable as the Twister game spinner. Before he joined forces with Jerry, people victimized by Richard's tantrums and other character flaws often posed *the* central question about Richard: Did he tank relationships on purpose, or did the company's "senior" partner presume friendship with him came with the stipulation that they'd have to shovel up his princely messes, as his mollycoddling family once had?

When Richard was in one of his "moods," workers learned it was smart to tiptoe around him. Some of this volatility wasn't his fault. Richard was probably manic-depressive, commonly known today in medical consults and Big Pharma ads as bipolar disorder. Nowhere was his dysfunctional brain chemistry more glaring than his feeble control over his anger and workplace exasperations. Provoked on a hectic day, Richard's temper pierced the ears of those unlucky to be around it. He'd peel rubber in the parking lot, honk at people lollygagging through crosswalks, or chuck small office equipment against his wall. Anything could set him off: an assistant unavoidably late to a meeting, the wrong paint sample. After a client once mentioned a slight error on one of his designs, he slammed the phone receiver down so violently that it splashed coffee onto the blueprints.

Underlings unnerved by his short fuse had to accept it, as did Jerry. Most wrote it off as the byproduct of an artistic temperament.

Then, in a blink, the likeable Richard snapped back as if he never vanished. He'd be the spontaneous Richard who ordered lunch for colleagues from a steakhouse and paid a taxi to deliver it; the compassionate Richard good for a pick-me-up phone call or gift to a despondent friend; the inspiring Richard who delighted in stoking creativity from his staff; the comedic Richard uncanny at impersonating Johnny Mathis and Monty Python characters, or retelling an only-in-LA anecdote.

Jerry, over the years, was accustomed to haggling with older men who figured they could bulldoze him into submission, like the Popeye-ish landlord always out for a better deal, or his manipulative corporate bosses. But handling Richard's emotional pendulum was freighted with higher stakes as partners on whose backs rode so much. Jerry was aware of Richard's skeleton-rattling closet. A first failed marriage. A crash-and-burn parting with a previous employer. Mother issues. Missed expectations. Whispered melodrama about him.

Thing was, Jerry pledged to overlook what he could for the sake of reciprocal benefits. As much as he groused about his flakiness, he still admired Richard's velvet cachet, how he compartmentalized his troubles to seal crunch-time deals. As for Richard's checkered employment track record, Jerry bought into a construct: that *he* could help save Richard from himself by granting him a second (or third) chance to discover his better angels. Informing this was Jerry's realization that Richard gambled on him by quitting a salaried job for a startup with a virtual kid. In that way, they rescued each other. Justifications aside, he believed Richard deserved slack. Co-running a high-pressure firm during a recession, coupled with relocating into a new house with a pregnant wife, would've taxed the most even-keeled.

Jerry's propensity to give Richard wiggle room was not shared by all. In mid-1978, an interior designer named Kay Lang was reaching her limit with him. When she first answered to Richard, he maintained a decent hierarchy where everyone, more or less, worked harmoniously. But those lines of authority began to dissolve once Richard coyly flirted with her while also abdicating some of his responsibilities to assistants like her. When his clients started badgering Kay, insisting to know when their remodel would commence or prepaid furniture would arrive, she could only apologize so much. Then she heard rumors about in-house money problems.

The next time Kay saw Richard walk up the mansion's steps, her swan song was well-rehearsed. Cradling design binders up to her neck, she entered his office and dropped the load into his lap. Before he could singsong "good morning" or seek cooler heads, she announced her decision.

"I quit," she said in a blindside. "I can't take this anymore."

Her snap departure was worrisome. The inability of the company accountant to get to the bottom of why some residential remodels were over-ordering construction materials was a red flag not even Jerry's magical thinking could ignore. Financial ledgers were supposed to be exact to the decimal point, not head-scratching. Again, he was preoccupied by a nagging question that he never imagined asking: Was something fishy going on under his nose? He nearly tripped walking around the office flyspecking dubious invoices. At home, his mind skittered across scenarios he barely wanted to confront while Tammy, a hummingbird of energy, described her day over dinner.

During a project-update meeting, Jerry finally steeled the courage to confront Richard about the discrepancies. Did he know something he wasn't revealing about why CM-2 was hemorrhaging money by splurging on supplies the jobs didn't require?

Richard bristled at the insinuation he was being a Brutus a la the Ides of March.

"Wait!" he said. "You're suggesting that *I'm* involved? Me? Oh, come on. It's my business too, remember? Stealing from it would be ripping myself off. This is silly."

"I know. But what would you think if you were me?"

From his first response to his last, Richard professed ignorance, letting resentment harden his voice. He'd been running himself ragged for their cause, and now he was getting the fifth degree about paperwork the obtuse bookkeeper couldn't remedy? To him, the issue was too ridiculous to belabor, especially when there were companies to grow.

Jerry left their sit-down feeling neither relieved nor doomed. Just unresolved. Over the next few nights, he stayed late at the mansion, poring over the ledgers to compare expense entries with color-coded jobsite figures. No *ah-ha* revelation emerged, so he continued tapping a pen to his temple. If his deepest fear was true—that Richard was backstabbing him by bilking CM-2— there was one person who would have the lowdown.

One day, while Richard was out peddling space plans, Jerry told Howard that they needed to speak. This was Jerry's big-boy moment. Except for his hospital visit, he'd scarcely been alone with Howard in the months Howard was on staff. Gone frequently in the field, he was some-what of a ghost at Space Matters; few of the staff were very acquainted with him. When he was there, he was an aloof, keep-to-himself type disinterested in water-cooler chitchat. His hard-hat ethic hewed to the idea that you did your job, punched the clock, and went home.

Jerry tried not to stutter when he asked Howard to keep what they were about to discuss in confidence, which Howard agreed to.

For the next ten minutes, while they reviewed each construction site, he probed him about Richard's honesty. Had he seen any evidence of financial skullduggery? Kickbacks? Skimming? Doctored invoices? Howard's standard reply was that he hadn't observed anything underhanded and, like Richard himself, resented being in the hotbox of suspicion.

"Anything else?" Howard said.

"No."

Jerry shoved his files back in his desk to signal they were done. Howard, though, strangely remained. From his chair across from Jerry's desk, he lit a cigarette. Then he exhaled a smoky lungful directly toward Jerry.

"You should still watch him," Howard said, inspecting the fleck of tobacco he picked off his lip.

"What do you mean?" Jerry said.

"You heard me."

"But I'm confused. You just said he wasn't doing anything wrong?"

"Let's just say there's more than one Richard in Richard."

"Am I missing something? Because you're making me think I should hire a lawyer."

"What you're missing is the point. I've dealt with lots of people like Richard during my career. They can start believing their own bullshit when they get moving too quick."

"I thought Richard's been burning the candle. CM-2, a new house, a kid on the way…"

"Jerry," Howard interrupted. "Figure it out for yourself. You're smart."

He sighed relief, overjoyed by what he did *not* hear: concrete proof Richard was playing him for a sucker. It must have been Richard's style that rubbed Howard the wrong way—the two-dollar words, the happy hour glad-handing that irritated Howard's Budweiser-and-bar-nut mindset after that they'd hung out. Yes. That had to be it. Besides, Howard would be implicating himself if he was lying. He might be inscrutable, crude among the well-mannered, but he had an industry reputation to maintain and a vested stake in the company.

Seizing on that, Jerry felt better. Flawed accounting—that's what this was.

"Hold it for a sec," he told Howard as Howard pushed off his chair to go. "I want to show you something I think you'll get a kick out of."

Grinning, Jerry wiggled his hand into the office plant on the corner of his desk. From the top of the soil he lifted up a small, black dictation-recording device whose spools were still spinning. He hoped that Howard would interpret it as a hardball tactic by someone brave enough to play detective for the good of the firm. That he was no marshmallow out of his league managing everything here.

If Howard's vinegary expression was any barometer, Jerry and his people-reading skills misread the situation. The foreman looked down at the gizmo in Jerry's palm as if it were a steaming dog turd and strode out of the room without comment.

"Thanks for your time," Jerry said weakly.

He refused to let that failed display of bravado, or the nagging sense that this was not the end of the intrigue, depress him. What he needed more immediately was time to recharge his drained batteries. Jetting away with his wife and baby son to Waikiki for lazy time under the tropical sun was his remedy. Hands weary from gripping blueprints and clients' hands got to clasp fruity cocktails and suntan lotion. The blue waters washed away kinks in his neck.

Back home in LA, tanner than when he left, the same problems greeted him, but so did the rewards of carving a name for oneself.

•••

DURING A PARTNERS' MEETING in November 1978, Jerry broached again the gremlin in their books: CM-2's still in explicably high invoices. Richard told him to quit being a namby-pamby. There was a real problem to tackle.

"What are you talking about?" Jerry said, cocking an eyebrow.

"I'll tell you. While you were at your appointment, Howard quit."

"He *what?*"

"He quit. And he made quite the little scene too."

Richard detailed it. Before he stomped out the door, Howard typed up a resignation letter, snapping down furiously on the keys of his IBM Selectric typewriter. He then walked the one-page document over to Richard, slapping it into his midsection.

"There!" he said in a hushed growl near the reception area. "We're official."

Richard said he asked Howard to step into a side room in case there was going to be fireworks. Inside there, Howard fumed, snorting how he expected to be repaid for every dime he was owed. On his list were any charges, authorized or not, that his credit line covered, back salary he was due, as well as $35,000 to buy out his one-third stake in CM-2. Added up, they were on the hook for $45,000. And he demanded his money now! Space Matters' leading men, he charged, had buttered him up solely to rip him off.

Tempers flared further as Richard disputed that anyone had been cheated. There'd be no speedy payback, either. This wasn't Johnson & Johnson. Small firms like theirs lacked that type of liquidity; it's why they needed his credit lines to begin with.

To Howard, on this his final day at Fremont Place, Richard was deflecting, making excuses, shoveling malarkey. Ignore these debts, he told him, and his phalanx of lawyers would make him and Jerry ever regret hanging out a shingle. They'd slap liens on every project to starve their cash flow. Consider themselves warned.

With that last word, Richard said, Howard stormed out, slamming the mansion's front door. The next sound was the groan of his car tearing away onto Wilshire.

Jerry was woozy picturing Howard's face, and felt worse quickly gaming out the implications. He began picking anxiously at a scab on his arm, thinking the episode could mark the beginning of the end for CM-2. If they couldn't pay off the vendors that they'd taken care of before with Howard's credit lines, how, in God's name, were they supposed to rustle up $50,000 that *he* insisted he was owed? Compounding matters were the holes his exit dug for them. They not only lost their field supervisor, they lost the contractor's license that kept their construction jobs legit.

"Great," Jerry said, puffing air out of his cheeks. "We haven't been this behind the eight ball since we were a two-man shop on Pico Boulevard."

Easy, Richard told him. Easy. Don't confuse a speed bump for a catastrophe. In the down economy, there'd be a glut of available supervisors ravenous for work. As for Howard, Richard speculated that he was saber rattling about siccing lawyers on them. Howard was with the company for only what, seven, eight months? In all likelihood, he would either fade into the woodwork or accept a fraction of what he claimed he was owed. He needed to work again; hell-raisers are picked last.

Richard's cool logic was just what Jerry needed, his words cottony reassurance that they would weather this just fine. As they discussed the companies' post-Howard era, Richard casually remarked that they were better off without him anyway.

"What do you mean?" Jerry asked. "The guy could run a site."

"True," Richard said. "But there are things about Howard that you don't want to know."

"Like what?"

"Stuff."

"Stop being cryptic. You can't leave someone hanging after that comment."

"Well, there's a cruel side to him that can slip out. He's also got secrets from before he was here. I don't know the specifics."

"It's funny you mention secrets, Richard. He told me that you were the one with them."

Richard called that a divide-and-conquer maneuver.

"I don't care if he tried smearing me," he added. "That's wasting our time. What we need to do is concentrate on finding a replacement and keeping our projects moving. Comb your Rolodex. Next year could be gigantic for us."

"I will. But don't you think you should've confided to me earlier that Howard was not the person I thought?"

"Yeah, maybe. I knew you'd overreact."

CHAPTER FOUR
STAIRWAY TO PARTING

NOVEMBER WAS RICHARD'S SEASON of leavings. First, it was CM-2's aggrieved foreman who walked out on him. Now it was someone else professing disgust with his character. Only he was wed to this one, and they'd just commemorated their second anniversary.

Usually in cases of marital strife, it's the husband who packs a suitcase while his estranged spouse stays put in the house, nursing despair. But this case wasn't usual. Neither of the couple publicized their split much beyond family and friends. Their breaking point would've sounded far-fetched, paranoid even, so they candy-coated it as a "mutual separation."

Up until then, it was a satisfying marriage between two people with fun-loving, compatible dispositions. The fifteen-year age gap between them was narrowed by Paige's spunky maturity and Richard's quest to avert tedious middle age. Both could be combustible, obstinate personalities, especially Richard, and they quarreled and made up with welder's heat.

Out in public, they were a smiling postcard for LA's pretty people. Diners at chic restaurants could be excused for comparing them to James Brolin and Cheryl Ladd, all lovey-dovey at a side table, for thinking Neil Simon should've cast them in a rom-com. While neither were Hollywooders, one could argue they were a modern fairy-tale: the aging, eligible bachelor who'd swept a young, country girl off her sandals.

It was the happily-ever-after business where the Richard-Paige storybook lost its binding.

They had met in an unglamorous parking lot at the West Hollywood apartment complex that they unwittingly shared, this around the time Richard and Jerry were logging fourteen-hour days at their start-up. Richard, with his allergy to rules, parked his beige, two-tone Cougar in Paige's designated slot one day and left. When Paige drove up in her yellow Volkswagen Bug with the flower-power stickers on it, she discovered someone claimed her spot. When she could find no hint of the presumptuous jerk outside, she tromped into the building—and right into the jaunty scofflaw.

"What gives you the right to park there?" she asked. "Who do you think you are?"

Richard's reaction spoke volumes. He yanked the woman whose name he just learned into his arms and kissed her. Before the encounter was over, Paige agreed to a date.

Three whirlwind months later, on Halloween, they married at the flamingo-pink Beverly Hills Hotel and honeymooned in Mexico. Paige was twenty-four when she became Mrs. Richard Kasparov. He was pushing forty.

She'd come from a tight-knit, middle-class family in Nevada City, a tiny, former Gold Rush town sixty miles northeast of Sacramento. Hers was a working-class upbringing with three brothers, a bartender father, a waitress mother, and the typical issues nobody called dysfunctional in the seventies. Paige was an athletic kid that her softball teammates nicknamed "slugger." After graduating from state college, she aspired to be a teacher or fashion designer, both areas where she showed talent, and trekked south to LA to develop it.

One area where she already stood out was her head-turning appearance. Even in a land where foxy blondes practically grew on palm trees, Paige's God-given beauty—smoky eyes, sculpted cheekbones, "Charlie's Angels" smile—was the exception, easy fodder for an Eagles's ballad about a ravishing, saucy newcomer wowing the

LA in-crowd. For a small-town girl, she acclimated swiftly to the big city. In her formative years here, she partied through the nights, lived madcap moments, and watched a girlfriend date Rod Stewart; she'd gone out with a hotel scion herself. Meld all that with her Christian roots and she might as well have been a ten-thousand-watt radio signal for Richard, a non-observing Jew drawn to fair-haired shiksas.

If he had soft hands into adulthood, you could trace it to a childhood where physical exertion was not required and chores were just as optional. He'd grown up in upscale West LA, home of pampered children, famous parents, and grand expectations. Beverly Hills's motto—"If you don't like us, we'll buy you out"—carried truck with him. He went to good schools, was given a car, and, like Jerry, showed an early aptitude for drawing. Later he attended the prestigious University of Southern California School of Architecture, though nobody ever recalls spotting a diploma on the wall.

Richard's father was a hard-nosed, bootstrapping businessman disappointed that his son wasn't more athletic rather than being the creative, sensitive type that he was. When he died of a heart attack at a relatively early age, it seared in Richard a fatalistic belief that he might too.

After USC, Richard worked his way up at various space-planning companies, gaining technical experience and learning salesmanship. In was in the mid-1960s, before Vietnam and the counterculture upended society, that he married his first wife, an intelligent, caring, dark-haired secretary from Long Beach. Their union lasted nine tumultuous years, producing an adorable daughter who probably wished her father were more attentive and an ex-wife glad to be rid of him.

Paige, for this reason, was Richard's pearly opportunity to illustrate that he could, at long last, be the stand-up family man whom everyone was waiting to see; that beneath his *bon vivant* panache, underneath those old demons, resided an evolved human. He himself recognized that if he whiffed on a reboot with someone as vibrant and stunning as her, his odds of finding happiness elsewhere would sink into statistical oblivion. To make it work, he heaped pressure on himself to surround his young wife with material comforts.

From their West Hollywood apartment complex southwest of Universal Studios, the newlyweds settled into a house on Wonderland Avenue in Laurel Canyon, a twisty, wooded enclave known as a beehive of singer-songwriters, actors, and Bohemians. Though a fashionable place to live, it happened to be near the site of a quadruple-murder involving ex-porn star John Holmes—bloodshed depicted in the 1997 movie *Boogie Nights*.

Richard and Paige decamped again once Space Matters began turning a profit, this time into a comfortable, two-story home set back from the street on Chandler Avenue in Van Nuys. Their new locale, in the heart of the San Fernando Valley, was more freeway-bisected, crowded, and pedestrian than where they'd been. Still, it offered all the amenities of suburbia: supermarkets, a private high school (Notre Dame) that a future child might attend, banks, a Chinese food "palace," gas stations, a psychic. If you didn't require marble fountains or define your self-worth by zip code, as Richard often did, bliss was attainable in Van Nuys.

Paige's first signpost that domesticity would be more nettlesome than she imagined flared up upon learning that she was pregnant. She was over the moon, ecstatic tears streaming down cheeks. Not Richard. Instead of strutting about Space Matters with a virile grin, doling out the stogies, he was emotionally flat-lined. Paige tried snapping him out of his detachment with big eyes hopeful for mutual excitement. Given Richard's pathological fear of being boxed in, this was a tough sell.

It wasn't surprising then that as Paige's baby bulge grew, her mind drifted. What, she asked herself, would life be like ten years from now in a relationship with a periodic nihilist who gnawed at the chains of commitment like a bleeding wolf in a trap? It sounded exhausting to her, if unsustainable.

The day she was wheeled into the labor room to give birth to her first child stamped an exclamation point on her concerns. On this milestone occasion, Richard was nowhere to be found. Paige, consequently, made her pre-delivery prayer about gender, asking God to send her a daughter. Since she could be a single mother raising this child, a girl seemed easier than a boy who'd course with testosterone and mischief in his teenage years. The moment she laid eyes on her healthy, redheaded little girl, Rebecca, she knew the stars had granted her wish.

Richard reappeared the day after, apologizing for his cowardly absence at the hospital. He told Paige exactly what she wanted to hear: that he was prepared to be a good father if she'd let him. This would also be his last time fleeing into the psychological wilderness, his favorite place to escape when the crush of grown-up duties made him sweat.

"Forgive me," he said. "I'll be different."

Paige agreed to give it a whirl for everyone's sake. She even attempted looking past the trysts she was positive that he'd carried on despite his denials. One of his affairs was with a Space Matters designer named Sharon, whom Paige became suspicious about when she phoned Richard for help after spilling Crazy Glue in an eye. Another time, a pregnant Paige found them nuzzling at Don Ricardo's Mexican restaurant. She threw a chair at Richard but missed.

With their new understanding, though, their marriage flourished as never before. There was a baby in the house, a wife back to her svelte, pre-pregnancy 114 pounds, and, most fundamentally, a husband acting like his scoundrel days were retired.

In the end, it would be others looming about that'd be too much for Paige to absolve.

•••

THE CALLS BEGAN IN the heat of the summer, not long after they arranged all the furniture. As soon as Richard drove off to work at Space Matters, usually in the 9:00 a.m. to 10:00 a.m. range, the same creditor rang the house phone over and over. Though the man nicknamed Pat was calling *about* Richard, it was actually Paige he sought as the lady of the house. His theme never varied: her husband owed him thousands of dollars from a side business venture, and she needed to shake common sense into him to make him honor it.

For Paige, it wasn't so much someone claiming Richard was stiffing them—because who knew how many debts he had accumulated before he met her, or in deal-cutting sessions away from Fremont Place? It was the disturbing regularity by which Pat phoned that frightened her.

"Richard owes me," he'd say. "Make him pay."

Click.

When no money was transacted, Pat's cadence grew icier.

"He better pay me, Paige, or there's *going* to be a problem."

She generally said little back. Judging by the timing of the calls, she could have sworn Pat deployed a spy outside to monitor their driveway. Some days only seconds ticked by from the moment Richard's Cougar backed out to the phone jangling. When Paige scanned the block for a beady-eyed accomplice watching them, all she saw were the typical morning pulses of suburbia: moms in station wagons, gardeners pushing lawnmowers. Goosebumps dotted her arms.

Even so, she tried ignoring the calls, sometimes plugging her ears when the phone rang. Richard said Pat was practicing the art of nuisance-making to collect pennies on the dollar. He foresaw that Pat would tucker out, maybe take this loan-shark shtick elsewhere. Yet the calls persisted, and with them Paige's hope that the pressure campaign would magically stop. What, she asked Richard, if they escalated from daily harassment to direct confrontation?

In the same phlegmatic tone he rolled out with Jerry, he reassured her that he'd never permit that to occur. Things curdled between Pat and him, and now Pat was attempting to squeeze him by exaggerating what he was due. In a show of good faith that he would resolve his debt, Richard lent him their Datsun 280-Z, the Japanese sports car that he originally purchased for Paige to drive. Pat, though, was never satisfied. Now he grumbled that Richard bamboozled him a second time by ceasing payments on the car; this prompted the bank that financed it to threaten repossessing the vehicle unless payments resumed.

Whether that was true or a fabrication to turbo-charge Howard's bluster, Richard did not distinguish. And why should he? To him, Pat was little more than a parasite who fed off its host until it was hollowed out. He regretted having any professional contact with him.

Richard happened to be there the next time Pat called. He snagged the receiver, walked into the kitchen, and barked at his creditor for ten minutes for scaring his wife on a subject that didn't involve her. After chewing him out and hanging up, Richard comforted Paige that Pat got the message. Yeah, he'd got it all right. Pat waited two days to phone Paige to say that her spouse was the vermin. The contempt started with him.

The following morning over breakfast, it was Paige this time doing the yelling. Pat's calls were poisoning the house.

"Get him out of our lives!" she screamed. "You hear me? *Out of our lives!*"

Her outburst ricocheted off the walls without dislodging Richard's hardheaded stance. He believed that Paige was exaggerating the threat—and underestimating the effect of post-childbirth hormones on her disposition.

An afternoon months later would lay waste to that assumption.

•••

ISABEL'S EYES WERE ALWAYS sensitive to shadows. The flicker of movement near the ground-floor window was no exception for the Guatemalan housekeeper who watched Richard and Paige's baby when they were gone. Curious about the origin of whatever interrupted the afternoon sunlight—a skittering cloud, a crow, a low-flying Cessna en route to Van Nuys airport—the squat, middle-aged woman stopped dusting near the bar to pinpoint it.

When she straightened up to get a clear view, a pit opened up in her gut. The shade passing across the window was a man—a man skulking up the exterior stairs connecting the backyard to the second-floor patio. In a room attached to it was the most precious thing in the house: her employer's infant.

The duster plopped out of Isabel's palm as she galloped up the inner staircase. She ran into the master bedroom, thankful to see no sign of the intruder. Then she jogged into the nursery, even more thankful to see Rebecca asleep in her crib.

¡Gracias a Dios!

When she looked out the window, she realized her gratitude was premature. Standing on the landing was a muscular, light-haired man in dark clothing. He was trying to break in. And making progress at it.

One of his hands gripped the handle of the sliding-glass door, trying to jimmy it open over its claw-like metal latch. The other fiddled with the metal frame keeping it locked.

From Isabel's lungs came a bloodcurdling shriek. The trespasser snapped his head up to determine its source while his hands stayed busy. Isabel's terror lifted up again after that. The man didn't scamper off the premises like a cat burglar restricting himself to unoccupied homes. The glass between them must've seemed as hardy as cellophane.

Her eyes swept the nursery for anything to weaponize, seeing nothing useful. What was she supposed to do if he wormed inside: club him over the head with the diaper-changing table? They were feet apart, the housekeeper and the man loudly jiggling the door. Instinct told Isabel it was the child he was after.

Just when she might've been tempted to grab Rebecca and sprint out the front door, she spotted something upright in a corner. The wooden broomstick handle about four inches long and a half-inch in diameter was missing its straw whisks. Intentionally. When Richard and Paige were away overnight, they would position the cylinder in the door track as a homemade burglary deterrent.

In one blurry motion, the chocolate-skinned nanny snatched the pole, dropped it into the slot, and listened to its hollow thump on the metal. Sliding the door was impossible now.

The question was what the would-be-kidnapper would do. If he were tenacious, he could wrap a hand in his jacket and punch the glass. Or just shatter it with a hard kick. He would be in the baby's room before all the shards settled. He'd then be off with the child, after doling out punishment to her.

For a few more chest-pounding seconds, Isabel waited for his choice: abduction or withdrawal. To her vast surprise, he chose to go, backing away from the immovable door and leaving the same way that he entered: the stairs.

When Paige arrived home from her Ventura Boulevard interior-design shop, Isabel recounted the entire, harrowing incident using choppy English and air-slashing hands. Every detail made a teary Paige clutch Rebecca closer. She and Isabel went around the house, double-checking that all the doors were locked and windows latched. Richard, once he got home from Space Matters, barely gulped a breath before being confronted by a fusillade of questions from his shaken wife. Should they contact a security company to install a burglar alarm? File a police report? Take other precautions?

Richard, again playing the unflappable head of household, tried talking reason to her. He said it was premature to be overly spooked about this, and that the intruder was unlikely to press his luck in a return visit. His guess: the man was a drug addict searching for a purse or jewelry to steal to feed his habit. Paige pushed back on the theory. If he were a dopamine-starved opportunist, why did he keep trying to bust in after noticing Isabel? Whatever Richard told her wasn't enough, for she slept that evening with Rebecca in her arms.

Shortly before Thanksgiving, feeling a red line crossed, Paige made the declaration that floored Richard. The next time the phone rang he'd have to answer it. She was pushing the ejection button on their marriage and taking Rebecca to someplace where they felt safe.

CHAPTER FIVE
DWEEB AT THE POLO LOUNGE

WEEKS LATER, WHEN SHE pressed Jerry's doorbell, the once hardpack ground beneath Paige's feet was actively crumbling. In leaving Richard, she vacated a cozy home, a two-income lifestyle, and regular daycare, all this before they even planted roots in Van Nuys. With no place to go, she beseeched friends for any empty space they could offer her and the baby. Money tight, she'd also reverted to subsisting on Kraft macaroni and cheese, her old college staple.

About Paige's only blessing was not trembling when the phone rang, but that would fade too.

Landing on Jerry's doorstep, on the western flank of the San Fernando Valley, was an ironic humiliation for her. Before they'd split, she and Richard snickered privately about Jerry, as if they were popular high school kids ridiculing the class nerd. They mocked him as a spaz and a twerp, a curly-haired weasel they struggled to be around for more than twenty minutes at a clip. They likened his habit of rubbing his palms together when he was antsy or about to close a deal to a praying mantis.

At Space Matters, there existed two loosely defined camps loyal to different bosses. Some on staff, knowing little about Jerry's upside-down childhood, or the corporate oppression he endured out of school, perceived him as Paige did: a contract-hungry schemer with more responsibility than he could handle. A Uriah Heep with an art degree. The more reserved, less flashy employees aligned themselves to

Jerry. They saw in his facility for mathematics, ergonomics, and design glimmers of a wunderkind who, as a brainteaser, could've packed a hundred cars into a garage designed for seventy. Some believed he should be solving payload questions for NASA or free-associating the next Rubik's Cube. For them, flamboyant Richard was the cagey one whose word you best not take at face value.

A planner once seduced by Richard's "extraordinary" abilities was burned by that. This planner, who'd enjoyed getting high with Richard listening to Tangerine Dream, a German electronic music band, did something inadvisable. He told Richard that he and his wife would be attending an upcoming Stevie Wonder concert in Long Beach. Richard, ever trying to play Johnny on the spot, insisted he could get them better seats through "a ticket connection." When he came up embarrassingly empty-handed, he promised to treat them to a hotel room near the venue. Checking in there, they were tickled to see he'd sent them a bottle of champagne. At checkout, however, this planner could've kicked himself for trusting Richard, who prepaid nothing.

For all these divergent views of them, for all the gibes spoken at home, Richard and Jerry had produced a robust alchemy together in a hotly competitive field. They didn't squabble in front of the staff. Didn't play politics. Didn't snipe. They grew the business up from nothing as Young Turks, landing deals that surprised the priggish architectural establishment. With Jerry's eagle eye for efficiencies and Richard's skill for presentation, their strengths complemented each other like a pair of odd-couple musicians able to churn out catchy tunes.

Paige, after once batting her eyes coquettishly at Richard in public, now stood on a doorstep in Northridge poised to forge a détente with Jerry, someone she knew only through shallow impressions and catty epithets. Economic circumstances had cornered her, so she phoned him, saying he'd want to hear what she had to say in person because it was urgent—and disturbing.

Jerry invited her in, studying Paige's sunken, rawboned face. It was the worst he'd ever seen her, far different than her appearance at a recent birthday here just after he and Tammy moved in. As before, there were few window coverings or decorative flourishes because all the Schneiderman's money went into acquiring the property. The clapboard tract home was the largest model on its twisting block, a white-painted, green-trimmed number with wood columns and a picket fence outside. It contained five bedrooms, a master suite, a bonus room, a three-car garage, excellent natural light, a pool, and an oversized television antenna. While no pre-McMansion, the residence shouted Yuppie mobility.

Paige, a wad of crumpled tissues in her sweater pocket, trailed Jerry into the egg-white kitchen, where Tammy was slicing the crust from a peanut-butter-and jelly sandwich and brewing coffee. She motioned them to sit down at the table so Paige could elaborate on the matter she asserted couldn't wait. Jerry steered her to a chair, feeling all thumbs. The closest contact he experienced with her was a glancing, courtesy kiss. The partners and their spouses, outwardly warm to one another but never truly close, had only socialized twice before. Once was on a trip to a Medieval Renaissance Faire where Jerry wore passé bellbottoms, the other a "Remember the Alamo"-themed party thrown by the owners of that eyesore Victorian.

Jerry always conceived of her marriage to Richard as a contemporary *My Fair Lady*, him the older, professorial Henry Higgins character, her unsophisticated Eliza Doolittle. Under Richard's wing, Paige evolved from wearing hot pants and ponytails to shopping at Beverly Hills clothiers like Alan Austin; from driving a hippy-ish VW bug to a polished Audi.

From her chair, Paige let out a sob, sniffled into her tissue, plopping her head into her hands. It was like seeing the disintegration of a former Miss America after being stripped of her crown. Tammy handed them coffee, and everyone took sips. In a minute, shaky-voiced Paige explained her dilemma. Richard's ongoing refusal to pay the majority of the $265-a-month, court-ordered child support shoved her to the brink of destitution. Nearly broke, she'd been evicted from the first place she leased after the breakup and moved in with the baby to a small rental close to them; the owner, the husband of a girlfriend, mercifully gave her discounted rent. Should that arrangement fold, Paige said she would be plum out of Plan Bs in LA and return to Northern California before malnutrition set in.

According to her, Richard's actions were fueled not by principle or his own budgetary woes. He dug in his heels in hot spite because of her temerity to walk out on him.

Jerry was in his office, forested in haphazard piles of blueprints and paperwork, when Paige called to arrange this meeting. To get him to agree to it, she downplayed her domestic troubles and uttered five words that Jerry was loath to hear.

"Richard is stealing from you," she said, teary-voiced.

Stealing? His mind peeled away from his body. He'd been thrown off a roof onto a block of ice. If Paige was right, the hunch he didn't want to accept was accurate. His partner, mentor, and supposed friend was a traitor dabbed in sandalwood cologne.

Watch him…there's more than one Richard in Richard, Howard said.

Since hearing Paige's bombshell sentence, Jerry was a wreck, sleepwalking through his days, repulsed by food, berating himself for naivete. Inquiries by a few CM-2 clients curious about why Richard altered how he billed them should've galvanized Jerry to action. But he stayed moored in fantasyland, telling himself the irreconcilable accounting was a mistake. Now that he knew otherwise, there was no room for self-pity. He needed to grasp the mechanics and scope of Richard's deceptions. If it was pervasive, it could be a neutron bomb that bankrupted Space Matters and its spinoffs, polluted his own reputation, and jettisoned his guiltless staff into the unemployment line during a bleak job market.

"Tell me everything," Jerry said to Paige. Give him a path.

At wit's end, she began, but she omitted two pieces of information about why her home was now too treacherous for her to continue living in: Pat's relentless calls about Richard's side debt, and the intruder on the balcony after her daughter. This would come back to haunt many.

Paige said she learned about what Richard was up to when she'd snuck back into the house to collect more of her and Rebecca's possessions for the long haul. On her way out, she gave into temptation to snoop. Rooting through Richard's desk, scouring for nothing in particular, she noticed a bulging dossier at the back of a drawer. She fished it out, opening it in her lap. It was tantamount to a swindler's journal. Inside were copies of checks for tens of thousands of dollars made out to him personally by CM-2 clients and others whose names she didn't recognize. On the note line of the checks were words like "home remodeling" and "redesign." Next to each invoice amount in the ledger was a coded series of numbers and letters. Richard's deviousness was well organized.

Jerry asked Paige to repeat what she uncovered, psychologically wounding as it was to hear again. If what she was describing was accurate, Richard's shenanigans were there all along in the bookkeeping muddle. He'd over-ordered—on CM-2's tab—lumber, drywall, vinyl, metal studs, paint, and whatnot, using some for legitimate purposes, the rest for illegitimate ones generating him pure profit. Then he lied about it. Richard's criminal *coup de grace*: having clients write checks to him or the outfit he never told Jerry he was starting, Kasparov & Company.

Listening to her reveal this last insult, Jerry felt not so much queasy as flush. The man who gushed about all those "wonderful things" they would accomplish at Don Ricardo's Mexican restaurant was operating a shadow business primed with stolen inventory. Their partnership was a mirage, a con. Richard was no different than others who'd regarded Jerry as a nebbish squirt from North Hollywood upon whom they could feather their nests.

At that kitchen table ringed with three twenty-somethings, Jerry presided, if shakily, by outlining the obvious counterattack to turn Richard's duplicity against him. It was an unsavory request with noble goals. Paige needed to sneak back into the house to grab the file so they could Xerox it and use it as leverage to compel Richard to confess to Jerry and pay the child support Paige deserved. After they copied the ledger's contents, she'd return it to Richard's desk without him being any wiser.

If he somehow caught wind beforehand, Jerry guessed that he'd destroy the incriminating paper trail. They needed to grab it now. Like today.

Paige, crying again, listened to Jerry explain how Richard's secret ledger was *their* secret weapon. She told him that she understood that, but she wasn't sure that she could go through with it. She'd be crossing a Rubicon. She'd be acting seditiously with the person to whom she'd vowed "I do." She'd be even more of a rat, and in tandem with someone she'd once disparaged as "a weasel."

Tammy, watching Paige at war with herself, elbowed Jerry in a fashion that communicated he needed to be more sensitive to her plight. As a young mother, she empathized with Paige's divided loyalties making her choose between feeding her daughter and sticking it to that little girl's father. As Jerry's wife, she needed him to do whatever it took to preserve their future, a future entwined with Space Matters.

Resetting himself, Jerry looked Paige square in the eye to reiterate that Richard was responsible for putting them in a position of getting justice by clandestine means. Even under pressure, Paige still wavered with cold feet. Whatever Richard's dastardly acts, she acknowledged that her love for him still blazed. Another thing left unsaid by her: the prospect of reentering the house, after the terrifying things that'd happened in there, would be a white-knuckle challenge.

After more tense back and forth, Paige said "fine" in a voice of choking resignation. She'd do it. Jerry grinned ruefully, which was better than slumping despondently in his chair. Tammy, the quick-minded Midwesterner who spoke at a kinetic speed, who believed good outweighed evil in the world, didn't bother asking if anyone wanted coffee refills. They'd execute Operation Bust Richard that afternoon while he was tied up in meetings.

Using her house key, Paige beelined to his desk. In and out in a jiffy, she wedged the Manila folder with the ledger inside under her arm and jumped into her car. A few minutes later she met Jerry and Tammy at the prearranged site: a Ralphs supermarket parking lot near the house. Next door to it was a copy shop. Paige and Tammy chatted about their children while Jerry perspired near the droning Xerox machine. What were the two mothers supposed to gab about: whether either of them had seen *Grease*, or if Tammy knew a good divorce lawyer?

Jerry jogged out when he was done, handing the original folder to Paige. He told her that when he was ready to spring the evidence on Richard, he would give her a heads-up so she could take the findings to court. Paige nodded she understood and drove back to return the papers with a bunched expression.

•••

THE DOORMAN IN THE burgundy polyester uniform at the front of the Beverly Hills Hotel greeted Jerry with a practiced nod, military crisp. You needed to watch closely for the once-over that he performed after, as if Jerry was a four-eyed poindexter crashing the bitchin' people's ball.

Jerry maintained his smile, despite the rush of self-consciousness he felt in these rarefied environs. It was time to stop letting strangers mistake his social awkwardness for meekness.

"Welcome to the Beverly Hills Hotel," the doorman said, reaching for the ornate door handle. "Your first time here, sir?"

"Hardly," Jerry said, straightening the unobliging collar of his best suit.

He had attended a pair of weddings here: his sister's and Richard's. He'd even treated a high-rolling client to a meal at the celebrity-frequented spot.

"Very good, sir. I assume, then, you remember the way to the hostess station."

"Of course."

Jerry wanted to tell the acned punk in epaulets to take a flying leap for his patronizing comment. By then, the doorman would've stopped caring anyway. He was toadying over the arrival of an actor whose presence no one questioned.

A hostess in a billowy dress escorted Jerry to the table he had requested in advance. He was seated just inside the glass walls from the garden patio, the sun glistening off the eye-blinding silverware. It was 1:08 p.m., and the place was buzzing with agents, producers, insurance-brokers-to-the-stars, coke-dealers-to-the-famous, fashion photographers, and perhaps a Laker or two. Outside, the parking lot was Germany on parade, jam-packed with BMWs, Mercedes-Benzes, and Audis. Indoors, the menu was Continental down to the pricy, exquisitely prepared selections served on monogrammed accoutrements.

Everyone in LA knew the grub was a fig leaf for the Polo Lounge's true nutritional value: just being seen at the Polo Lounge.

Jerry, best he could, tried drowning out the room's husky laughs and tittering voices while he rehearsed his role in the upcoming theatrics. He mentally recited his lines while quaffing three glasses of iced tea to quench a nervous thirst. A hullabaloo at the table behind him over who botched some hotshot's pâté was empty noise. He was stuck in his own head when Benjamin Wynn, his business attorney, tapped him on the shoulder.

"Finally," Jerry said, "a friendly face. Iced tea?"

Benjamin was a rangy, skeletal man with dog-legged sideburns that lent him the appearance of Ichabod Crane in a tailored suit. Though only thirty-two, his regal nose, shoulder dandruff drifts, and intellectual deportment made him look fifty. Depending on how this gambit went, the two would later either celebrate triumph or head downtown to the District Attorney's office to press fraud and embezzlement charges against Richard. Jerry, remembering Paige's swollen face that day at his kitchen table, wasn't sure how Richard tolerated mirrors. He and Benjamin practiced another dry run before the main act.

Until today, Jerry never would've been able to muster the spine to lure Richard into a trap, particularly here. But this was about the New Jerry refusing to be anyone's pawn anymore. This was about not darting to the men's room to alleviate intestinal cramps. Richard, it was now obvious, divided people into three finite categories: those he could suck up to for business and social climbing, those so mesmerized by his charms they forgave his transgressions, and everybody else. Like disposable Jerry.

Richard's infectious laugh heralded his arrival. Somebody from a table close to the entrance must've spotted him and waved him over for a quick hello. The Polo Lounge was his natural habitat, so it was understandable. He grew up around West LA kids whose parents worked in the movie industry, high-end real estate, and other top-tax-bracket professions, then mixed with them as an adult. He spoke their language. Shopped at the same posh retailers. Ingested the same drugs. Where he diverged with them was in his laggard economic station. Here he was nearing forty, a non-millionaire living in the bourgeoisie San Fernando Valley, while classmates and old chums resided in marble-and-wainscot mansions on the affluent side of the San Diego (405) Freeway. Though some were trust-fund babies, others weren't, and this resentment of underachieving must've tempted him into mendacious spaces to compensate.

Ever the salesman, he walked up to Jerry in a tan suit and toothy smile, as if he just rolled out of hedge-happy Bel-Air. Their immaculate table was set with more forks and glasses than there were practical uses. A matronly woman over-spritzed with Chanel at a nearby table ogled the man half an hour late to this working lunch.

Richard shook hands with Jerry's tablemate, whom Jerry introduced as a property owner soliciting space-planning bids. He apologized for being behind schedule, fabricating another baroque lie about how he'd been waylaid at the office; Jerry and Benjamin pretended they believed him.

"You won't believe this happened," he said. "As I was getting ready to leave..."

Seamlessly, Richard transitioned into a sales pitch about what Space Matters could do for Benjamin. Near the end of his remarks, he put a bow on the presentation with his hallmark move. He ripped off a sheaf of graph paper and sketched a rendition of the plan they recently composed for another client, doing it upside down so Benjamin could study it without having to crane his neck.

What a talent, Jerry thought. *And what a waste.*

When he was done drawing, Richard handed Benjamin his business card, asking him to shoot off any questions. Benjamin answered he had none, and Richard reclined in his chair, acting like he'd bagged another sale.

But Benjamin was done with the charade. He dipped his hand into his briefcase and fished out a multi-page document stapled onto a blue backing.

"Richard," he said. "It's my turn to show you some papers."

He passed them over the table to Richard, who grasped them with a quizzical brow.

"You see, I'm Jerry's personal lawyer, and *you've* just been served."

Richard's body language spoke the dialect of someone who realized they'd walked into a cage of their own making. He puckered his mouth, then contorted his upper body sideways to reduce his surface exposure. At that fraught moment, the waitress glided over to the table to see if everybody had picked out what they wanted. Richard, gobsmacked, mistakenly placed the threatened lawsuit, not his menu, onto the tray. The waitress glanced at the papers with a bemused expression. It would've been hilarious in a different situation.

"What's this?" she said with a smirk, handing Richard back his formal notice of litigation. "Sir, I think it belongs to you. I just need your menu if you know what you'd like."

Richard replied that he would be skipping an entree. Jerry and Benjamin were hungrier. They ordered and the waitress flitted off.

"You better take this seriously," Benjamin said. "When you read through the entire suit, you'll see we've attached your assets, including your place in Van Nuys. The smart move would be for you to resolve this immediately, without a lawsuit, by giving up your share of the companies to Jerry. If you don't, the consequences will be devastating. Have I made myself understood?"

Richard mumbled to Benjamin that he did.

"I'm sorry it came to this," Jerry added. "But I'm mostly sorry you did this to me."

The dialogue ground to a screeching halt. What else was there to say? From the forensic sleuthing that Jerry and Benjamin completed since Paige's revelation, they had compiled demonstrable proof that Richard stole from the get-go. On the same August day that they filed the CM-2 "Doing-Business-As" form with the county, Richard filed a similar form for Kasparov & Company. His whole luxury-home-remodeling proposition was a swindle by any other name.

Richard, sidelining the silver tongue that endlessly bailed him out, was dazed. He didn't stomp out in protest, holler that Jerry mischaracterized his actions, or try concocting a preposterous explanation to wiggle free. He sat there in silence for a few minutes until he declared he needed to go like someone remembering they left the gas stove on at home. When he lumbered out of the Polo Lounge, there was no slowing to talk to any old pals. The show was over.

Afterward, Jerry and Benjamin stayed for lunch at the fancy table set for three. Once the plates were cleared, the two placed imaginary bets on Richard's next move. Benjamin believed he would buckle; Jerry wasn't sure he'd acquiesce without resistance, believing that a lawsuit might be necessary. Around 3:00 p.m., Benjamin congratulated Jerry for his bravery and departed for his Westwood office. Jerry remained, saying he'd pay the tab.

Crisscrossing emotions ping-ponged through him sitting alone in the window seat: adrenaline for his tactical victory, apprehension about what tomorrow would bring, pangs of wistfulness for what was lost. He decided he'd hang around the Polo Lounge status junkies longer to observe the scene. He'd be useless at the mansion the rest of the afternoon anyway.

Bill paid, he removed his suit jacket and began strolling along the Beverly Hill Hotel's botanical pathways fragrant with pink cherry blossoms. Maybe it was their sweet scent, but his history with Richard came whistling back.

At their inception three years earlier, they'd worked out of a spartan, one-room office in the nine-thousand block of Pico Boulevard. Its contents: two drafting desks, a pair of chairs, and nothing for guests. To distinguish themselves from competitors, they branded themselves the "fastest space planners in town," gunslingers with a T square, if you will. They'd meet prospective clients during the day and draw all night to impress them. With little money for rent, they bartered by sketching designs for the landlord's other spaces. Wearying as those days of five o'clock shadows and too much coffee (and other stimulants) were, they were equally gratifying as down payments on bigger dreams.

Now that those were kablooey, Jerry could only ask *why* Richard diverted close to $150,000; he could only surmise *where* the money went, and whether Richard was really that narcissistic or simply incapable of corralling his greed; and *what* his motivation was for stealing. Was it to cocoon Paige in a sapphire lifestyle so she'd avert her eyes from younger men or richer gentlemen, or something else buried inside him?

That Richard betrayed him knowing the gamble Jerry took to give Space Matters a running start only pushed the dagger deeper.

On the threshold of quitting his last corporate job to become his own boss, Jerry had fused craftiness with risk. One by one, he took his twenty or so clients to lunch. With puppy-dog eyes, he sought their opinions about whether he should he stay in his thankless position there or venture out on his own. The property owners, many of them wrinkly curmudgeons who scraped for every square foot in their portfolio, were flattered that Jerry treasured what they said. Which he did—as well as knowing that some egos needed to be stroked. It was the brashest deed an introvert like him ever devised.

Predictably, Jerry's now ex-boss was apoplectic hearing that his former employee had poached fifteen clients. On a day in April 1976—the same day Jerry married Tammy and he and Richard formally launched Space Matters—this man phoned Jerry at his honeymoon suite at the Plaza Hotel in New York. Over the line, he shouted at eardrum-bleeding levels. He threatened to sue Jerry, maybe even kill him. Blackballing him from the industry would be going too soft. Yet Jerry didn't cower. People with aces in the hole don't need to.

Through the grapevine, he knew that one of Tammy's cousins sublet an apartment to the concubine of his very married former supervisor. When he got his mistress pregnant, he bribed her into undergoing an abortion by purchasing her a new BMW, which he financed through a kickback from a colleague. So, after he railed at Jerry, calling him an "ungrateful punk" who would pay for his sneaky deed, Jerry calmly mentioned the woman and shady BMW. That stopped the yelling. The man knew he'd been checkmated.

Jerry now circled round on the path back toward the Polo Lounge. He came upon a tinted window reflecting his image. It struck him that he looked older, less unblemished, perhaps stronger. Confronting Richard, the blow-dried snake in the grass, illustrated he could go this alone. Walking out to his car that afternoon, somehow upbeat, he persuaded himself his crucible was over.

•••

NEARING FIFTY, HOWARD SAW no use in moral victories like Jerry, nor any benefit to "free himself from the past" like Richard once attempted through the trendy Human Potential Movement. Given a coupon to an "est" seminar sweeping LA, he would've trashed it. His priority was clambering out of the financial sinkhole in which those users at Space Matters shoved him.

By January 1979, two months after he quit, Howard made good on his pledge to unleash hell on his former employers. His attack-dog lawyers filed mechanic liens against every CM-2 jobsite to put their knees on the company's throat. Still, they agreed to settlement talks, meaning that Jerry and Benjamin planted themselves across a conference-room table from Howard at the offices of Marc Frankel and Ronald Allen. It was on a fleabag stretch of Beverly Boulevard north of downtown as nasty as them.

Allen, a bullnecked, florid figure in a pinstriped suit, took the lead trying to browbeat Jerry into submission. In a bombastic voice meant to cow the youngest one in the room, Allen presented an ultimatum: either Jerry resolve their client's $50,000 debt, five grand more than he originally demanded, or they'd napalm him with a lawsuit salted with embarrassing details.

Jerry could just about detect black smoke coiling from Howard's ears whenever his representatives explained the damage, both specific and reputational, that Richard inflicted on Howard's credit lines by plundering them. Though Howard kept his lip buttoned most of the time here, he did volunteer one insight. He didn't bust his hump all these years in construction to be flimflammed by a charismatic "liar and thief."

Jerry couldn't wait to get away from these heavy-handed, bumptious lawyers. But he learned some eye-opening details about the extent of his ex-partner's six-figure larceny. And, with his own lawsuit against Richard filed, it was better to mediate this case than face a two-front legal battle. With his consent, Benjamin offered a compromise: if Howard rescinded the liens, Jerry would sign over to him the entire interest in CM-2, giving Howard a whole company for his mistreatment. Ever since he allowed Richard to talk him into home remodeling, nothing was the same. Howard's men quickly shot down the proposal, enjoying saying no. Their client wanted money, not a fraud-riddled firm on life support. Expect a lawsuit, they said.

Coinciding with this was Howard's decision to mail to Jerry at Space Matters and his wife in Northridge a personal letter that read more like a jeremiad. In it, he expressed outrage that nobody returned the personal possessions he left at the company when he walked out in a huff: his IBM typewriter, three table-model adding machines, four handheld calculators, a printout calculator, and, oddly enough for a workplace, a multi-piece stereo system. In biting sentences dripping in victimhood, he also insisted somebody get busy reversing his financial ruin.

> *Dear Jerry,*
>
> *...I feel quite confident that your answer to this situation will be...,* *'I am very sorry, Howard, but I do not know anything about it.' Well, good, old, honest Jerry, please don't give me anymore of your bullshit. At one time I went for [it] when you were telling me about your partner, Richard Kasparov. I even agreed with you regarding his [shady] character and business practices...I want you to pay attention to everything I am going to say at this point. Somewhere along the way you developed the opinion that I just fell off the pumpkin truck... Let me inform you, Jerry, that I have more time in the pay line than you have in the chow line. And I will be damned and go to Hell before I will stand like a tall dog and let you or members of your firm screw us. That, my old friend, you can bet on... At the present time my wife is suffering very much, and is under the care of a doctor because of the nervous condition she is under. We are still receiving threatening calls and letters resulting from your [companies'] failure to pay the material bills. I would appreciate you starting to work and getting some correspondence to those people involved. I would suggest that you do this very quickly...so there is no question that you are at least making an attempt to cooperate and resolve this fucking mess you have gotten into. I will tell you one more time, Jerry, to get off your ass and get something done... Since my wife is now [affected], I do not like [this] at all.*
>
> *Very truly yours,*
> *Howard L. Garrett*

Legal bullying aside, Jerry felt awful about the stress that Howard's words laid bare. There *were* grounds for him to lash out about, what with creditors hounding him for debts he didn't rack up, an anxious wife, and missing stuff he'd worked hard to earn. Richard could've easily returned those items; it would've required only stuffing a couple of boxes and a quick phone call to a delivery company. But Richard never missed an opportunity to be punitive to someone who he felt insulted or deserted by, or who questioned him. No wonder Howard was acting like a violin string perilously close to snapping.

Mercifully, without any warning, Howard's zeal to bleed Jerry into concessions stopped in its tracks. After weeks of "admit this, stipulate that," his lawyers communicated they were ending their scorched-earth strategy because Howard directed them to settle the dispute for a paltry $7,000. He was also dropping his contention, flimsy as it was, that his consent to put up his valuable contractor's license entitled him to a fat cut of whatever CM-2 was worth, post red ink.

Jerry, by agreeing to the deal he assumed was cut because Richard was Howard's primary financial target, had survived this great unraveling, the one that began with Howard's exit and ended with the revelation of Richard's secret ledger. There were still hotspot fires to douse that Richard's chicanery started with those scam remodels, but at least Space Matters was standing above the embers.

CHAPTER SIX
PAT'S BRIGHT IDEA

AMONG THE INGENIOUS NEW products of 1979 blitzing into the American marketplace were some culture-shifters: the Sony Walkman (one-shade: banana yellow), the McDonald's Happy Meal, and Atari's "Asteroid" video game. On deck were voicemail and personal computers.

While certainly no technologist, the businessman nicknamed Pat hungered to add his contribution. It just wouldn't be encased in plastics or cardboard. It would be jacketed in throwback metal.

His experimental incubator to gauge his concept's real-world value rested on the sinewy shoulders of an unlikely individual. Pat and Robert "Frenchy" Gaines Freeman had made acquaintances in a confined venue where innovation took a backseat to the indelicacies of incarceration. Pat then was in the San Bernardino jail on a felony charge, Robert on a more pedestrian burglary. A year-plus later Pat was exonerated, but Robert was back behind bars after another arrest. That's when Robert's wife, Elena, phoned Pat seeking a holiday-time kindness: would he, in this time of giving, post her husband's $3,000 bail so the couple could spend Christmas together? They'd reimburse him once they weren't counting their pennies.

Pat answered that she'd come to the right place. Wish granted. Off he motored, a good Samaritan with a cigarette between his teeth and an entrepreneurial vision crystallizing by the freeway mile.

No traditional headhunter would've given someone with Robert's credentials—a criminal record, a heroin addiction he was struggling to kick, and few marketable skills—so much as a glance. But where others saw degenerate loser, Pat saw potential in the bluff thirty-six-year-old who never held down anything approaching gainful employment. For him, Robert's chiseled physique (from prison weightlifting), bisexual proclivities, Aryan Brotherhood ties, and second-story skills were assets to mold or, should things get hairy, railroad him. In Pat's cold-eyed, business calculation, he was the ideal underling—assuming he'd take the job.

In recruitment, Pat provided sweeteners. He drove Robert, free of charge, to San Francisco so he could open presents under the tree. Before departing, he tossed him a surprise: the keys of the car he'd taken him in—a metallic blue, 1975 El Camino, which Pat cherried-up with a white camper shell and chrome-magnesium wheels.

"This is yours," he said. "Do with it as you want. But when I tell you I need it, I want it back immediately, okay, like that day."

"Understood," Robert said. And, "God bless you!"

If he didn't know it then, he would soon: Pat's bigheartedness implied reciprocity. A few days after Christmas, he instructed Robert to return the El Camino to Southern California in order for him to hear out Pat's exploratory-business proposal. Four hundred miles later, Robert pulled up, saying he was all ears to the man he hoped would continue doling out the freebies.

Pat began leaking the outlines of his bright idea while driving his guest around the festive wreaths and oversized candy canes arrayed on Pasadena's retail showcase, Lake Avenue. He divulged more at his apartment on Del Mar Avenue, which was just south of where flower-bedecked floats in the Tournament of Roses Parade would roll on New Year's Day. (This year's theme was especially escapist for America's surly mood: "Our Wonderful, Wonderful World of Sports.") Pat sprinkled additional details as they browsed a liquor store for refreshments.

After this job pitch, Pat asked Robert whether he was interested. It paid $5,000, and he was keen to get started. Robert's answer was disappointingly ambiguous. As eager as he was to repay Pat's generosity, and to collect the fat salary the man was dangling, he had reservations. The position required a skill set that surpassed his current abilities and experience. Wasn't there someone else better qualified than him?

"No," Pat said. "If you're as grateful as you contend, you'll sign up." He'd train him.

Robert played Pat's enlistment coyly, saying he needed to discuss the proposition with his wife in the Bay Area. Please do, Pat replied; happy wife, happy life. As a bonus, Pat let him take the El Camino, this time with his Mobil gas card. But Robert's phone started ringing too and didn't stop. In the calls, Pat reiterated that he needed an answer; all this largesse was transactional. Message received, Robert responded, figuring he could always wiggle out of the box Pat was trying to squeeze him into—after he milked Pat for more. For now, he gave him what he yearned to hear.

Yes, he'd be the contract assassin in this budding murder-for-profit corporation.

Now that they'd formalized a professional relationship, how should he refer to him: boss, mister, something else? Pat, Robert knew, was a nickname that came and went. Pat instructed him to use the old-fashioned name the construction world knew him by.

Howard is fine, he told him. Just say it discreetly.

•••

ON REFLECTION, HE REALLY owed the brain trust at Fremont Avenue his everlasting gratitude for awakening him to the possible, to lush opportunity lodged into certain moments. Specifically, they'd taught him that you should snatch the reins of your own destiny before someone else hijacked it. If Jerry and Richard hadn't misused his contractor's license—or drown him in debt, or taint his credit, or send his wife into the emotional gutter—who knows if this insight would've dawned on him before he was too old to commoditize it? By fleecing him for cash as they did, they lit a fire in his belly to stop allowing LA's top-down real-estate culture to treat him like so much Styrofoam. He was done being a tool-belt Joe Everyman who devoted himself to the vaporous promise of upward mobility. Done with skimpy paychecks and management power trips.

His brief time at Space Matters provided him with another insight as well. It clarified where to focus the first phase of his new generation company—one dedicated to murdering wealthy, white-collars in the property business too spineless to fight back. If there was anything Howard knew, it was that Jerry Schneiderman and Richard Kasparov were soft—Charmin soft. And they were not the paupers that their attorneys asserted.

Like any entrepreneur, Howard regarded this first operation as a pilot project to evaluate for future endeavors. The effort was two-pronged. After Robert killed the first Space Matters partner, his company would extort and eliminate the other one, the rest of his family if required, to acquire the tens of thousands of dollars they expected. Howard's business philosophy was constructed on three bedrock doctrines. One: always have a patsy with a violent record and rabid fear of him to do the dirty work; two: be out of town with a provable alibi when the blood splattered; and three: never overlook the tiniest detail that could lead to your downfall.

Howard just needed to turn the launch key, though a management consultant might've admonished him that by acting so soon, with a grudge dominant in the equation, it would point the finger at himself given his financial disputes with his former employer. True as that was, Howard could fashion a counterargument. He was a proven savant exonerating himself from heinous activity. Hubristic—not him. A corpse left burning in the desert and a first wife who perished under murky circumstances said not to underestimate him.

Quickly, he and his wife, an hourglass-shaped, Thrifty Drug Store manager unaware of her husband's plot, hit the road in Richard's lent-out Datsun 280Z. For alibi by distance, Howard chose Robert's neck of the woods in San Francisco. They should've just flown. Howard's murder franchise got off to the lamest of starts when the Datsun's engine blew up halfway there in Fresno. Because repairs would take too long for his purposes, they caught a Greyhound bus the rest of the way.

Up at their hotel, Howard drummed his fingers waiting for Robert to call him with good news. It never came, and Howard deduced why. Not only did his inaugural employee fail to pull a trigger in the San Fernando Valley, he didn't even travel from the Bay Area to give it a try. Peeved, Howard buttonholed Robert about the imperative of him keeping his word. If he was harboring second thoughts, spit it out. If he was going to be wishy-washy, Howard'd hire someone he could bank on. The face-to-face reprimand must've been effective, for Robert recommitted himself to fulfilling what Howard was browbeating him to accomplish.

Two weeks later, in early 1979, Howard hailed Robert to LA to be schooled in the finer points of professional assassinations. Howard, management trainer, swung his charge by the house where he needed to prove his worth. Parked there at the curb, he patiently explained the facets of the neighborhood that his apprentice had to grasp, and how he wanted the job carried out with bang-bang efficiency. When he returned here on his own, Howard told Robert to nonchalantly walk up the driveway, as if he were a pizza deliveryman, and either knock on the front door or ring the doorbell. After their quarry opened it, Robert was to shoot him point-blank in the head using the .45-caliber pistol that Howard would lend him. It was contingencies next. Should the door be slammed in his face, Robert should blast through it, muscle inside, and murder *everybody* in there. Howard echoed his grisly order: leave no witnesses—or fingerprints, for that matter.

Howard, a believer in options, devised another scenario: executing their man off-site. They'd impersonate a wealthy homeowner supposedly impressed by the remodeling work that CM-2 performed for Dr. Joseph Marmet. The phony property owner would book him for a site visit at a remote address; a lonely stretch of Mulholland Drive would do. When the target showed up with his drafting pencil, Robert would show him the last thing he'd see on earth: the muzzle flash of the .45.

Let's go with plan number one, Howard said.

Those words ringing in his ears, Robert made the long trek across numerous freeways to the appropriate street one night and rapped on the door. Nobody answered. On his second trip, he repeated the same steps and received the same results. Apprised, Howard shook his head: they were 0 for 2. Consequently, the next time Robert rolled up to the address, headlights off in the dark, Howard sat next to him. He wanted to do some reconnaissance, as well as offer Robert another tutorial. As luck would have it, somebody was home, but there could be no murder with the boss present.

Hoping a fourth time there would be their breakthrough, Howard leaped on a celebratory excuse to remove himself from LA. With his wife's birthday looming, he'd whisk Carol to Las Vegas from January 27 to February 2. If a homicide detective grilled him, he'd say he was there to treat her to roulette games, a steak dinner, heck, maybe a Johnny Cash concert too. The trickle of independent construction jobs he wrangled since leaving Space Matters could wait for a few days of decadence. As to a Valley homicide, how precisely could he be involved if he was 230 miles away in Nevada? Moreover, why would he concoct something so stupidly self-sabotaging when he was fixing to sue his previous employer for fuck-you money?

Personal alibi: check. Up next: what else he could do to complicate life for forensic bloodhounds. One task was kid's stuff for a carpenter like him. With a hammer, saw, and file, he flattened the barrel of his .45-caliber pistol to prevent bullets discharged out it from revealing telltale marks tracing it to his state-registered handgun. He then gave it back to Robert, reminding him to safeguard the keepsake. Long ago, a Royal Canadian Mountie presented the weapon as a collector's item to Howard's father, who later bestowed it on his son for nostalgia. Had either been alive, imagine their horror realizing its purpose outside of its glass cabinet.

Financing was Howard's final loose end to tie up before blazing off to Vegas. For the money exchange, he knew a place where no one would suspect a thing: a forlorn gas station in Ontario, a working-class city just across the eastern LA County line in San Bernardino. He was waiting in the 280Z when Robert, who grew up in Ontario and was staying with his sister in town, arrived in the El Camino, which was effectively the company car now. Both men disembarked, and Howard set his briefcase on the sport car's warm hood. From inside the case, he withdrew eight one-hundred-dollar bills, more cash than Robert ever saw at one time.

"Take it," Howard said. "And listen up."

Robert was to spend the money to buy the transportation required to make this an unsolvable case. He was to fork out some of it to purchase a jalopy from a used-car lot in Long Beach. This, Howard said, was *the* vehicle to take to the murder site. After the killing was over, he should drive it to a nearby motel and dump it for another beater he had already purchased and pre-positioned. From there it was Robert's choice: he could return to San Francisco in that second car, or go to Los Angeles International Airport for a flight up north.

Shoot, ditch a vehicle, and flee: your basic, three-step execution.

If some Curious George got nosy about the dough, Robert should lie that his boss advanced it to purchase concrete for a "construction job" deep in Orange County.

Before they went their separate ways, Howard gave Robert a signed blank check for miscellaneous expenses and a stiff order. After the target was dead, Robert needed to promptly call him at the Las Vegas Hilton to notify him. Howard said he was prepared to remain there for as long as it took! Just don't force him to cross the Mojave Desert for home if he screwed up.

"You got it?" Howard asked. Robert nodded that he did. As his employer continually reminded him, the people he wanted gone pushed him into this pit with creditors and bill collectors. It was only fair he should put them in a different hole in return. Jerry, Howard groused, really should've settled with him.

He split, leaving Robert at that Godforsaken gas station with a fistful of money and a passenger studying his every move through the El Camino's windshield. Ros Ann Dyer was a twenty-nine-year-old single mother from nearby Mount Baldy who worked in advertising. She'd begun dating Robert after they'd hooked up at a local nightclub. When she inquired about what he did, he answered that he was a "contractor apprentice." His night hours, backwater meeting spots, and slippery details about what the position entailed made her dubious, though. Having just watched him pocket a wad of cash for a supposed construction project a county away, Ros made a lighthearted crack.

"That's a lot of money," she quipped as Robert scooted behind the wheel. "What? Do you have to kill somebody for that?"

Before her black humor settled on the dashboard, the blood drained out of Robert's complexion as if he'd seen a ghost. Ros, in noticing his reaction, must've realized that her comment yanked back the covers on something dark. And that she might've yucked *herself* into danger. Be it for self-preservation or decency, she broke up with him weeks later.

By then, Robert should've broken up with himself.

On top of everything Howard put into his arms was a final piece of hardware, a heavy one at that. It was a shotgun—Howard's registered shotgun—for supplemental firepower. If the home of the man they were after was more fortified than they anticipated, and Howard's Dirty-Harry-esque .45-caliber pistol was insufficient, that big gun would come in handy. Robert just needed to saw off the barrel to make it easier to camouflage and harder for police to link to the crime. Robert said he'd do it, the only reply Howard tolerated anymore.

He carried the weapon outside, probably into the yard at his sister's Ontario residence, and grabbed a hacksaw; to the east, Howard and Carol zipped off to Las Vegas for Howard's future excuse. Robert ripped the saw's aluminum teeth across the iron muzzle, producing a screechy whine comparable to fingernails on a chalkboard. Then again, nails don't incite what happened next, or create its ripple effect.

The saw's movement caused the shotgun to accidentally discharge with an air-bursting crackle.

Bah-wusssh.

By the time the boom petered out, Robert grabbed his face, uncertain if all its components were still there. He felt around. His eye—his lacerated eye! The blast had sent flying a tiny, razor-sharp metallic shaving from the saw-point of the barrel into the fleshy meat of his eyeball. Within minutes it was swollen shut, stabbing him with a white-hot pain so deep into his skull that he would've welcomed passing out. By dinner, Robert could barely see out of the puffy socket.

What was he supposed to do? Howard was nearing the end of his rope, and Robert needed urgent medical care before an infection set in. Before the accident transmogrified him into a Cyclops walking around with a glass eye and no prospects. After a batch of calls and scrambling around, he visited a doctor who plucked out the sliver from his tender cornea and prescribed him medication.

Metaphorically speaking, a painful foreign object remained in him. Howard's long, black claws were sunk deep into Robert's flesh, there for profit and extortion, for sick revenge and last laughs. He expected someone who never killed anyone before to eliminate two men who'd never done boo to him, and possibly their innocent families. Should other measures fail to secure his blood money, his employer snickered about kidnapping and maiming a child. And it was all to commence in the next few days. If Robert wiped out everyone on Howard's shit list, history would rate his body count in the same breath as a serial killer or the Manson Family butchery.

He'd never go along, pleading with Howard to rethink his business MO *before* he stomped the 280Z's gas pedal toward Sin City. From the second police strung up the crime-scene tape around Jerry's and Richard's homes, he'd be the common-denominator suspect. Violently kidnapping a child, Robert noted, would also drag the FBI into it. Howard politely heard him out and then shook his head. Both targets, he believed, had accumulated enough enemies to keep detectives occupied for months. Plus, this: he wasn't paying Robert a salary, when he was hurting financially, to play Jiminy Cricket to refresh his conscience. He was paying him to slaughter whomever he chose.

So, yeah, that teensy shaving mired Robert at the crossroad of bad options, options that would define him forever. His life was worth more than this, a life heretofore spent more behind bars than outside of them, a life of robbery and burglary that began at seventeen while his peers got drunk or lost their virginity at their disco proms. But his blurry vision brought him an epiphany. Harming others had mostly hurt him. One way or another, he needed to unlatch Howard's claws before they dug through muscle and reached soul.

Question was, how?

•••

NORMALLY IN CONTROL OF his molten temper, Howard must've battled with himself not to punch his fist through his Nevada hotel room upon learning what happened. Nobody he wanted dead was, and the man who'd blown it yet again bolted town in his El Camino. Veins popping, patience waning, he and Carol drove to San Francisco in the 280Z on Valentine's Day weekend to compel Robert to honor the commitment he gave weeks ago. If Howard was forced to drag him down the Golden State Freeway by the nostrils to do it, he would. For a second time now, he found Robert in the Haight-Ashbury neighborhood that was his refuge.

The questions came fast. "Why'd you disappear? How'd you mess it up again? Where's the $800 I gave you?"

Robert, once more, apologized to an enraged figure who rarely raised his voice. He explained that the shotgun discharged while he was sawing off the barrel, and how his inflamed eye had left him seeing a barren future. Since scurrying here, however, he realized it'd been the wrong course of action. He'd given his word, and a contract was a contract. Next, he vowed there'd be no more blunders, no more excuses, recommitting to murders that in his heart he had no intention of *ever* committing. He was filibustering a madman.

Howard seemed to buy the artifice of his reinvigorated hitman. But he didn't trust it entirely because he insisted on immediately driving him down to LA to take care of business. Robert smiled in agreement, probably to hide his shaking knees. To wedge in buffers in case Howard was lying about offering him another chance, Robert asked if they could give a lift to a couple of friends. Howard, aware every favor one grants consigns the giver clout, said sure. On February 15, 1979, he, Robert, and his two chums—one a cross-dressing thief that Robert was likely in a sexual relationship with while in jail, the other a knucklehead junkie—climbed into the El Camino. That automobile knew more about what its owner was capable of than any of its passengers.

Robert the next day was back where he least wanted: at Howard's Pasadena apartment on the shortest of leashes. There he received another remedial lesson on being an assassin and how the revised sequence would play out. Because Howard already went to the Bay Area and Las Vegas for alibis, he was considering someplace sleepier this time, like Santa Barbara or Vacaville. Until he gave the signal for the fourth attempt on the Space Matters' partner, Robert was to stay local and not even think about skedaddling home. Robert left for his sister's place in Ontario with a black cloud hanging low.

Out there, equidistant from desert and mountains, the LA dream felt several galaxies removed. Unlike Van Nuys, Pasadena, or Guccified West Los Angeles, the California sun was dimmer in Ontario, the opportunities less abundant. Rather than tiled, backyard swimming pools, people here deposited castoff cars on weed-choked lawns. It wasn't always this dreary. Ontario, as its neighbors, had undergone breakneck growth at the turn of the twentieth century. The city erected health resorts, citrus fields, olive groves. "Iowa under Palm

Trees" was the civic slogan—West Coast weather with midwestern sensibility. Hearing the call, General Electric and defense companies came, and subdivisions followed. But the future was rust. When some of the factories padlocked, the town of ninety thousand boasted only a speedway and a second-rate airport owned by LA city hall. Gangs, some spawned from Latino families who'd once hoed local farmland, recruited well from the disenfranchised castoffs. By the late 1970s, Ontario was stagnating, stuck on its haunches without ever enjoying a prime. It was not all that different from Robert.

Back in his old digs, Lady Luck quickly frowned on him. While he slept, his junkie friend snuck off in Howard's El Camino on an impromptu trip to score drugs. Before he reached his dealer, unfortunately, he plowed Howard's pride and joy into another vehicle and ditched the car. Authorities investigating the hit-and-run found the Chevy and towed it to an impound lot until the accident was resolved. When Robert had no choice but to tell Howard, Howard himself could barely see straight. He couldn't have his vehicle attracting unwanted police attention so close to their first killing for profit. He howled in anger at such a decibel that Robert fretted Howard might kill his friend that very day.

Robert now owed him more than ever, and Howard snatched the leverage. The evening of the hit-and-run, he pressed Robert for a connection to sell him heroin or cocaine for personal relaxation. If anyone should appreciate the immense stress he was under, it was him. Don't worry, Robert assured his employer. He knew a guy. Johnny Williams, an old childhood friend from around here, had a reliable dealer. So did Johnny's brother, who fraternized with the local Hells Angels. Robert volunteered to take it a step further too. How about if he threw a narcotics party in Howard's name that night?

Sure enough, Howard showed up on Maitland Street anxious for a good high. In doing so, Robert knew *he'd* be breathing another day.

Johnny's room was a converted bedroom inside his father's garage. For him and his chums, those four walls represented sanctuary, a musty-aired haven from which to get loaded, scheme, and condemn worldly adversaries. In attendance this session were Howard, Johnny, Robert, and Jamie Jones, the orange-hair-cropped drag queen who'd ridden down to LA in the El Camino. (The junkie involved in the hit-and-run with the El Camino wisely declined the invitation.) If you tried listing the criminal charges everyone there had tallied over their lives, your Bic pen would run dry. Inside Johnny's makeshift drug den, needles plunged into skin, straws vacuumed up powder, pot smoke lingered, and bottles probably opened. Howard, meanwhile, sat on the bed, contentedly buzzed, gratified about this newly discovered pipeline for highs through a man he basically owned.

Though impaired himself, Robert could still think. About how badly he wanted away from this phony benefactor, who had gotten him out of jail with an ulterior motive. About what that metal shaving that nearly blinded him signified. About arranging the pixels of an escape plan that nobody would detect—an escape plan that came to him that blurry evening. He would become an actor performing for an audience of one. He'd trick Howard into believing he was finally embracing what it meant to be his lead assassin and manager.

In front of this eye-dilated crowd, Robert launched into an impromptu lecture about the underpinnings of Howard's murder-for-profit venture, like a team leader at an informal seminar. He spoke about the meticulously planned operations, which had circled some six men sitting on substantial wealth to execute. He spoke about compensation by the hit, monthly stipends between them, and other perks, all with low risk of incarceration.

Howard grinned listening to Robert's surprise presentation, believing his assassin had turned the corner from ambivalence to action. Yes, this was all coming together. Surveying everyone in the garage, he also felt power. He was older, smarter, meaner, more devious, and, comparatively speaking, a Rockefeller next to these losers. He owned business licenses and called millionaire executives by their first names. Robert, Johnny, and company, by contrast, were lucky the state issued them drivers licenses at the asinine rate at which they shuttled in and out of California's prison system. Howard, a panther tattoo on his left arm, a skull figure on his right, could do pretty much anything he wanted with them.

After he drove home to Pasadena, probably with narcotics to go, Robert continued his pretense as Howard's number two with more money talk. If Johnny and Jamie joined him on the company's maiden job, they would pocket $2,500 apiece! What Robert excluded in his recruiting pitch to the heroin boys was the most important part: he was dealing himself out.

CHAPTER SEVEN
CLAW REMOVAL

FOR SPACE PLANNERS DEPENDENT on light, both fluorescent and natural, to brighten dark spaces on their blueprints, Richard and Jerry were falling prey to optical illusions. When they peered out at their own circumstances, in a no-man's land between their fractured partnership and fresh beginnings for themselves, they only seized upon the glare reflecting their own troubles, neglecting to be on the lookout for scaly things sneaking toward them.

Jerry, up to his padded elbows in crises, was a blinkered young man. There was a staff to manage by himself, legal bills stacking up, and Paul Fegen's properties to sketch. His most galling chore, untangling CM-2's legitimate jobs from the ones corrupted by Richard's avarice, was also the most painstaking.

Richard, now being counseled by the attorney his long-enabling mother was chipping in to pay, had a substantially lighter workload. He lost his appetite to contest Jerry's lawsuit, agreeing in principle to the covenant that Jerry and Benjamin insisted on when they ambushed him at the Polo Lounge. He'd yield his entire interest in *all* the companies in return for Jerry withdrawing his suit and threat to contact the District Attorney's office. The last thing he needed was to sustain huge, punitive damages, or to watch the media brand him as a debonair con artist. Until he signed the final dissolution papers, he was eating plenty of crow, including assisting Jerry, in person, to sort out the mess he made at the spinoff he'd once trumpeted as a million-dollar initiative.

For Jerry, every second in the proximity of his lanky, bearded ex-partner was teeth gnashing.

When we're done, he thought, *I'll never have to see his lying face again.*

Jerry's mistrust of him bordered on the febrile. In fact, if Richard was scheduled to visit Fremont Place to sit in a room to earmark the paperwork he'd doctored, shy, levelheaded Jerry acted downright paranoid. Before Richard's arrival, he would scuttle around the office directing employees to hide in their desk drawers any job spreadsheets, ledgers, or other sensitive materials that Richard might usurp to his advantage if he glimpsed them.

There was little pushback to Jerry's hysterical moments, even among the hipper types previously loyal to Richard. Everyone had heard that he swindled Jerry, and in doing so, them by proxy. Nobody tugged Richard aside so he might recount his version of the scandal. It was the opposite. After he entered, they cast suspicious glances and spied his movements. For someone with Richard's vanity—someone quick to emphasize that he resided in "Los Angeles," not gauche Van Nuys—it must've been 500 PSI worth of embarrassment.

Despite those bruises to his ego, he refused to sink into a rabbit hole of depression and listlessness as he did after his first marriage collapsed in the early 1970s. Beautiful loser? Not him. He was hardly even forty in a town where the disgraced were rewarded with second chances, a town pontooned on self-reinvention. Maybe it wasn't too late to seek redemption by contrition with some of those he'd exploited or disillusioned. At least he was seeing a Pico Boulevard psychiatrist before he hit rock bottom. Dabbling in the past with est and other self-help fads—feel-good psychology whose salves of enlightenment burned off quickly—left him incomplete. Lying on a shrink's couch heightened his chances this time of emerging whole.

Intending, as he did, to win Paige back, he needed to be different. Why not express that with presents? At Christmas, early on in their separation, he purchased a $400 women's Cartier watch for her and clothes for baby Rebecca. Paige, then fighting to keep a roof over their heads, was bewildered. What, she asked with a scoff, was she supposed to do with a Cartier, official timepiece of the affluent, while he was withholding so much of her court-ordered child support that she could barely afford an In-N-Out Burger for dinner? His gift for Rebecca, meantime—blue attire for a girl—seemed to indicate he was deluding himself about her gender. To Paige, his head was orbiting Jupiter when it needed grounding on Earth.

At Space Matters, there was but one woman who remained steadfast to Richard circa 1979. Brie Levine was a statuesque woman who favored tight pants and loose tops, a free spirit with dark hair and the smile of an Italian actress. She had dated Richard years earlier, seeing in him a sweet if damaged soul whose mercurial outbursts would've driven others to delist their phone numbers. They'd been attending couple's therapy in Topanga Canyon, supposedly in a committed relationship, when Richard dropped her cold by announcing that he was marrying Paige—in two days. After Brie's tears dried, she resumed a friendship with him, which Richard later repaid by hiring her as the company's unofficial office manager. Her job: bringing order to the pell-mell filing system and fuzzy procedures. Now that he periodically spent time in a building where he was stigmatized as a pariah, Richard was thankful for Brie's grace.

As time passed, she deduced the obvious: Richard's outward assurance that he would bounce back was a fig leaf that only fooled him. The same mesmeric personality that, on his best day, made space planning sexy was unraveling in public. The cowlicked hair, wrinkled clothes, and whiff of aimlessness cataloged it. Lurid rumors that circulated reinforced that narrative. A client who still rooted for Richard disclosed that he previously tried selling him a baggy of Quaaludes from the stash he squirreled away in his desk. Another customer divulged that when he went to fetch his newspaper one recent morning, Richard was parked on his driveway, asleep in his car. Was it because he was too wasted to drive and needed someplace to crash, or something else?

At one of his next visits to the mansion, Richard dropped any pretense that he was taking his downfall in stride: shoulders slumped, eyes lightless, brave face evaporated. When Brie noticed his unmasked dejection, she hurried down the staircase to comfort him. Richard, by then fatigued with her pep talks, growled to leave him alone. He wanted to get to where he was going. Which, at that moment, was pretty much nowhere.

By February, there were few people clamoring for Richard's company besides his mother, sister, and the blonde he was seeing on the side. His fundamentals sounded like a candidate for an antidepressant: unemployed, alienated from his ex-partner, separated from wife number two, and self-medicating with weed and coke. His Mercury Cougar, the chariot he was normally so fussy about that he would park it blocks from dust sources, was coated in grit. His psychiatrist must've reached the same conclusion that Brie had.

Richard was lost—curtain-pulling, don't-shave-for-days lost.

•••

WHILE HE STRUGGLED FOR reasons to get up in the morning, and Jerry ticked down the days before he never uttered his name again, Howard Garrett's reluctant assassin pirouetted around a single question: How could he slip out of his commitment without sliding a noose around his own neck? Robert Freeman, after thinking hard, settled on a placeholder measure. He'd pretend to play along with Howard's murder-for-profit enterprise until he found a trapdoor out of it. To do so, he would have to deceive not only Howard but also the friend joining him now on assassination attempts. Where Robert dreaded the idea of going through with it, his friend itched to spill blood.

At thirty-seven, Johnny Harold Williams was about Robert's age but missed out on his good looks. He was bantam-size and addict-thin, with caterpillar eyebrows and a cube of immovable brown hair. Blocky black glasses as wide as his face rested under a trapezoidal-shaped forehead. Johnny's natural expression was a fixed sneer, for he enjoyed appearing tough and never counted much to smile about anyway. His six-page rap sheet was an homage to miscreant versatility: car thefts, forgery, statutory rape, drug possession, even a fish-and-game violation.

Who knows how Johnny could've turned out if another family raised him? At a young age, he scored high on intelligence tests and evinced signs of a photographic memory. Uncanny, his father once noted, how Johnny could recite paragraphs verbatim from books years after reading them. He might well have parlayed those gifts into a fruitful life, too, if not for the misfortune that redirected his trajectory. It occurred in boyhood, when Johnny's mother was driving him to see his dad, then a long-distance trucker returning from the road. On the way there, the car door creaked open, and Johnny tumbled out of a vehicle traveling at forty-five miles per hour, whacking his head on the blacktop. Doctors believed the neurological damage sparked the epilepsy requiring him to take medication for life.

Whether by illness or nature, villainy percolated in him around adolescence. Boy Scouts and college applications were for the kids on the rich side of LA; for him, it was juvenile hall and parole agents. Prison guards or worse might've been in the offing had he been prosecuted in his late teens for killing three people in gang violence around his native Ontario. People fired at him, it was said, so Johnny returned fire more accurately. Not once did police question him. Johnny, still a smart cookie despite his brain injury, must've gathered that society's belief in justice for all excluded dead kids from wasteland towns.

On the heels of the garage drug party, where he got to know Howard, Johnny began riding shotgun with Robert on the fifty-plus-mile trip east from Ontario to the Valley. As incentive, Howard upped the payday on the hit to $10,000; Robert was to peel off a quarter of that to any cohort who assisted him. Johnny needed cash, but he salivated to prove himself to his new boss just as much. For this reason, it was him, not Robert, who sauntered up to the target's front door and knocked. It was Johnny who received what Robert did before:

no response from an empty house. A flustered Howard commanded them to try again.

On their next murder trip, they got what they wanted: a reaction from inside. After Johnny knocked, a light flashed on, and a man and a woman peeked their heads out the window to see who was there in the dark. Johnny fingered his weapon, hoping to see the door crack open next. It didn't. The people inside, perhaps assuming it was ding-dong-ditch-playing teenagers or pamphlet-bearing Jehovah Witnesses wanting their time, backed away from the widow. When a glowering Johnny relayed what happened to Robert, Robert faked disappointment to disguise his relief that bid number five ended in failure.

Howard, knowing talent when he saw it, decreed a management shakeup, even so. Johnny, from now on, would be *his* second-in-command and his preferred triggerman. Unlike his peers, Johnny was fearless, took direction well, and demonstrated enthusiasm to learn the ropes of engineering unsolvable homicides. Robert could not have been more thrilled to be replaced. After all, he'd gingerly tried enacting it.

They began meeting alone, Johnny and Howard, so Howard could educate him on a deeper level about the roots of his business and its expansion plans. Through Johnny's friend network, Howard added a pair of employees in Jamie Jones and another man named Hector "Chaser" Villa. Like Robert and Johnny, Howard paid them stipends to keep them loyal and attentive. Unlike in January, when he could've gnawed metal in frustration, he was in buoyant spirits now. The killings were slated to begin using a different shooter, and his El Camino was back in his garage.

If Robert believed he was off the hook since Johnny was in ascension, he'd misjudged Howard's definition of obligation. It was only fulfilled when Howard said it was.

A February evening of terror and guilt eradicated any doubt that he could turn in his pink slip. That night, Howard and Johnny popped up at Robert's mother's home in search of a murder weapon. Howard had heard "the old lady" named Hazel, who was closer to his age than senior citizen status, kept a shotgun there for protection. He explained to her that he needed to borrow it to handle a "serious situation" in LA. Asked pretty please if she would lend it to them, considering all the generosity he'd bestowed on her son, the woman, to Howard's astonishment, replied sorry. She'd like to help, but the rifle *was* registered with authorities. She apologized if he'd wasted his time laboring under a misperception.

Howard, who'd decided against using his own shotgun—the one whose barrel Robert almost lost an eye sawing off—brooded and steamed. His gut told him that she was playing cat-and-mouse to stonewall him, using an excuse precooked-up by Robert. That's all right, Mrs. Freeman, he said. Excuse him while he spoke to her son.

Alone with Robert, Howard expressed his displeasure, then his willingness to return *here* later to take it out on his mother. If he wanted to avoid that, he insisted that Robert arrange transportation for Johnny and Jamie to you know where. Nobody was taking the El Camino, and neither of them was going. Robert winced, unsure what to do. The only person that he could think of under Howard's piercing glare was his sister's boyfriend, Mark, a noncriminal who had a car. Whatever Robert told him must've been persuasive, for soon Mark was carrying Johnny and an associate across three rain-slickened freeways, late at night, for a hazy reason.

The chilly rain continued to fall as Howard's men stepped out of the car at midnight. They'd bundled up, anticipating this moist weather. What caught them flat-footed was the unidentified vehicle parked in front of the target's place.

"It looks like he has company tonight," Johnny said. "I don't know if we ought to stop by or not."

But he did know this. He was no waffler like Robert. And he wanted to validate Howard's faith in him. So, he puffed out his chest, informing Mark that he could take off. They'd find their own lift back to Ontario.

Johnny, once again, walked up to the well-trod entryway with the poise of an Amway salesman. And, just as the time before last, it was déjà vu, nobody responding after he knocked. He returned to Jamie, bedeviled that they'd struck out again.

Hold on, said Jamie, whom police later speculated was taking estrogen injections as part of a transition from male to female. Something occurred to him. What if he gussied himself up in his favorite skirt, blouse, lipstick, and accessories to trick the man they were hunting into believing that it was a woman in distress ringing his doorbell—a woman packing a .32 revolver in her purse? Johnny listened, marveling at Jamie's impromptu idea.

Until Jamie said whoops. He just realized that he didn't bring the ladies' clothes he needed for his gender-fueled ploy. Well, where were they? Johnny asked. Locked inside the camper shell of Howard's El Camino in Pasadena, Jamie answered. Then why didn't you lead with that? Johnny said. Jamie shrugged.

A glint lit up Johnny's eyes, though. A glint that Jamie's half-baked notion wasn't totally worthless. Not at all. Walking up and knocking had, over half a dozen attempts, elicited either silence or faces in a window unwilling to open the door to uninvited annoyances. If, however, they fabricated an entirely plausible scenario, their man was bound to drop his guard.

Moments later, Johnny started up the driveway, subterfuge ready, while Jamie stood to the side. Johnny planned to knock and wait for a response. If anyone inside the house stirred, he'd holler that he'd just ate it in a motorcycle accident and needed to call for help. Their mark, with an ounce of compassion, would turn a doorknob into his own demise. At last!

Johnny's knuckles were inches from the door when real life derailed their make-believe one. Down the block, a woman in a domestic sedan collided with a woman in a Mustang in a metal-crunching smash-up that awoke part of the neighborhood. Johnny and Jamie froze on their insoles, jaws open. Thwarted again?

Not necessarily if they adapted, Johnny realized. Since their target probably heard the wreck, it made their sham scenario about being in a motorcycle spill that much more credible. Quickly, he rang the doorbell. Yes! Two faces looked down at them from an upstairs window.

"Hey, Mister—there's been an accident," Johnny shouted through the drizzle. "Can we use your phone to call the cops?"

The people in the window said nothing. Then, as before, they receded from the driveway sightline.

There was no time for cursing, not stranded so far from Ontario after another snake-bit mission. As always, Johnny kept his composure, another quality in him that Howard admired. He walked over to the accident scene like other lookey-loos, sidling up next to a man in a Pontiac Firebird to ask a favor. Could he possibly drop him and a buddy off at Corky's, a fifties-style diner not far away? The Pontiac man agreed. Inside the restaurant, Johnny phoned his elderly father to pick them up in the distant town.

Howard was speechless, though unsurprised, when notified of this latest failure. It could give a guy an ulcer, but they'd just have to plow ahead like all startups grooving a path. It wasn't like he was idle, either. There was a problematic employee for him to manage before he reassessed what to do in the Valley.

The day after Johnny's escapades in the rain, Robert traveled from Ontario to downtown LA for a court hearing on an old charge. After the judge postponed it, he drove toward the future that he envisioned for the new him: to J&B Produce Company, where he hoped to take a physical qualifying him to become a long-distance truck driver. Among side benefits, it would put time zones between him and a certain someone.

It also might've been the world's most combustible fairy-tale. Sitting in the waiting room, clipboard in hands, Robert looked up to see *him* step into the room. Howard sauntered over to Robert, looming for a second, cheeks purpling in suppressed rage.

"I have wasted enough fucking time with you," Howard said in front of the other J&B job applicants. "I have places to go and people to see, and I am not spending any more time here. Come on. Let's go."

Robert departed with the gait of someone being marched off to a Soviet gulag. There'd be no commanding any sixteen-wheeler anytime soon. Howard steered the El Camino onto the freeway and told his captive passenger he had something explosive to lay on him. Something that Robert might not believe but better remember. Ready?

In the plainest of voices, Howard said that Robert's old pal Johnny just volunteered to murder *him* because he chickened out of their first job and knew too much about their general intentions. Johnny, Howard added, was so psyched to do it that he didn't want a cent.

"How could you run around with people who called themselves your friend when they would offer to kill you for free?" Howard asked. "Does that sit well with you?"

His only reprieve, Howard said, was to stop the pussyfooting around and start taking the initiative to check off this box. After all, you gave your word.

Robert knew for a while that Howard was more venomous than the sexual predators, robbers, and white supremacists he knocked around with in prison and out. But what he appreciated now was who Howard was: a walking reptile who hid in the open behind the legitimacy of his California contractor's license to make you believe he was Joe Six-Pack. In truth, he'd stalk whatever whetted his palate. Deny him something he yearned to digest, and he'd swim into your waters to feast on the contents. Heaven help you if he knew your weaknesses—drugs, embezzlement, gay sex, fear of reincarceration. He'd paddle in stealthily, with the blackest of eyes, anxious to lunge at you or anyone you held dear. Of course Howard wasn't innocent of the felony rap that he said he was when they met in the San Bernardino lockup. He was guilty from the day he was born.

Robert understood what he needed to do. He had to bolt LA. Not for a week. Not for a few months to let Howard's claws retract. This would be ditching LA forever, as if the city sloughed into the Pacific after the Big One. Believing he could merely replace himself as Howard's chosen hitman with Johnny was hazardous dreamland.

Without hinting about his plans, Robert pigeonholed Johnny about what Howard told him in the Chevy. Is it true? he asked. You're foaming at the mouth to kill me—for free? This is your thanks for me introducing you to him? Nah, Johnny said. He was just blowing smoke to impress the boss into giving him money before he'd earned it.

Robert said cool, though he knew his old bespectacled chum was lying through his teeth. Why? He'd already learned that Johnny recently tugged aside Robert's *own* stepbrother, Nathaniel, to inquire if he wanted to make ten grand. There wasn't much to it, Johnny explained to him. All he needed to do was to help Howard and him snuff out Robert, his sister, Janice, and their mother in an all-in-the-family triple homicide. Nathan flatly said he wasn't interested. Then Nathan's half-sibling said see you later.

Howard's first employee roared away in the only conveyance at his disposal: the knobby wheels of the El Camino. And none too soon. Pulling out of Ontario, he could've sworn he heard someone fire a potshot at him. Hours later, he walked through the door of the San Francisco apartment he shared with his wife, Elena. He might not be truck-driving, but he could start a new life. In a couple of days when he went to check on the car that he'd parked on his street, that same life flashed before his eyes. A thief had swiped Howard's car. What was it about it that imperiled so many people?

He and Elena discussed how to handle a delicate situation for which there was no how-to guide. The only solution, it seemed to Robert, was to dissemble their way out of it because telling Howard the truth meant provoking the inner animal of someone pre-riled up. Best, he said, if she phoned him at his Pasadena apartment to say this: someone must've hot-wired the Chevy, and Robert was so devastated about messing up again that he took off without indicating where he was going. Prepare yourself, Robert cautioned her.

Howard was silent while Elena read from the agreed-upon script. He said nothing as she described how upset Robert was, even as Robert secretly listened in on the receiver. He heard her recommend that he report the El Camino stolen to the police or his insurance company to recover his loss. After she was finished speaking came a pause on the line and a flicker of hope that Howard would evoke a spirit of forgiveness.

A flicker: with him?

Howard exploded, yapping threats that made them feel as if his poisonous claws were flexing through the transmission lines.

"Your husband is a sonofabitch, and you know now he is a dead sonofabitch," he shrieked.

A weeping Elena tried interrupting the barrage to talk sense to him. It was futile.

"*A dead man*, you hear me," Howard said. "He stole my car!"

In the ensuing days, Howard started calling Robert's sister to pinpoint her brother's whereabouts, allegedly for employment purposes.

"He has a job to do," he told her. "Have him call me."

When Robert never called, Howard switched to guilt.

"I was good enough to get him out of jail, Janice, and now he won't do the work that I've already paid for. I'll ask you again: Where is Bob? San Francisco?"

Janice said who knew?

Getting nowhere with his verbal bullying, he and Carol took off for Haight-Ashbury, mecca of the sixties' psychedelic free-love movement, in one of their other vehicles. Robert hadn't given Howard his current address, smartly so, but Howard knew where he hung out and, by sheer luck, spotted Robert entering a building. As much as Howard must've wanted to disembowel him, he wanted his hallowed El Camino back more.

He and Carol continued searching for it on streets and in alleys, around red cable cars and behind mossy brick buildings. Then, like clouds parting, there it was, shiny blue on a curb not far from where the joyriding car thief must've returned it.

Howard plucked out his spare key. Robert would be hearing from him again.

CHAPTER EIGHT
PAWN SHOP PERFIDY

WHEN CALIFORNIA'S TANGERINE SUN burst through the gloomy skies, it coincided with Johnny's latest stroke of criminal originality. Nothing needed to be sawed off or filed down for his concept to take hold. No, just broken into, as in the residence on the leafy block that repelled them before like a deflector shield in a cycle of failure.

A new face was present with him in the Valley today—Chaser Villa, a bony man of Hispanic descent undersized like Johnny but without his natural growl for depravity. They made their move in broad daylight, when no one was home, just as Johnny designed. They slipped onto the property through a gate along the narrow side of the yard and slinked into the backyard. They then clambered up the stairs to the second-story deck, where Howard's manager knew just what to do. He bashed the bathroom window with a screwdriver to gain entry.

Neither burglar carried a gun. Why would they? They weren't here for bloodshed; Johnny's plot was too shrewd for that. As he knew from memorizing portions of the California penal code, the courts would sentence them to extra prison time if they were caught with a deadly weapon.

He and Chaser now roamed the place that Paige ditched with her baby after the string of menacing calls by Pat—a.k.a. Howard—over Richard's side debt to him. Their boss had already briefed them there was no alarm system or guard dog to fret over, meaning they didn't have to agonize in deciding what to filch. When they collected the loot they wanted, it included items similar to what Howard was yet to retrieve from Space Matters: a typewriter and stereo components. Also going out in their arms were assorted trinkets and the crème de la crème of their haul: Richard's expensive yellow Cartier watch. Nobody from Johnny's block probably held one before, unless it was at an estate sale.

Richard discovered his ransacked house upon returning from a two-day trip, to where nobody knows. Whoever broke through the glass window exited impudently through the front door. He filed a police report, then apparently took no other precautions. In his inventory of what was pilfered, his distracted head neglected to even register the missing Cartier, which he'd bought with the one he'd gotten for Paige in his impulse-makeup bid to her.

Days later, around March 12, Johnny manifested his knack for beastly plotting by turning something harmless into something lethal. He had his father, Carl, take him to Euclid Loan and Jewelry, a pawnshop in downtown Ontario a short hop from the town's railroad tracks. The reason? Johnny needed to go rifle shopping—rifle shopping as a convicted felon forbidden from owning a firearm. But his dad, with his unblemished record, was the perfect straw buyer. As to what Johnny aimed to do with the rifle, he stayed mum, and Carl Williams probably didn't want to inquire.

At the pawnshop, Johnny told his dad to trade Richard's Cartier and the fifty dollars cash that Howard gave him earlier for the gun making him lick his lips. It was a .30-caliber M-1 rifle, which was originally manufactured for American paratroopers jumping into combat in Europe and Asia during World War II. Its semiautomatic firing mechanism and other features gave the infantrymen and paratroopers gripping it a decided edge over enemies saddled with bolt-action has-beens. Army General George Patton, who'd taken it to Axis forces in the Mediterranean, France, and Germany, once raved the M-1 was "the greatest battle implement ever devised."

He'd receive no argument from Johnny, an excellent marksman euphoric about owning a piece of military history. The Cartier got him that, plus a five-round ammunition clip. There was one transaction Johnny bartered for himself at Euclid Loan and Jewelry, trading Richard's IBM Selectric II for $75. In his current existence, he had about as much use for a quality typewriter as he did a Ralph Lauren tuxedo.

Longing to use it, he took the M-1 outside the next day to saw off its barrel. That night he test-fired it by pumping rounds into a neighbor's beater car. The action was fine, so the future hitman calibrated it for a close-range blast.

His timing was impeccable. Howard on the following day announced to him, Chaser, and Jamie that he was tweaking phase one of his master plan. They were going to briefly postpone the murder-for-profit job in the Valley for a closer one that he expected to be a confidence-building cinch. They needed a success, and Howard said he knew the right prey to notch one.

As he told the crew, the franchise was poised for brisk business after completion of these first missions. Phase Two would see them pillaging a Beverly Hills contractor reckless enough to keep $180,000 in company payroll at home. Down the punch list was another Beverly Hills businessman who stored $500,000 at his residence, and then a vulnerable target in Santa Barbara. Howard tabulated that if every job paid off to the max, he could walk away with close to $800,000, making more in a few months of debauchery than he had hoarded in twenty years in the LA construction trade.

Johnny almost busted his buttons hearing this news. He could've been an Army sniper or Olympic skeet shooter if his mugshot hadn't been snapped so often. He loved caressing the M-1's cold steel and fiddling with the trigger mechanism. He took pride cleaning and oiling the barrel.

Howard's passion for guns was half of Johnny's. As a busy CEO with logistics to map, he needed to be a tactical thinker. If he typed up a memo, it would be to remind his employees to stay extra cautious as they prepared to act. They already exhausted their quota of mulligans, and without revenue, even the saintliest of businesses shrivel up.

•••

ON AN OTHERWISE FORGETTABLE day around then, as Los Angeles talk radio dug into the year's hot-button names—Ayatollah Khomeini, Patty Hearst, Ronald Reagan, Sid Vicious—Jerry steered the car that looked too old for him into the parking lot of the steel-and-glass Glendale Federal Building in Beverly Hills. Paul Fegen, Space Matters's most prolific client, wasn't revolutionizing office leasing in some archaic, concrete hulk.

Jerry was here for his regular meeting with Fegen, as if there was anything regular about a real-estate mogul who turned personal exhibitionism into a second vocation. Over to the side of the garage, Jerry saw Fegen's two Excaliburs, high-price luxury cars modeled after the 1920s-era Mercedes-Benz SS. One of the automobiles was purple, the other candy-apple green. Fegen often drove them in matching coats.

He took the elevator to the penthouse floor, entering a fifty-feet-by-sixty-feet suite larger than some small Miracle Mile manses. The walls were bare except for tacked-up Christmas cards and news articles about Mr. F.

Yawn. Jerry had seen it all before, including the unorthodox business attire. Fegen sat behind a desk in boots, tights, and a Renaissance-style shirt as if he were a middle-aged buccaneer. The clothes accented his bright-eyed face, though it was his signature hairdo that was the attention-grabber: hippie-long brown locks that curtained down Fegen's neck from the sides of a receding hairline. Jerry likened him to "a balding Jesus"—if Jesus fostered a circus-like atmosphere with shades of a cult personality. Close by him was the German shepherd he taught tricks to, and the unicycle he pedaled around for amusement when bored. On the other side of his office wall was Fegen's small battalion of attractive secretaries, many of whom were Eurasian, and all of whom were trained to fetch him pencils sharpened to obsessive specifications. Other times he shouted "press" at them to retrieve his media-clippings file so he could grandstand for a newcomer.

All business, Jerry fanned out half a dozen preliminary sketches for Fegen to examine. His distracted mind sometimes whisked him to distant universes, but he always returned when a leasing project required diligence. Jerry gripped the first blueprint, one for a Houston skyscraper, and detailed his vision for its layout.

"Impressive," Fegen said. "I like where you put the doors. Now tell me about the hallways."

He had known Jerry since 1975, eventually pegging him as a "genius" out of the thousands of people he encountered during his fanciful life. Whether one regarded him as a needy oddball or the archetype of originality, Fegen demonstrated not only how profitable it could be reinventing oneself, but also how riotously entertaining. The son of a milkman, he helped put himself through college working as a juggling clown. After a stint as a personal-injury attorney, he began honing his skills outside the law by renting and renovating office space, his own building in Beverly Hills a petri dish to determine if the math penciled out. Before long Fegen was leasing unprecedented amounts of space, primarily for law firms. His technique grew so popular, and so copycatted, it earned its own moniker: The Fegen Suite.

Off hours he was an accomplished amateur magician, yet there was no sleight of hand to his moneymaking philosophy. He winnowed it down to the science of salesmanship and economy. Fegen and his associates would approach building owners, some of them strapped with unoccupied, cash-draining properties, and propose pre-leasing entire floors. If they heard yes, they would reshape the space into nicely done, efficiently contoured professional suites. Wasted square footage here was taboo. In Fegen's model, solo-practicing attorneys and law firms were typically arrayed on the perimeter of a floor, with a central reception area in the middle. Tenants shared everything nonproprietary: secretaries, law libraries, telephone operators, kitchens. By maximizing each inch of rentable area, landlords made more with less.

Today's WeWork modular office was the late seventies Fegen Suite. What he cleverly marketed as low-cost luxury tapped into voracious demand. Fegen's empire subleased more office space than any competitor in the world. Its holdings stretched from California to Texas and required a six-hundred-person workforce.

The only piece missing was a fertile mind able to churn out the floorplans. Jerry's audition for the role literally began at shoe level when one of Fegen's projects required bulk indoor carpeting. Appreciating this chance, Jerry rustled it up speedily and at a bargain price. Blown away at how he'd managed it, Fegen designated Jerry his go-to space planner, a plum gig that others would've loved to nail down. Over the years, Jerry crafted more square footage for Fegen's properties—seven million square feet—than *all* the commercial square footage in LA's Century City combined.

Until they met, Jerry had never associated with somebody as uniquely confident or as unabashedly narcissistic as Fegen. Even in a freewheeling California—you know the tropes: macrobiotic diets, hot yoga, dog therapists, boardroom cocaine—tycoons generally don't drive exotic cars outfitted with microphones so they could flirt with young women, or plaster sequins on their cheeks for laughs. Nor do they commission stained-glass windows of themselves at their homes. Fegen was an icon of self-creation, once proclaiming that he intended to go to his grave at one hundred certain there'd never be another like him.

How could there be? Celebrity and crowds enthralled him as much as full-occupancy office towers. In 1971, Jimi Hendrix and David Bowie performed at his house; later in the decade, Devo entertained guests. Where Fegen truly etched his legend, however, were the soirees he threw at four-diamond hotels like the Century Plaza. Here, a sea of partygoers told to dress in certain colors (purple, black, and white) witnessed a famous Hollywood stylist cut Fegen's famously weird hair. Never one to shrink from self-congratulation, he claimed partial inspiration for the 1968 comedy "I Love You, Alice B. Toklas!" about an Aquarius-age lawyer, played by Peter Sellers, and his "groovy" brownies.

Besides the barrel of work he provided for the company, Bald Jesus gave Jerry something else. He'd proved that anyone, regardless of background or fetish, could strike it rich in real estate with enough dynamic belief.

CHAPTER NINE
SHORT MEN IN TRENCHCOATS

O NCE UPON A TIME, when he still believed the sun shined on him, Howard would've been mortified had anyone accused him of dispatching little monsters to attack the émigré family that he tried connecting to the American dream. He would've chopped off his own pinkie before scrawling a list of others, starting with Jerry and Richard, for his minions to shoot in their heads.

So why did an old-school construction chief with a trick back, neurotic wife, and a union card decide to mortgage his soul? It *was* the disease that produced no tumors or coronaries, the disease that you couldn't see—a tarry black resentment toward those more prosperous than him in his skewed accounting. While no one ever confused Howard with a choir boy, few could've dreamed that this bitterness would darken his heart from troublemaking to wicked; that his grievances would transport him to an alternative reality where he brainwashed himself into believing that his victims warranted the cruelty he was about to serve them.

Earlier in the 1970s, the Argentinian family that immigrated to the same Arcadia neighborhood where he lived considered him part of their welcoming party. Luis, patriarch of the group, was a smallish, fleshy-faced man, a jack-of-all-trades who was especially mechanically inclined. With his wife and kids sardined into an apartment, he wasn't averse to grunt labor, though. Howard, impressed by his work ethic, stuffed money into Luis's pockets every chance he could. When he required weekend yard cleanup at his Coronado Drive home, he paid Luis to do it. When his construction projects required demolition, Luis got the call.

After becoming better acquainted, Luis came to realize that there were different Howards. There was the jobsite professional insistent on quality work. There was the hard-partying blue collar that guzzled champagne as he raced his old Corvette 100 miles per hour on the hairpin Arroyo Seco Freeway. Then there was the compassionate Howard, who would don a holiday costume to make hardscrabble kids giggle.

His mother, Mabel, practiced this same helping-hands philosophy. The heavyset woman with the horn-rimmed glasses and difficulty moving around delighted at digging into her purse for the Buonsanti's. One Christmas, she bought Luis's brood a sleigh's worth of toys and threw in secondhand clothes. Grateful for everything, Luis and his wife named Mabel the godmother to their youngest son, Maurice. It was easy to root for a tightknit, hardworking clan like theirs to succeed.

Years passed and Luis's tenacity achieved just that. His break-through: purchasing an auto body repair shop in Arcadia. After he'd banged out enough dents and replaced enough crumpled hoods, the entrepreneur in Luis coveted fresh opportunities in real estate. He began flipping homes before it became the cottage industry it is today, fixing up and unloading two derelict properties for a nifty profit. Now he hungered to flip more, a lot more, and reasoned that Howard, with his trove of experience and connections, would make the ideal partner. Howard even performed work on one of the spec houses.

On the same day that Howard's men burglarized that residence in the Valley, Luis revisited with his generous friend the theme of them flipping houses together full-time. Howard brought his El Camino into Luis's shop for body work, so what better time to discuss it? Luis told him that he circled the next house he hoped to acquire, but also requested assistance. Economic assistance. He needed Howard's help finding a bank willing to provide him with a low-interest loan. As a backup in case he couldn't secure a lender to finance the transaction, Luis knew a solution.

"I have fifty-five thousand in my house," he said in broken English. "I'll use that."

Howard, elated to hear Luis repeat that he had money in his house, promised to ask around. Luis smiled in his salt-of-the-earth way.

Then, abruptly, Howard veered the conversation to his El Camino, which showed front-end damage and a mashed rear fender. He acted prickly about his car, griping about how some people abused it. Just recently, he told Luis, an ex-friend ran off with the Chevy to San Francisco without his blessing. When he got it back, there were "strange" items in the camper shell that he did not recognize. He was so disturbed by them that he refused to touch them.

Luis was perplexed about why Howard was spilling all this to him, unable to peer through the smokescreen being lit. His comment about the items in the camper was a foundational one to frame Robert Freeman should any of his own murderous plots go awry. His other motive: manufacturing an alibi for the El Camino when his goons pillaged the man standing *next* to him.

Blind to it all, Luis lent him a light green Fiat four-door, one chum to another. It marked his final day of innocence.

At dusk the following day, Howard sat ensconced in another vehicle down the street from Luis's green-speckled house in Monrovia, a bedroom suburb east of Arcadia where the clapboard houses were well tended and flag ownership high. The lookout car that he planned to ditch later gave him the anonymity he desired as the plot's mastermind. Hours earlier, with the aid of Johnny and a compatriot, he stole a 1976 Buick Riviera from the underground parking lot of the Roosevelt building in downtown LA once the parking attendant split for the evening. Howard, having worked construction at the historic property for years, knew its layout and tenants well. Hence, this wasn't any random car. It belonged to Bruce Friedman, one of Howard's many lawyers, who rented an office there. The Buick's vanity license plate said it all: J-U-R-Y. The keys were left in it.

From the Roosevelt, the three headed east, first stopping at a mall to buy latex gloves and duct tape, and then to Bob's Coffee Shop in Monrovia for a pre-operation briefing.

At 8:30 p.m. inside the house of Buonsanti, Luis's family, along with his shop foreman and wife, nibbled appetizers while waiting for their late supper. It was just another dull Wednesday evening in Jimmy Carter's America. Everybody was in the front of the house except for Luis's eldest boy, Sergio. The high-school freshman remained in his back bedroom, watching prime-time sitcoms instead of engaging in the pre-dinner social hour. Sergio's eight-year-old kid brother, Maurice, was out with the grown-ups. So was his big sister, Sandra, a vivacious brunette looking forward to graduation as an eighteen-year-old high-school senior.

When the doorbell rang, Sandra answered it, anticipating seeing her boyfriend in the entryway. Uh-uh: it was a pair of short men in long, dark coats standing there, framed against the night. One (Johnny) wore shaggy hair and a goatee out of place with his brown suede shoes. The other was Howard's latest hire, who was smaller than Johnny and even stranger looking. "Crazy Eddy," as his friends called him, wore his brown-reddish hair in a comb-over, likely to obscure violet facial bruises from a recent scrap. Johnny spoke first.

"We're here to pick up the car," he said. "Can we speak with Luis?"

The car, Sandra inquired? She'd hung around her dad's shop before and never heard of a customer traveling to their house on business. The men noticed Sandra's baffled expression.

"You better go get your dad then," Johnny said.

She passed the message along, and Luis was as confused as his daughter. The only person he could imagine with the chutzpah to surface here was a Cuban customer so finicky about his car that he once requested Luis drive it home to reduce its chances of being dinged or stolen from his shop. Luis realized his Cuban-customer hypothesis was wrong as soon he stepped outside.

"We're here to get an estimate," Johnny said, changing their story.

Before Luis could announce they must be mixed up, the men pirouetted on the stoop. When they whipped around, their orange-gloved hands clutched rifles, one of them a sawed-off M-1, the other a shotgun, that they'd hidden before under their trenchcoats. Seeing the guns, Luis rushed back inside while Sandra tried slamming the door. Howard's representatives were too fast. They jammed their rifle butts into the arch and shouldered their way in, knocking father and daughter backward.

Pandemonium erupted in the room where appetizer plates had just been passed around. Luis darted toward the kitchen, reverting to his native Spanish.

"*Es un robo*," he yelled to no one in particular. "¡*Llama a la policía!* ¡Policía!"

He snagged the kitchen phone to dial the operator while continuing to shout "¡policía!" as if he expected armed officers would parachute in from a helicopter. Crazy Eddy tracked him there, waving a gun at him and ordering him to set the phone down.

He and Johnny rounded up Luis, his wife, Norma, their daughter, and their youngest son. Next, they pulled the Granados, friends of the Buonsanti's unlucky to be in the house, out from behind the bar where the couple hid. Then they steered everyone into the living room, forcing them to their knees.

Shut up, they said. Keep still.

The intruders counted heads, and afterward Johnny peeled off for a quick search of the interior.

"Where's the other kid?" he asked upon returning. "There's one missing."

Luis's near-hysterical wife volunteered the reason why.

"He's at Boy Scouts—a Boy Scouts meeting," Norma said. "He won't be back until later."

Johnny took her word, believing that they would be long gone by the time the boy walked in. The intrigue was what Sergio would find: a bloodbath, shaken hostages, a home in flames? Johnny and Crazy

Eddy weren't positive themselves on this question. Howard stressed robbery here but encouraged gore if necessary. What should they do if they met resistance, Johnny had asked?

"Just pull the trigger," Howard said glibly.

He abhorred recalcitrant hostages as much as disloyalty from his employees. As the number two here, Johnny was vested with the latitude to do whatever was necessary to walk out with the cash that Howard believed was "in the house." If Luis was still clamming up after seeing his family manhandled, Howard told Johnny to shoot Luis's wife. If that failed to get Luis talking, Johnny was to shoot the children, one by one.

Crazy Eddy began placing strips of duct tape over the mouths and eyes of the captives except Luis. Johnny trailed, taping hands behind backs and ankles together.

"Why are you here?" Luis said, begging.

"You'll find out," Johnny said. "Shut up."

"You can take anything, okay?" Luis said. "Just don't kill nobody!"

Johnny walked over to the kneeling, groveling head of household.

"*You* know what we want," he said.

"No, no, no," Luis said, complaining they were being too vague about their demands. "This is a mistake."

He whimpered that he would give them $1,300 cash. Johnny repeated they were here for something else without specifying it was that fifty-five thousand.

"Hurry up," Johnny ordered Crazy Eddy, who was busy applying the restraints. "Let's get this over with."

Norma piped up, repeating the men were there in error. They didn't appreciate her petition, and told her to be quiet, Johnny in English, Crazy Eddy in Spanish. When she simmered down, Luis resumed his beseeching and questions.

Johnny returned to binding hands and feet. He understood they didn't have forever, and that Howard expected him to emerge with a satchel of money. At Bob's Coffee Shop beforehand, Howard told Johnny that Luis was not the heart-of-gold breadwinner that everybody thought. Luis, he said, paid his workers under the table to avoid taxes, that some of his grease monkeys might've been illegal aliens from Mexico, and there could be stolen cars at his garage. Because of that, Luis would not want the US Immigration Service or IRS prying into his file cabinets. He would probably be too scared to even report to authorities any money taken in a robbery.

What Howard never bothered to inform Johnny was that he was smearing Luis's integrity minus a shred of proof.

"Don't you have kids?" a teary Norma asked. "Don't you see what this is doing to us?"

Crazy Eddy admitted he had children, even as he continued taping Luis, father of three.

Little Maurice now spoke up for the first time, repeating like an adult his father's plea for level heads.

"Guys," he said in voice muffled with duct tape. "Take it easy."

Luis assumed they were about to be gunned down execution style over a mistaken identity in the comfy confines of his living room. How could they not be? The little hoodlums didn't bother to shield their faces with masks, meaning they didn't expect anyone would be pointing then out later in a police lineup. They'd be dead.

Sandra, his daughter, carried her own trepidation as Howard's men leered at her and her mother when they weren't binding: the two would rape them before this ended.

But surprise. The Buonsantis had some say in their destiny with Norma's risky but credible-sounding lie. Her oldest son wasn't at some convenient Boy Scouts meeting. He was in his bedroom, watching *Laverne & Shirley* in a pair of boxer shorts and T-shirt, when the intruders burst in and his panicked father shrieked for the police.

Oh, fuck, the fourteen-year-old thought.

He needed to muster courage. Needed to ignore the terror clamping his windpipe. But to do what? Brandish his bee-bee gun at the bad guys? Create a distraction? When he heard whimpering from the front of the house, he realized those tactics were too passive to keep the lamenting from becoming screams of pain. His idea: throw on some pants and unlatch his window.

Sergio dove out headfirst, tumbling about eight feet on account of the home's steep grade. He sprinted to a neighbor's house, rapped on the Clines's back door, and rocked nervously back and forth waiting for someone to answer. And then waited some more. Picturing what could be happening inside his house, Sergio let himself in, much to the shock of a fifty-something couple who didn't hear him knocking. He apologized for the rude entry but said diabolical men were holding his family at gunpoint. Got a phone? Dennis Cline dialed the Monrovia Police Department because Sergio's fingers were shaking too hard to do it. He handed Sergio the phone, and the boy summarized to police what was unfolding.

"*Hurry!*" he added.

The response time was phenomenal for a bucolic, low-crime city where emergency calls often involved black bears wandering down from the foothills to rummage in people's garbage or take a dip in their hot tubs. Within minutes, a patrol car with two officers flew up Hillcrest Avenue, siren off. Blazing up the road, one of them noticed a grizzled-looking man sitting inside a parked Buick. As soon as they passed him, he abandoned the car and disappeared phantom-like up somebody's side yard.

Sergio was the next person the officers encountered. He stood on the Clines's house patio, pacing and crying. Seeing the black-and-white car, he pointed toward his house.

"They got 'em in there!" he shouted.

Johnny was the first to detect the cruiser rolling up to the curb. The officers would be reaching for their holsters next.

"Here come the pigs," he told Crazy Eddy.

They confabbed about what to do in front of captives whose terror was klieg-lit by the whites of their eyes. Johnny's impulse was to mow down the first cop dumb enough to enter without blasting his way in. Cucumber cool, he aimed his M-1 at it the front door, waiting for the handle to jiggle as his cue to shoot. Crazy Eddy was no cowboy like Johnny, wanting zero part of a firefight with authorities. His inclination was to escape, like that instant. The two goons were at loggerheads, split between valor and retreat.

The Buonsanti's poodles weighed in next, yipping and barking, sensing the officers' arrival outside, if not the anxiety dripping from the ceiling inside. The animals' frenetic carrying on seemed to snap Johnny out of his reverie for a gun battle, which would've pitted his powerful, vintage rifle against the cops' skimpy revolvers. He exhaled and posed himself a hypothetical: *What would Howard advise?* It'd probably be act strategically. Nobody was liable to get rich off future murder-for-profit operations after a police shootout. It'd be either body bags or handcuffs.

Johnny stopped pointing his M-1.

"How do we get out of here?" he asked his detainees. "Is there a back door?"

Sandra, able to speak beneath the slapdash tape-job over her lips, projected as loudly as she could.

"Toward the dogs!" she said.

Crazy Eddy may have asked whether they bite, but neither he nor Johnny lingered for a response. They lit out of the rear door, trampling a grave-stake fence rimming the property and leaving a gaggle of raggedly-breathing people behind.

Sandra straggled to her feet and waddled to the entryway. The duct tape around her ankles loosened, and she managed to unlock the front door to meet the police on the lawn.

"They're going out the back door!" she said, pointing.

The officers dashed into the house, ordering the Buonsantis and the guests to run next door while they conducted a room-by-room search. They appeared pale following their sweep. The restraints and the descriptions of the men's firepower was big-city criminality, not some rare holdup in quaint Monrovia. One close-range bullet from an M-1 would've blown someone's chest apart. Backup arrived, and the consensus was that the robbers vacated the neighborhood by foot. The danger was over.

With Monrovia PD poised to chase after them, Crazy Eddy separated from Johnny in the Buonsanti's backyard, fleeing in the dusk to remove himself from the scene. Johnny took the opposite approach.

The Buonsantis and Granados wept, hugged, and thanked God that Sergio got away to bugle the cavalry. If he hadn't been in the rear watching *Laverne & Shirley*, a comedy about a pair of spunky, working girls from 1950s Milwaukee—a show whose gibberish theme song warbled *Schlemiel, schlimazel, hasenpfeffer incorporated*—half a dozen people might well be massacred.

Later that evening, after they had deemed the property secure, Monrovia police bore down on a possible person of interest. They listened for slipups in his account. They poked into his background. Not all victims are guiltless. Right, Luis?

"What did you do to have this happen?" they asked him. "What's the real story? You in the drug business?"

Luis was numb. First, Johnny interrogated him with that huge rifle in his face, now the police with their notepads. Near midnight, officers drove him to his body shop on Las Tunas Drive. Could a customer of yours, they asked, have choreographed this? The only foggy linkage that came to Luis was Howard's unsolicited comment about the peculiar stuff in his El Camino. He doubted someone as decent as Howard would do such a thing, and felt guilty about mentioning him to the men with the badges. But this was *his* life being jacked around.

Detectives made Luis unlock the vehicle with the Garrett & Associates decal on the side doors. Yet there was nothing hinky inside, only a set of carpentry tools and blueprints. The Howard connection was weak.

The stolen Buick, conversely, was an evidentiary Easter basket. In plain view, scattered around the floor mats and seats, were a rifle box containing a carbine-clip and instructions for it, as well as a parking claim-check, cigarettes, and various papers. A license plate check for J-U-R-Y confirmed that it was reported taken from the Roosevelt Building that afternoon. As to who swiped it, or masterminded the house invasion, police missed any tie to the El Camino.

The police did recommend that Luis's traumatized family sleep elsewhere to play it safe. His group was home the next morning, hoping in time that they could erase from their memories those mangy, gun-toting creeps and their "we're here for the car" charade. None of them realized they should've kept miles away, for Johnny was closer than the most paranoid could've shivered about.

Instead of running headlong into a cordon of blue, he'd lobbed himself over the backyard wall dividing the Buonsanti's property from their neighbors and crawled into the neighbor's small pool shed. Kept his escaped so simple it was complex. As Monrovia police canvassed that area, flashlights beaming, revolvers drawn, he sat in the enclosure with his M-1 cocked, still itching for a fight. But the officers never gave him one. The enclosure must've seemed too audacious, too obvious a place to hole up. Johnny grew so bored waiting for a confrontation that never roared that he dozed off.

When he awoke, he popped his head outside, mindful of where he was, and walked down Hillcrest Avenue to Bob's Coffee Shop as if he were a local. When Howard picked him up, probably in the Fiat that Luis lent him out of the goodness in his heart, Johnny expected to be torn asunder after another stumblebum raid. Surprisingly, Howard was genial, loose even, chortling about the terror they'd visited on his "friend" despite its failure to net even one hundred dollars. That Howard once dressed up as Santa Claus as a Christmas surprise for Luis's kids or chugged bubbly with him after a day schlepping drywall gave him no sentimental regret. It generated more braying about how they rat-fucked the Argentinian.

Luis was suffering for that, presiding over a family spooked about the invaders paying them a second visit. They deserved protection. They'd earned peace of mind. So, the day after those men shouldered in, he purchased a .30-30 rifle from J. C. Penney. Next he installed a motion detector alarm system.

Good thing too, because that night at about 3:00 a.m. his new alarm blared. Luis grabbed his department-store rifle and crept toward the living room. That's when he saw a shadow flicker and heard a ruffle.

Oh, my God, they're back!

He didn't hesitate to identify or warn whoever was inside. He fired. Nobody else in the house of shattered nerves, thankfully, heard it.

The next morning, Maurice went through his normal routine in an abnormal time. He filled a bowl up with cereal, sitting down in the living room to watch cartoons. Bugs Bunny or Wiley E. Coyote would've appeared too—had there not been a spiky hole in the set's glass screen.

"What happened to the television?" he asked in wonderment.

"Dad shot it last night," Sergio, his big brother, answered deadpan.

And why did he fire? One of the yipping dogs shook its head, tripping the alarm.

Howard stopped by the repair shop later that same day, ostensibly to whine but really for intel collection. He bitched to Luis, who looked five years older overnight, that the loaner Fiat was worthless. Thing was barely drivable, he said; all four tires were worn thin. Luis apologized, explaining his mind was someplace else after those fifteen minutes of duct tape and ultimatums. He kept tight-lipped about the police's search of the El Camino, still remorseful he mentioned his friend.

Howard listened like a sympathetic uncle as Luis described the incident for him. How he was so jittery afterward that he fired a wild shot inside his darkened house at a motion, he was embarrassed to admit, that was probably caused by one of his dogs scratching its ears.

"I'm so sorry, man, really," Howard said. "That's just awful."

He opined that Luis was smart to buy a gun and alarm system, what with so many hoodlums preying on innocent people nowadays. After consoling him for the crime that his employees brought into Luis' living room, Howard drove off in his repaired El Camino, smirking.

•••

BACK IN PASADENA, HOWARD reoriented himself on their business in the Valley.

Not Johnny. Not now. He remained obsessed about finishing what they started in Monrovia. He pined for another chance to murder Luis, even if he never saw the man's face before the assault; he would stalk him all the way to Buenos Aires if he must. The specter of revenge against the cops who responded to the break-in put another homicidal gleam in his eye. Those aspirations, though, would just have to wait.

He and Chaser were soon at a local Chevy dealer, feigning interest in buying a black GMC "four-wheel drive" truck. At the lot, Johnny bombarded the car salesman with technical questions about the pre-sport utility vehicle. Does it lumber in traffic? What about the shocks? Pickup? If it handled as well in a test-drive as it looked there, he'd whip out his checkbook. By all means, take it for a spin, the salesman said. He only needed a valid driver's license. They supplied him one, presumably fake.

Hours later Robert Freeman stood on a Haight-Ashbury sidewalk, jawboning with a knot of apparently gay men. He was in his element, bisexual conquistador that he was, married to one woman, dating others, all the while engaging in male liaisons, in jail and out. Not even that eclectic love life gave him what he could've used just then: eyes in the back of his head.

Cruising up behind him was a truck occupied by a pair of recognizable faces who'd already recognized him. Johnny ordered Chaser to park the car around the corner and to keep the engine running. Depending on the commotion they were about to generate, they might need to hightail it out of there like they'd just robbed a bank.

Minutes later, Johnny's footfalls wove him around pedestrians and past colorful storefronts, bringing him closer to the gruesome cabaret that he yearned for: a daylight execution of Robert, whose back was turned. Johnny's fingers curled the .357 Smith & Wesson, which Howard had lent him from his mini arsenal, after Johnny wouldn't pipe down about taking care of his yellow-bellied, car-stealing, deal-welching erstwhile "friend." Howard relented so long as the operation in no way jeopardized their profitable business ahead with Space Matters.

The hitman who replaced Robert on Howard's management pyramid believed in his bones *today* was his day. Why else, in a city of millions, did they happen to spot him out in public if kismet wasn't in their corner? This was to be a quick slug in the rear of the skull. Afterward, Johnny would stride back to the GMC, perfectly composed, as he did from the shed next to the Buonsanti's; Chaser then would guide the car back onto the freeway, LA bound. In Johnny's thinking, Robert's acquaintances would be too petrified to give chase or reconstruct his description. Everyone there remembered how many died in the Harvey Milk execution five months ago.

Yes, this time it was going to happen. Johnny's eyes swept the block for any last-minute deal-stoppers, feet shuffling toward his target. He could click the safety off the .357.

Then he cursed under his breath when he would've preferred hollering Jesus F. Christ.

Out of nowhere, a San Francisco Police Department patrol car materialized, and it wasn't scooting off on another call. It idled next to Robert as if it were in on the universe's joke. An excruciating decision sat in Johnny's lap: pull the trigger for the endorphin rush and glory, hoping it didn't provoke a gunfight with the SFPD, or bide his time for another day?

What would Howard do?

Grudgingly, he tucked the .357 back into his jacket and trudged toward the stolen truck. Seeing Johnny's hangdog expression, Chaser knew that it was going to be a long trip home, though one without sirens in the rearview mirror. Home from another missed chance, they ditched the GMC supposedly out for a test drive.

Howard should've expected this outcome would be the same as the others. But he was also a carpenter at heart and understood basic math: the laws of probability would eventually reward him.

CHAPTER TEN
THE DELICACY OF GLASS

RICHARD, BY ONE YARDSTICK, had done the extraordinary by March. He rediscovered his buoyancy, flouting the pesky currents of self-destruction that sucked him beneath the roiling surf before. Depression? Not this time. Suicide? Ridiculous. It was time to get out of his bathrobe and back into the world.

His skin glowed with a healthier sheen now that spring roses readied to bud after a torrential winter. Nibbles for Kasparov & Co. design work portended sketching for underused hands. Richard, humbled after weeks of self-inventory and therapy, determined to rid his DNA of the moody narcissist in him, felt like a man lighter after shedding undesired old skin.

Easter was three weeks away. He would resurrect himself.

And his blueprint for a better tomorrow started today, at Paige's door. In recent weeks, they dined out at a bistro and gotten together elsewhere to discuss reconciliation. Paige, exhausted from moving, and missing him, now leaned toward halting her initial steps toward divorce. Despite reams of evidence that her spouse betrayed Jerry, she questioned, with the aid of Richard's propaganda on the subject, if Jerry manipulated *her* by embellishing the scope of Richard's fraud. During their talks, they pondered relocating to San Francisco, away from the smiling assholes of LA and their own choppy history there. Richard was willing to go. If he could survive the loneliest winter of his existence, he could acclimate to any place, temptations and all.

With things looking decidedly up, he anticipated Paige greeting him with a luscious smile when he knocked on her rental home on Saturday, March 24. It was to be Rebecca's day out with daddy. Yet Paige was anything but smiling. She was despondent and shaking, as if she'd just heard awful news.

"What's wrong?" Richard asked on the stoop. "The baby okay?"

"She's fine."

"Then what? Something's going on."

"I'll tell you what. I just got an anonymous phone call from a woman who said there was a contract out on you, Richard! A fucking *murder* contract. Somebody wants you dead."

"A murder contract? Please," he said after a pause. "This is a joke, right?"

"I wish it was."

"When did this happen?"

Paige said the phone rang around 11:00 a.m. as she was feeding Rebecca in her highchair.

"And how did this mysterious caller know how to reach you? You've already moved twice."

Paige wasn't sure but suggested the Yellow Pages.

"And that's it?"

"What do you mean that's it? This woman asked to speak with you, and I told her we weren't living together."

"So?"

"She wanted to know if I was married to an architect. I said you were a space designer."

"Why did that matter?"

"Because she wanted to make sure that you were the right person to warn. Haven't you been listening to what I said?"

"Yes, and so far you're making too big of a production out of it. Sounds to me like a prank call. A hoax."

Paige was quivering before. Now frustration rucked her brow.

"You're just not getting it if that's what you think," she said. "This lady said, 'Why don't you name the people who don't like your husband?'"

"And did you?"

"No. She told me to tell you that you should go around 'making nice to people,' and that you should be careful. She wanted your number, actually, but I refused to give it to her."

Richard stared at Paige as if she were a mental patient.

"What the hell does that mean, 'go around making nice,' huh?"

"I don't know. But you better quit asking questions and start getting to the bottom of this."

"Well, I can't get to the bottom of something when you're telling me that somebody wants me dead! That's crazy. Who would want to murder me? Tell me. I can't wait to hear."

"That call wasn't for nothing. This woman asked about *you*— Richard Kasparov. She sounded nervous herself."

Dead air hung between them before Richard reacted as he often did upon learning about blowback from his past: he spurted bile at anyone in target range.

"There was no call, was there, Paige?" he said. "Admit it! *You* made this whole story up."

He pantomimed a shoving gesture, next, to imply she was sandbagging him.

"You're pandering to the court for money," he continued. "Very sneaky of you."

Paige's welling eyes filled with indignation, the panicky kind.

"I'm confused," she said. "How could you believe I'd go from discussing getting back together to suddenly lying about this? I'm scared, alright? Remember the man on the deck with Isabel? I'm pleading with you, Richard. Don't be stubborn. Go to the police! Figure out who's after you. This could be your life we're talking about."

"Quit saying that. Where's my daughter? That's what I need to know."

"You're certifiable if you think I'm letting Rebecca leave with you after receiving a call saying somebody wants you dead. No mother on earth would agree to that."

"I'll ask again," Richard said, crimson-cheeked and cross-armed. "Where is she?"

"Same answer. She's not here."

Voices ratcheted up. Each stepped farther away from the other.

"Is she with Erica across the street? I'm her father, in case you forgot, not some schmuck. I have rights."

"Sorry. I have a duty to keep my daughter safe."

"If that's the way you want to play it, the next phone call you'll be receiving will be from my lawyer, not some made-up woman. I'll see you in court. I don't have to take this shit."

Richard pivoted around, storming toward Erica's home with a body language that'd clear out a crowded post office. Erica, though, cracked her door to intercept him.

"Turn around, Richard—you can stop right there," she shouted from her porch. "The baby ain't coming with you."

"The hell she's not. I hope you know the law…"

"I hope you know," Erica interrupted, "that I hate your guts and you're going to fucking die if you don't watch it. Now get *off* my property!"

Had anybody noticed Richard's pallor as he returned to his Cougar, they would have seen it was no longer maroon as it was during his verbal combat with Paige. Forehead to chin, he was ghostly white.

Auf Wiedersehn, reconciliation.

Even before her torrid fight with him, Paige had already beat Richard to a lawyer. After the nameless woman contacted her, she wasted no time contacting her attorney to ask what to do. He told her to reach out to the LAPD, an understaffed department stretched thin during a record crime year, especially for murders; in 1978 alone, there were a quarter million unanswered emergency calls. The officer who picked up Paige's call was useless himself. Sympathetic as he was about her predicament, he said there wasn't any action the department could take. The reason? The anonymous tip contained too little evidence of "a specific threat." Besides, the cop was reluctant to fill a report out, this being the weekend shift.

Back on the horn again, Paige described this bureaucratic shrug of the shoulders to her attorney. So, he phoned Richard's, and, after bickering, they agreed that a judge would referee Richard's rights to see his daughter.

Sometime that Saturday, Paige phoned Jerry's wife about the supposed price on Richard's head. Tammy was incredulous.

"Paige, this is 1979," she said. "These things don't happen."

•••

BY MONDAY, RICHARD COULD not care less about anything over the horizon.

Early that morning, the woman he was seeing in Paige's absence phoned him, and he was never more appreciative. He needed someone whose pants he could still charm off, and Susan Sullivan was that candidate; to her, Richard was no ostracized gray fox. He was a dashing gent supportive of her career aspirations. Plus, like others, he owed her money. In their brief conversation, Susan raised that touchy subject; he was late paying her for the clerical work that she'd done for him since his partnership dissolution with Jerry. Bills, she said, were clogging her mailbox.

They'd met when a temp agency referred her to Space Matters to fill in as the office receptionist. Right away, Richard's indefatigable libido noticed that the leggy newcomer had the sex appeal of a *Penthouse* magazine model, not the mothball scent of a dowager who typed sixty words a minute. Susan, all the same, was confined in an office where Richard was regarded as an embezzling Judas. Because of that, Susan's ongoing fealty to him made her both his one true believer and sexual analgesic. It was Jerry, Richard carped, who spoiled things, even as Jerry rooted him out of the company.

Whether *he* believed this self-serving, parallel universe account, no one can say. But he assured Susan that he would call her later that day about getting together to sort out his debts to her, while also budgeting time for romance. Right now, he told her, he needed to make a "client meeting."

This one was a whopper. The meeting to which he referred was his appointment to sign the final paperwork granting Jerry full control of the companies—the companies that they grew together from seedlings to maturity. Included in there: the home-remodeling spinoff that Richard conned because he couldn't help himself.

Post signature, Richard traipsed from Jerry's lawyer's office a hollowed-out man, not unlike a condemned building after the first dynamite blast. Only random frontage now remained, and even that skeletal frame will teeter without temporary buttressing.

He reached Susan at home just after 4:00 p.m. to discuss a rendezvous time. They set one, Richard in need of no-questions-asked TLC, Susan that check for her secretarial work. Before they hung up, she inquired whether he read the script she gave him, the script with the part for which she was auditioning. Susan didn't intend on being a temp secretary forever; she intended on being a Hollywood actress. Richard, to no surprise, replied that he didn't get to it yet, but he would by tonight. Definitely. So head over.

Susan arrived about 8:45 p.m. in the midst of another sloppy rainstorm. Richard stood tall in the entryway, presenting a resilient facade, not one gasping for answers about what the future held. Behind him, logs crackled in the fireplace. Upstairs in the master bedroom, the college basketball national championship game pitting Magic Johnson against Larry Bird in a clash of future sports megastars flickered on TV. Not that Richard was ever much interested in sports, or exercise; his idea of a workout, Paige used to joke, was a vigorous day shopping at Neiman Marcus.

They walked up the stairs, entered the master bedroom, and kissed. Richard then switched off the game and turned on his gallantry. He announced that she deserved a fine dinner on him, and that he would hear no objections. Sounded lovely, Susan said, but she wasn't prepared for anything fancy in a wrinkled dress. Richard, bewhiskered aphrodisiac, suggested how she could smooth out the creases. Just take it off and hang it on the doorknob. She did as suggested.

Disrobed, Susan wrapped herself in a vine around him on the bed until they melted onto the floor. There, body heat rose. Dopamine bubbled. Richard's mouth made the first real move, just not toward lips, bra, or panties.

On the floor of his bedroom, he queried Susan about, of all things, her finances: rent, car, salary, credit cards—the math of high-cost L.A. If she needed to economize, she could move in here. Look at all this space! He'd broached the idea of cohabitation before in recent weeks, a backup plan in case Paige snubbed his entreaty for a third chance. Susan, as before, responded that while it was flattering to be asked, she treasured her independence and would need to demur.

Still, she was sure glad to be in his arms now.

They shifted onto the bed for some rainy night sex, but the juices of two people with reasons to be preoccupied weren't flowing. Richard withdrew to slather on Vaseline, and still the arousal meter registered low when they went back at it. He recommended that they postpone their search for crescendos until after he treated her to dinner. No need to rush. Good idea, Susan said. While she applied her makeup, Richard switched on the TV—to a beauty pageant. The Magic-versus-Larry title game was over, anyway.

They were in his Cougar in search of a late dinner by 9:30 p.m. The first place they tried, Albian's on Ventura Boulevard, was closed. Passing it, Richard briefly forgot whom he was with, noting that Paige helped decorate the interior of an adjacent building. They drove next to La Serre, also on Ventura Boulevard, and found an open kitchen. Inside, Richard ordered impulsively: artichoke hearts, beef, strawberries. They were back in the house by 11:15 p.m.

Susan sat downstairs near the waning fire, sketching with a borrowed pad and pen. Her purse and sweater rested near the front door, revealing ambivalence about whether she'd spend the night. Ten minutes later, the drifting scent of incense wafted into her headspace. She followed the aroma upstairs to the bedroom. Richard, pied piper, was setting the mood.

He was leaned up against the headboard reading her script when she strolled in. He tossed her his pajama top and invited her to join him, perhaps grinning about the next carnal hours. She disrobed, slipped on his top, and jiggled beside him. Richard's king-size bed was a colorful expanse, fitted with blue sheets and a brown-and-white comforter. Susan took the manuscript from him and requested his undivided attention, as if that were possible. She needed to rehearse her lines for that upcoming audition.

Richard told her by all means. He would be her audience of one.

•••

JOHNNY, SHARP AS HE was sociopathic, realized the bugle would be tooted soon. He just assumed it would blow sometime other than during a near monsoonal rain, which he and Chaser used as an excuse to take flight on a time-bending heroin cloud.

Howard, who phoned Johnny just about the time that Richard left for dinner, was disinterested that he was wrecking their chemical adventure. The money at stake wasn't going to magically parachute into anyone's bank account.

"Let's go take him," he said in a gravely rasp.

Like now! Howard didn't dial his triggerman from Pasadena. He called from a public phone at a bar in Johnny's shabby hometown on a night he must've marked.

Works for him, Johnny said, trying to shake off his buzz, knowing he maintained no wiggle room to object. Carping, flaky behavior, and unsolicited opinions got you exiled to Howard's doghouse, a hazardous place to be sentenced. Ask Robert Freeman about his occupancy there.

Everyone grabbed his weapon of choice. Howard tucked the .357 that his wife, Carol, gave him for his birthday. Johnny's selection was the object of his affection: the pawned M-1 paratrooper rifle and the carbine clip, which he stashed under his bed. Chaser scooped up his pistol, a peashooter by comparison.

Howard picked them up at Johnny's in the El Camino, which itself was a proclamation. Unwilling to abide delay and debacle any longer, he'd ripped up his earlier blueprints for effective murder for profit—the out-of-town alibi for himself; the junker car to throw police off their scent. That Richard remained living three months after he signed a contract on him was burning Howard up, making him nuts. One could invite a double ulcer from this cavalcade of failure, where irritation led to aggravation to barely containable rage. His only remedy: to personally supervise the job, knowing he could always frame his lackeys.

For those keeping score at home, they'd confirmed that they were the most hapless of assassins. Twice, Robert had never bothered to show up at Richard's home, once after Robert's shotgun-barrel-sawing mishap. On the two occasions he made it there, the target wasn't home. After Howard replaced him, Johnny fared no better on multiple attempts, including his clever ruse about the pretend motorcycle mishap. Altogether, they had whiffed seven, eight times, maybe more. If that didn't define a clusterfuck in the slang dictionary, what did? Howard realized he needed to revise his training.

Rolling west at this hour, in these conditions, traffic was light, so the usual aureole of red brake lights was reduced to scattered pink dots. Inside the tobacco-reeking cab, with little chatter among the men, the air was filled with the hypnotic swoosh of Howard's windshield wipers. This afforded him time to scheme and his heroin-fogged underlings a chance to sober up. Next to them on the dark, slick concrete were big rigs hauling consumer products and dour workers traveling to graveyard shift jobs.

If anyone flipped on the all-news radio stations, ones like KNX or KFWB with golden-throated newscasters and clacking typewriter soundtracks, they would've heard about an eventful day in the world. Gasoline prices were now forecast to surge in the wake of an Arab-OPEC decision to dramatically raise crude oil prices, this after two embargoes in the decade. Talking heads predicted that there'd be a free-for-all on the global markets and more pain at the gas pump during the stagnant economy.

Competing news burbled out of Salt Lake City, Utah, where the Michigan State Spartans just defeated the Indiana State Sycamores for the NCAA men's basketball championship. Until now, the title game and the tournament funneling it were high holy days only for Vegas bookies and sports fanatics. Not anymore. The 1979 matchup attracted a record audience that'd transform the college basketball playoffs into the big money, bracket-filling gambling juggernaut that it is today. "March Madness" was being born. In the game, the college player of the year, a rangy white-bread forward from French Lick, Indiana, named Larry Bird, was hogtied by the Spartan's double-teaming defense. The hero of the championship was from Michigan State, a 6'9" man-child whose marquee ball handling skills and high-wattage smile solidified his nickname: "Magic." The NBA's LA Lakers would soon draft Earvin Johnson as their franchise player—heaven-sent news for a futuristic city boiling with personal grudges.

But it was the storm in normally sun-kissed LA that dominated the news cycle. Rain was lashing the area from the sagebrush high desert around Palm Spring to Malibu's curvy coast. The year's precipitation totals were already challenging records etched in 1969, when a giant swarm of warm Pacific Ocean water propelled such destruction— landsides, $400 million in property damage, ninety-one deaths—it still felt like urban myth. From the sounds of the radio updates, whole stretches of Laurel and Coldwater Canyons were now underwater. Wherever you went, palm trees were bent backward, power lines drooped, and milkshake-thick mudslides flirted with becoming highway avalanches. If this wasn't the storm of the century, it was making a case for runner-up.

Southern Californians as a whole never learned to drive adroitly in soupy weather. People weren't used to it, and auto-body shops like Luis's benefited afterward. Tonight, as the hydroplane spinouts and fender benders littering the freeway shoulders attested, many steered with the herky-jerky reflexes of a novice ice skater. Howard whizzed past, seeing mortal weakness everywhere.

Two-thirds of the way to its destination, the El Camino streaked along the Ventura (101) Freeway through Glendale. It rounded the emerald Verdugo Mountains speckled by white graves at Forest Lawn ccemeteries. It cut through Burbank, headquarters of Walt Disney Company and Warner Brothers, Hollywood's dream factories, and by the Cahuenga Pass. Just over the onyx horizon was America's suburb: an infinite flatland of single-family houses, mom-and-pop stores, grease-soaked machine shops, and the domicile of a certain Space Matters partner. The Valley welcomed all.

At the exit just before the concrete ribbons of the San Diego Freeway, Howard off-ramped north on Woodman Avenue, entering a section of Van Nuys known today as Sherman Oaks. Its commercial anchors—glass-paneled car lots, a General Motors plant; even Anheus-er-Busch Corporation's sudsy brewery—barely rated a mention on tourist maps by LA's gaudy standards.

Then again, Howard and his San Bernardino cronies were regional extraterrestrials here. One group's middle-class community was another's high-rent; one's inflation-shriveled paycheck would be another's lottery ticket. Nearing Richard's address, they wheeled past spacious homes with basketball hoops in the driveways and Spanish imitations crowned by terracotta roofs; by lime-green lawns of people born into the right gene pool and Porsches on stainless driveways. Breaks never sprinkled on these outsiders from the east seemed standard issue on Chandler Boulevard.

It was about 11:00 p.m., almost Johnny Carson hour, when Howard parked the El Camino around the corner from the residence that flummoxed them so regularly. Outside on the puddling sidewalk, they muffled their anticipation, acting as casual as could be. Their pretense was probably excessive, given the setting. Richard's street seemed as wide as an airport runway. A grassy median planted crookedly with pine, magnolias, and eucalyptus split it, keeping the sides of the block far apart. Homeowners' dense shrubbery gave trespassers extra shadows to dissolve into. Another positive: the backside of Richard's house pointed south, away from the street. They'd never knock on his front door again.

Before creeping into position, the men cupped their faces around the windows of the bottom level of the wood-and-stucco, ranch-style structure. Half-charred logs glowing orange in the fireplace were just what they hoped to see, tantalizing proof tonight was their night.

There was only one hitch: Richard's Cougar was missing from the driveway!

If Howard began muttering about voodoo doctors or guardian angels or Star Wars-esque force fields protecting his quarry, you couldn't argue.

They retreated from Richard's property to the car, dripping wet but not defeated. Unlike previous attempts, where they backtracked to Ontario, Howard said they would regroup here and see what happened. He aimed the El Camino toward Van Nuys Boulevard in the direction of Corky's, the Art Deco greasy spoon under whose V-shaped roof Johnny and Jamie trundled into a few weeks earlier. The trio spent forty-five minutes at a table avoiding loud discussion of why they were there. Everybody sipped coffee, and Howard ordered a bagel. Time-killing by the fry chefs: that's all this was.

Johnny drove back from Corky's and maybe him at the wheel was the lighter fuel they needed for their kindling. When they cruised by Richard's place this time, the Cougar *was* outside. Pulses galloped and eyes narrowed inside the Chevy as Howard directed Johnny to park it a few blocks away. It needed to be out of sight and pointed toward the Ventura Freeway for their getaway. Then they set out on foot again, rounding the corner onto that familiar boulevard.

At the house, they strode past the bushes fronting the property and hurried across the concrete apron, Johnny's boots squeaking *swuh, swuh* every step. Howard turned back, scolding him and Chaser that it would be radio silence from hereon. They weren't in some outland ghetto pa-powing with hourly gunfire. They were in the bosom of a low-crime, well-patrolled neighborhood.

They ducked by the garage, the one underneath the second-floor rooms, entering a narrow side yard partitioned with two sets of automatically closing gates; Johnny was conversant with the setup, having been here for the burglary that financed the intended murder weapon. At the base of the steps up to the deck, they hesitated to scan the grounds and resecure their hardware. All quiet so far. Johnny carried the long M-1 rifle under his coat protectively, as if it were a priceless phallic sculpture.

They slinked up the stairs, past the potted bougainvillea bush near the top of the landing, careful not to brush into any unexpected patio furniture that might give them away. Looking in for that first time, they might've been shivering in the fifty-two nip but they couldn't have been happier. They were close, deliciously close. A bare-chested Richard was lying on top of the bedspread ten feet away, within easy striking distance. Just one tug of Johnny's trigger and Howard's enterprise could finally say it was a going concern.

The single object between them and that benchmark was a thin sheet of glass, a rectangle of fortified silica that some nameless factory shipped out. It was probably the same brand of glass that the kidnapper pursuing Richard and Paige's baby daughter could've shattered four months ago had he not been foiled by the broom-wielding nanny.

The weather then was better than tonight. Every few seconds, a stiff breeze ruffled the men's waterlogged trousers. Raindrops dousing them like a sprinkler plinked Richard's roof with a drowsy patter. Down below, concentric ripples formed in Richard's pool. Electric blankets were made for these nights. Just not to Howard. To him, the storm could not have arrived at a more fortuitous moment. Between the gray cape it threw over the starry sky, and their obscured position, nobody was likely to spot them in pre-attack mode. Even busybodies who might've discerned something awry were cozy in bed. The showers tucked prying eyes inside.

Johnny and Chaser were certainly all for a wham-bam execution. Back in the comfort of the El Camino, they could warm their bluing fingers over the vents of the cranked-up heater, fantasizing about how long before they could get those same mitts on their heroin.

Being pressed up against that sliding-glass window was no picnic. It was a stressful fogbank. In the damp, scrunched up so close to that pane, they created steamy, Rorschach-shaped micro clouds just by exhaling. Johnny probably had to continually wipe the glass with his sleeve to maintain a decent sightline, while ensuring he did it inaudibly. If one of them so as much as sneezed or coughed or made something creak, the noise would ruin their element of surprise. They'd have to barge in then, killing Richard and the woman in a burst of gunfire likely to wake up the block. That or race back to the Chevy, cognizant they'd blown their final chance. Even Richard would yank his head out of the sands of denial then.

•••

INSIDE THE BEDROOM, SUSAN read from the script as Richard listened as raptly as his injured psyche would permit. On the deck outside, rain battered the men with their own mental impairments.

This, of course, included Howard, whose typically stoic expression in high-wire situations was almost unrecognizable now that he was ringside to serve Richard up a honking slab of just desert. The occasion perverted his face into a mask of primal, limbic-brain fury whose single directive was facilitating his transgressor's sweet annihilation. You could see its need for completion in Howard's glassy, bugged-out eyes and unblinking glower, in the protruding carotid arteries that throbbed from his neck like a boiling river about to spill over its banks. Had he twisted around to absorb what would've been impossible to forget, Johnny might've speculated that Howard was like him: an epileptic whose glitchy neural circuitry made him prone to trances. But Howard's spell was self-manufactured—a kind of flash-dried delirium that commandeered him like a split personality for a sacred piece of revenge. It was from this stupor that Howard clapped his palm on Johnny's narrow shoulder, stooped over him like a baseball umpire does a catcher, juiced to give the go-ahead.

Whenever that would be. Richard sensed something amiss. He wouldn't have jerked his head away from the flashy blonde in his pajama top toward the window where they squatted otherwise. In reaction, Johnny and Chaser played invisible while Howard continued staring.

Frozen, they watched Richard gazing out at eye level, praying his focus didn't drift down to shoe-top level. He appeared to be tuning into an innate survival antenna that he and Susan might have company. Not that any of his malevolent visitors were aware of it, but Richard could've also been hearkening to Paige's cuckoo-sounding warning from Saturday two days ago when she refused to let him take his daughter out.

Still, his gut hunch egging him on to check his surroundings had to contend with the immutable laws of optics, and those laws generally triumph. Yellow-white glare from the master bedroom's lamps and floor lights revealed only a single figure in the window— him—not the steam-panting hunters bowed at the edges. Looking off to the periphery in the pitch dark was useless. At that tick of the clock, the main radiance in the 13,000 block of the boulevard emanated from his *own* house. The refractory effect was that of a well-lit fishbowl, an ocular phenomenon advantageous for those looking in from the outside but hazardous to the fish.

Even so, the power to erase that advantage was only a finger flick away. If Richard cut the bedroom lights to eliminate the glare, he might've realized his intuition was correct and fled. Yet, no sooner did he glance out the window toward the disturbance he sensed was present than he turned his attention back to Susan. The men observing his every twitch, who confused the script she was reading for a book, survived their near-disastrous close call.

Every second that Richard resumed listening to her was a second closer to Howard squeezing Johnny's shoulder. The timing needed to be right, despite the fact that the few minutes they'd been out there elapsed like purgatory hours. They were about to be extended, too.

Richard spontaneously bounced off the bed, leaving open the possibility that the hairs on the back of his neck bristled again and he might make a run for it. Nothing about killing him was ever linear, though. True to this pattern, he walked the opposite direction of the sun deck, deeper into his bedroom. Johnny gripped his M-1 tighter.

The man it was intended for went to his dresser, opened a drawer, and removed a brown paper bag. Then he was at his closet, taking down a shoebox from its shelf. Returning to bed, Richard laid back down next to Susan. In a wink, the slender fingers endowed with all that starry talent—the fingers that should have helped enable him and Jerry to emblazon Space Matters' name on the top of a skyscraper—had pinched, tamped, and rolled an exemplary doobie. Afterward, he returned the brown bag and shoebox to their hiding spots and repositioned himself halfway down the bed.

There was a tasty anticipation to getting stoned on a drizzly night, especially after such a calamitous day. A numbing agent was his escape, not some stairs.

As Susan recited her lines, Richard lit the joint, inhaling a beefy first hit. Smoke coiled, and the pleasure trip was instant. He passed the doobie to Susan, who stopped her lines to toke off it, and handed it back to him. The burning red tip dimmed, but Richard didn't try relighting it, assuming he could later. Can you imagine the biting jokes spinning in the minds of the bottom feeders watching, knowing for him there would be no later?

Susan fell back into character. Richard situated himself diagonally across from her, lying on his stomach with his head near Susan's hips and his palms propping up his hunky chin. It was twenty minutes past midnight, and he was floating.

Suddenly from the bedroom's smoky placidity came a muffled thwack and shake that vibrated the mattress before petering off quickly.

Curious, Susan set down her script and asked Richard if he felt the disturbance. Could it have been a minor earthquake or wayward truck rumbling past? What about a sonic boom from the test flight of a new-generation bomber designed to penetrate Soviet air defenses? Susan readied herself for the juddering and thud to repeat. Neither did.

Since Richard never answered what he thought the source was, Susan nudged him again. He remained an un-budging lump. So she gently prodded him a second time: same result. It wasn't until Susan looked down the bed, near her pelvis, that his silence was explained. It wasn't the weed or her acting that made him doze off. If only it had.

No longer up on his elbows, Richard's face was mushed into the sheets. Around his head, scarlet fluid pooled into the mattress from a raw gash near his throat. *His throat!* Yet, Susan realized, he wasn't unconscious. He was moving like a convulsing animal laboring to find shelter before it died. Ever so slowly, he began crawling a few inches toward her on the right side of the bed.

The shooter had pulled off a tricky shot not every marksman could. His bullet whistled upward through the sliding-glass window, zoomed over Susan's outstretched legs, and struck Richard under the right side of his chin, close to his jugular. Its speed on impact was 1,700 miles per hour. In less time than it took to yawn, the projectile ripped open a star-shaped, half-inch-diameter wound that transformed the portion near his Adam's apple into fleshy hamburger. It continued traveling from there at a sharp angle, coming to rest in the left side of his brain. The fishbowl had doomed him.

Johnny's debut as a credentialed hitman also repurposed the bedroom into a slaughterhouse. Richard's blood and brain matter now stained his mattress. Caked his sheets. Sprayed his walls in a ghastly fantail. The bullet's jacket, sent aflutter after piercing the glass, landed in the folds of his bedspread.

And here was Susan, caught in a gruesome puzzle of time. One minute she was reading for an acting part in a snug bedroom, and next there was that wall-shaking thump. One minute she was with a man who wanted her to move in with him, banged her, bought her dinner, and split a joint, and now she bore witness as the life gurgled out of him. Once the reality sunk in, she cut loose a spine-tingling scream; legend held it could be heard blocks away.

When the echo faded, Susan confronted her own horror-movie moment: the washed-out breathing and scuffling of feet she heard from the landing yards away. Dreading what those noises boded for her, she tore into Richard's bathroom, but not before grabbing the master bedroom telephone to take with her. This space, though, was no haven. Carved into the bathroom wall was a window, outside of which was the deck where the shuffling—and bullet—originated. She might've been two feet from what she feared.

Her trembling fingers dialed her friend Nicholas Torrini at 12:30 a.m. "This is Susan," she said in a hushed voice. "I'm in terrible trouble."

"What?" Nicholas asked half asleep.

"I'm in the house of this man and he's been shot. I think he's dying. I'm hiding in his bathroom right now."

"Oh, Christ."

"Maybe whoever shot him wants to shoot me too. I don't know what to do," she said, hesitating for a moment to listen outside. "I think they're still here."

"The bathroom door is locked, right?

"Yes."

"Why didn't you call the police?"

"I don't know. I don't know. I just called you. You were the first person I thought of. Help me, Nicholas!"

"I will. But where are you? I mean, what's the address?"

"I don't know that, either. His house is on Chandler...between Fulton and Woodman [Avenues]. You're not going to hang up on me, are you?"

"No. Just stay on the line, okay? Don't go away. I'll use my other line to call the cops."

"Hurry!"

Nicholas phoned the LAPD directly; the flagship 911 emergency system hadn't yet been established. Initially, he got a robotic-sounding recording. When a live officer picked up, he informed Nicholas that he dialed the wrong LAPD dispatch number. Red tape does not bow, even to murder. The officer patched him through to the right colleague, who, like his peer, questioned why Susan didn't contact the department herself. Nicholas said to forget that. Just send someone out. There was a shooting! But this officer doubted gunplay could erupt in someplace as safe as Van Nuys. Nicholas assured him it did.

The officer asked Nicholas for the number that Susan was calling from, which forced him to jump back on his other line with her. After he passed it along, the officer immediately phoned her. All it got him, though, was one hair-pulling ring after another because Susan was too paranoid to click over to Richard's second line. If she disconnected herself, she could be marooned with whoever did this to Richard.

Luckily for Susan, Nicholas stayed calm. Using his two-line phone, he relayed the LAPD's instructions to her. She was to run outside, memorize the street address, and call them with it. Susan agreed, reluctantly, knowing it was either go along or take her chances with whatever it was crouched outside in the blackness. She scurried from the bathroom to the curb, then back into the bathroom. After she relayed the information, an officer told her to stay put; the department was sending out black-and-white patrol units and an ambulance.

Susan phoned Nicholas back while she waited, reporting that she could still hear Richard groaning despite the hole in his neck. Pretty soon there were sirens, followed by police whacking on Richard's front door.

"We're here," they yelled. "Open up."

Homicide detectives from the LAPD's Van Nuys division drove up half an hour later. By then it was 2:00 a.m.

Sometimes between then, detectives' aggressive grilling of her, and her plunge into shock, Susan told Nicholas what stuck with her.

"It's strange what goes on in your mind," she said. "Someone must be a very good shot."

•••

JOHNNY HAD A DILEMMA on his grand night. There on that darkened patio, he was unable to find the lone shell casing that might connect him to the killing, and he was disinclined to paw anything that might leave fingerprints. Delicately, he felt around his wet boots, near Howard's, and then the perforated window. Nothing.

Out of his trance, beautiful gruesomeness achieved, Howard was less bothered by Johnny's anxiety over the casing than ensuring that Richard stopped moving and the Southern California Rapid Transit District bus unloading late-night passengers nearby rolled away. For an interminable minute, when they weren't sure how quickly the LAPD would respond, he made them wait before they descended the stairs and galloped back to the El Camino.

From start to finish, the mission—*this* one, anyway—to execute Richard Kasparov lasted sixteen minutes. Johnny knew it because he checked the automobile's clock before they embarked.

There was one further task to complete before they called it a night and celebrated with their preferred intoxicants. From Richard's place, they took the freeway north toward Newhall. Chaser lived around here, so the direction made sense. Up by the scream-happy roller coasters of Magic Mountain, the amusement park on LA County's border with Ventura, Johnny, under orders, disassembled the rifle he wished he could've kept intact forever. Piece by metallic piece, he heaved most of the components out the window.

As Howard knew from experience, evidence destruction and escape were always an onramp away. The same freeways that Californians reviled for their gridlock and pileups, respiratory death and social isolation, were the perfect arterials for dirty deeds.

CHAPTER ELEVEN
ORIGINAL MARCH MADNESS

AROUND NOON ON TUESDAY, Jerry hunched over his desk, in the center of a paper blizzard, sketching as if the dark lines on his blueprint were all that mattered. Outside, the sun breaking through the aluminum-gray rain clouds had a sopping-wet city to warm. After the phone rang, none of that amounted to anything, for Jerry's planet had snapped off its axis.

Tammy just heard about it from a hysterical Paige shortly after the police notified her. Emergency-room doctors at Riverside Hospital in North Hollywood who tried to resuscitate Richard pronounced his time of death 1:30 a.m. By then, cracks extended outward from the bullet hole in his bedroom window like crystalline varicose veins.

An execution-style murder, of a space planner, in his own bed, off that tree-lined boulevard—Jerry expected someone to tell him it was a case of mistaken identity. That it involved another Richard.

The shock wave that spiraled through him made his hands clammy and head pound. Questions he never thought he'd pose stacked up in a logjam: who did this, what was the motive, and where would it stop? If Richard was killed, who was to say that *he* wasn't next, to say nothing of his fourteen-month-old son, Jude, or Tammy and the second child she was carrying?

Or, could this be the tip of a conspiracy: someone trying to frame him, in an inside job, for knocking off a partner whose trickery nearly capsized the company? Eliminate Richard. Incriminate him.

Both scenarios were horrifying, but an overheating mind digesting surreal news always settles somewhere. Jerry's decided that he and his family better take cover.

Within minutes of hanging up with Tammy, he was on the line with his attorney, frantic for advice. Benjamin had some. By that afternoon, Jerry sat in his West LA office answering homicide detectives' questions about Richard's enemies list, past and present. Listening to them lowered his panic level, for their protocol, their steady voiced experience, was something concrete in a haze of disbelief. It was after he was back in his car, slogging through the metal gnash of traffic, that a renewed sense of vulnerability cranked it back up.

When Jerry reached Northridge, where his family had lived for only two months, that crank couldn't wind any tighter. The spacious home, which he had been so proud to own at such a tender age, seemed more exposed than Richard's place. Windows were plastered everywhere!

He thumbed through the Yellow Pages looking for security guards able to begin immediately. A credible-enough seeming firm caught his eye, and Jerry explained to the manager how dire things were. At his insistence, the company that afternoon sent out a pair of lanky, longhaired men in their early thirties, both wearing leather jackets frayed at the elbows. They could have passed for rock-band roadies if you ignored the pistols swinging off their belts.

Even with that muscle there, Jerry kept visualizing the geometry of how Richard was shot, and worked the phone again. He contacted the office to have a Space Matters handyman race out to tack up shades on the windows still missing them. And, depressingly, most were on a structure whose street-facing exterior was a profusion of glass. Within a few hours, the Schneiderman's impromptu fortification was complete, with screens blocking interior views and the rent-a-guards providing a first line of defense. Jerry and Tammy assessed it all, reaching the same consensus: It wasn't nearly enough.

Distance. They needed distance and obscurity. To achieve it, they stuffed a few suitcases, collected their son, and, along with the guards,

141

piled into Tammy's red Cadillac Seville. The idea was to lie low at the home of one of her girlfriends for a few days until there was an arrest. Anxious to leave, Jerry keyed the ignition in her car as he had done countlessly before. But never had a thick plume of black smoke billowed from the front grill, like now.

"Everyone out of the car!" one of the guards shouted, suspecting the car may have been booby-trapped. "Go."

After some palpitations in a clumsy exit out of the sedan, they all stood far off to the side, out of any blast radius. In a minute of everyone catching their breaths, the longhairs with guns decided that it was safe for them to pop the hood to investigate. Jerry watched, heart only slightly less in mouth, as they studied the engine block, pointing here and there. Then their tense expressions slackened, and so did Jerry's. There were no plastic explosives, no ominous wires hooked to a battery. The men did point at a wisp of smoke over a splatch of hot oil on a head gasket, a clue the vehicle required a mechanic more than a bomb squad.

At Tammy's friend's house, where a dinner party was underway, she, Jerry, and Jude tromped in like suburban nomads, sheepishly waving at the staring guests.

They were back in Northridge two days later, as paranoid as before about the home's multiple windows. For peace of mind, they slept huddled together on the floor of the bonus room, away from any glass. Tammy, a Michigan girl from a solid, risk-averse Jewish family, was already pining for their old routine.

"I hate California!" she began saying. "This doesn't happen to normal people."

•••

NORMAL? EVEN THE MOST elastic conception of that shattered the second Richard's second-floor pane did.

A few days after the killing, his funeral was held at Hillside Memorial Park, a grassy cemetery accented with waterfalls and marble off the bumper-to-bumper 405 Freeway. According to Jewish tradition, the dead are to be laid to rest as soon as possible. Its ancient customs also forbid mourners from viewing the body. Paige, nonetheless, tried to skirt around a screen where his casket was parked for a private goodbye until Richard's mother stood in her path to block her. Later, when no was looking, she did manage to slip her wedding band into the coffin.

It was a remarkable feat, for her grief that day bordered on the catatonic. During the ceremony, she sat in the front pew of the chapel next to her friend Erica, away from black-clad in-laws who wanted little to do with her. As the gravity of it all sunk in, Paige sobbed and spaced out, wept some more, and then tasted bile. Amid the rabbi's solemn words, she at one point flew out the chapel's side door and vomited within earshot of the mourners. It was the perfect metaphor for an atrocious scene.

Neither she nor Jerry found much consoling amid the others' split emotions. Richard's family, when they weren't hugging, crying, or wailing about poor "Dick," glared conspicuously at them, some muttering under their breaths. Jerry, already feeling awkward, quickly deciphered the gist. He and Paige were *the* ones who enmeshed Richard with sub-humans who trafficked in murder. They were accomplices to his demise—condemnation by false association— no matter their own pain. As far as Jerry could tell, none of the Kasparovs pinned responsibility on the subject himself. His loved ones either martyred him as an innocent led astray into a dangerous crowd or behaved as if it were a car wreck or sudden illness that whisked him away too young. Nobody commented on what detectives found in Richard's wallet. Besides twenty-four dollars and two checks were five credit cards. One of them belonged to Jerry.

For Richard's now-fatherless children, those contradictions were for the adults to hack through. At the service's conclusion, Rachel, Richard's eight-year-old daughter from his first marriage, gave him a send-off by releasing the balloons she'd been clutching. The handkerchiefs emerged again as she did.

Jerry watched them drift and dart skyward, wincing inside about what no one here at Hillside Memorial was openly saying out of respect and fear: a murderer was running free. What they didn't know: that Richard himself had been aware that someone wanted him planted in a coffin like the one in which he now resided.

Last Monday, after he drove from his Van Nuys home to Benjamin's office to relinquish his stake in the companies, he did something that Jerry never anticipated. He'd prostrated himself, swallowing false bravado and apologizing without a single qualifier or petty justification. He voiced how sorry he was—immensely sorry— in a frog-choked voice. One bad decision segued to another before accumulating into a snowball of deceit.

Jerry accepted the apology, telling his ex-partner / onetime mentor that he wanted him to rebound. Wanted him to latch onto hope. They even enjoyed a brief stroll down memory lane. Those Pico Boulevard all-nighters, Paul Fegen's weirdo parties, hawking space designs to crabby landlords, mainstream cults, and executives with hair plugs; this was *their* history.

But the nostalgia faded, and Richard remarked something fatalistic, like someone who'd read a grim set of Tarot cards.

"If anything happens to me, and I'm not saying it will, make sure Paige and the baby have what they need," he said. "You know, check in on them once in a while. I know that sounds melodramatic."

Jerry recoiled at what he was hearing. It fed on what Tammy told him about Paige's contention: that someone phoned her to say that Richard had a price on his head. Jerry decided not to pry, figuring that Richard was about to leave town. For all the man's wretched behavior, Jerry still found so much about him to adore.

"Are you going someplace?" he asked.

"Not directly," he said. "I can't explain it; maybe in the future. Just promise me?"

Jerry promised.

"You sure you don't want to tell me?"

"Not today."

Richard issued his surprise apology and request nine hours before he was shot. It didn't make sense. If he were in mortal peril, why did he dawdle around Dodge? And if he didn't believe it, why did he ask Jerry to look in on his family?

As those balloons sailed above the mausoleum, Jerry appreciated that Robert died as much a riddle as a maze. And that *he'd* never felt so unwanted as he did now, cast unfairly as a villain by Richard's kin. The hour hand on his watch couldn't sweep fast enough.

Following the service, Richard's sister hosted the shiva, a Jewish wake part of the one-week mourning period for the departed, at her West LA residence. Jerry and Paige were *persona non grata* there too, especially Paige. Richard's high-strung relatives, while sympathetic to Paige's new standing as a widow and single mother, refused to comfort her with anything approaching standard compassion. To them, she remained the way-too-young, fast-lane wife, as opposed to Richard's first wife, whom they deemed a virtuous keeper. They didn't want Richard to marry a blonde gentile outside of their tribe. Consequently, cold gusts flapped her direction while guests huddled in cliques, plates loaded with sandwiches and mayo-drizzled salads.

Paige and Richard's mother were unlikely to bury hatchets anytime soon, either. After Paige left her son months back, a conversation that began peacefully between them devolved into a back and forth of screamed grievances. Paige berated, among Richard's other character defects, his stout refusal to pay child support. Mrs. Kasparov counterpunched, chirping that someone with Paige's "expensive" nails was in no position to complain. Just below the surface of these hostilities was Richard's fitful relationship with his roots. Ever since Paige met him, he chafed at his Judaism and family's compulsive behaviors like an uncomfortable saddle. Mostly, he resented his mother's heavy-handed love for him. Now that her only boy was a martyr, she was free to scorch earth. Taking in her granddaughter's red hair, she scathingly asked Paige if she was "sure" it was Richard's baby.

"How fucking dare you!" Paige responded before trooping out. "You babied [Richard]. You did everything for him. That's why he turned out like he did."

True as that may have been, this whole sordid affair never would've happened if Richard had taken reasonable precautions after hearing that mystery woman's portentous words.

•••

FOR PAIGE, TUESDAY, MARCH 27, was anything but another day in a turbulent year. That morning, two homicide detectives showed up at her Ventura Boulevard interior design shop and tapped on the locked front door. Paige, jumpy the last few months and alone in the storefront, was confused about their appearance. She went to the shop window, mouthing that the officers would need to wait there while she phoned LAPD headquarters to confirm their identities. Annoyed, one of the detectives pressed his badge up to the glass. Paige let them in.

Following protocol, they asked where she was the previous night. Paige answered that she was with a client, and questioned what this was about.

"A homicide involving your husband, I'm sorry to report," one of them responded.

Homicide? Paige was unacquainted with the term. With the officers' continued repetition of it, though, she deduced its macabre significance and began hyperventilating.

"Is Richard okay?" she asked, sputtering breaths. "What hospital is he at? What's his condition?"

The detectives had her exhale into a bag, but it stemmed little. Paige was free-falling into shock feet from her fabric swatches. She'd require someone to help her survive the next hours. Just then, Erica, the friend who'd forecast that Richard might get himself killed, returned from an appointment and contacted a doctor. He traveled right over, giving Paige a Valium shot to calm her down. That had no effect either. In her rubbery shape, the tranquilizer was about as potent as chamomile tea.

She was driven from the shop to her rental house with eyes rolling up in her head. On this blackest of days, she got relief only when Rebecca's nanny, Isabel, brought out the child. Seeing her daughter unharmed and alive, Paige exhaled, and the Valium did its job. She conked out on her bed, temporarily forgetting the new word in her lexicon.

When she awakened, she came to in a hellscape where heartache was ever-present and the shadows long. Where doing what no one else would could incite madness.

Someone needed to clean the bloodied master bedroom where her husband died now that the detectives were done culling evidence. The professional cleaning company hired to scrub it down backed out of the job after workers who visited the site said it repulsed them too much. Paige, who originally believed that Richard was shot through the chest, had to wipe down the brain blood spray in their stead. As if Ajax and bleach could expunge what that bullet wrought. Yet she did it, a wife down on hands and knees numbly sopping up the remains of the love of her life. She resisted the urge to weep, worrying that once she began, she might never cease.

•••

THEY WERE A SATURNINE group that day, eyes gravitating downward. At least at Langer's, they could drown their melancholy in the best pastrami sandwich in LA.

Jerry, Howard, and Bert, Jerry's second-in-command, were squished into a red vinyl booth to commiserate over a meal. The mood at Richard's service ping-ponged between sorrowful and delusional. Here around the brown laminate table and mustard selections, it was downright gloomy.

It was Howard's idea to meet at the popular deli across from a small urban lake in the Westlake district northwest of downtown. Langer's, a favorite grub spot for city hall officials and LAPD brass, traced back to the postwar era, when skyscrapers were few. Jerry was surprised that Howard organized this, and later guessed it was for an ulterior motive. Maybe he'd propose dropping his residual claims against the company in exchange for freelance work on Richard's unfinished remodels.

Well, Jerry guessed wrong. He tended to do that when it involved translating other people's mindsets. Howard was here just to remember their chum.

Only one newspaper, *The Valley News and Green Sheet*, later renamed *The Daily News of Los Angeles*, published an article about the murder, in a three-paragraph brief. The much larger *Los Angeles Times* wrote zilch. The *Green Sheet*'s late-filed story was blandly headlined, "Man Dies after Shooting." It reported that thirty-nine-year-old Kasparov perished from "a bullet fired from the second-floor sun deck of his Van Nuys" home. It ran under a piece about TV star/comedian Redd Foxx facing a $30,000 default judgement for allegedly pistol-whipping an associate.

"Flooding and Death" from the storm was the paper's lead story.

Howard mumbled into his pastrami about how scant on details the article was. Did anybody hear anything more? Bert answered no. Jerry did too, saying nothing about Richard's inkling he might be done for; some things should remain private. Nor did he mention speaking to the LAPD about potential suspects. Detectives wanted confidentiality.

Amid the complimentary pickles and signature number nineteen sandwiches bulked up with cole slaw and Swiss, the trio switched to happier memories about Richard and then conjectured about the future for Paige and Rebecca with him gone. No one pretended there were any silver linings. After lunch, Jerry and Bert shook hands with Howard and returned to their Miracle Mile office.

In Northridge, Jerry and Tammy had decisions to finalize about safeguarding their family in the slim chance a larger plot was afoot. After mulling their options, they let their schedule be their solution, albeit with one modification. They were already booked to fly to

Michigan to visit Tammy's family around Easter. When Tammy called her parents to educate them about what'd happened and see if they could travel out a few days earlier, they failed to grasp their daughter and son-in-law's desire to vacate California. Arrive on your original date, they said. No need splurging on changed plane fare.

The Schneidermans stayed on course, boarding their regularly scheduled flight. Tagging along with them was a rose-colored fantasy: that before they returned to the West Coast, a murderer would be in custody and a semblance of normalcy restored. No suspect was apprehended, so they altered their plans. Tammy and Jude would remain with Tammy's family in Ann Arbor outside of Detroit, meaning Jerry would leave on an LA-bound plane by himself.

At the airport, Tammy cried, stricken with second thoughts. Before Jerry clumped down the ramp, she pleaded for him to stay, even if only for a few days. Jerry, convinced that his shell-shocked company would flounder without him, said he had no choice.

•••

THE GNARLED HAND TAPPED on the door of the bookkeeper's office, where Jerry sat alone in a loop of uncertainties. The mystery of an assassinated ex-partner and a business polluted by his actions had to end sometime, didn't it?

It was an April morning, eight days after his return from Michigan, in a time of radioactivity and shattered glass ceilings. Back east, Pennsylvania's Three Mile Island nuclear power plant was suffering through the partial meltdown of a reactor core; mere days earlier, *The China Syndrome*, a movie about such a scenario, premiered in a case of art imitating life. Overseas, Margaret Thatcher was just elected England's first female prime minister in a major leap for women's rights.

Jerry, news junkie, ordinarily would've been on top of all this. Today he was distracted, overworked, and stressed out. Plus, Howard was standing there.

He appeared without an appointment, and decked out in monochrome: blue shirt, blue jeans, blue shoes, and blue-tinted sunglasses over his bluish-green eyes. Jerry couldn't decide what surprised him most: Howard's decision to step foot inside Space Matters after pledging he never would again or his outfit.

"I'd like to speak with you privately," he said softly from the door jam.

"Geez, Howard," Jerry said, brow knotted. "I wish you would've called first. I'm slammed. And I have to be downtown by noon. Can we talk now?"

Howard shook his head no.

"I'd prefer going someplace else," he said. "I was thinking that we could grab coffee."

Just then, an employee named Thomas walked in; Howard civilly asked him if they could have some privacy.

"Nobody will bother us here," Jerry said. "The room isn't bugged. That was just a one-time deal to find out about Richard's cheating. If you need to talk, shut the door."

Howard did, and within seconds underwent a metamorphosis that he was expert at hiding. His relaxed expression became something reptilian—burning eyes, recoiling jaw, disappearing lips. This wasn't so much a pre-bloodshed trance as mealtime. He jerked his chair up and bent forward, so close that his sharp chin loomed over the edge of the desk.

"*You* fucking Jews—you're all alike," Howard said in a smoky half-whisper. "Hitler should have just killed all of you."

Jerry couldn't respond. His tongue was epoxied to the bottom of his mouth.

"I used to think that Richard was the bad one, but now I know you're as much of a shit as he was. I also know you have one hundred and fifty thousand in life insurance coming due. I want half of it."

Jerry, scared Howard might lunge at him, forced himself to speak.

"I don't understand," he said in as regular a voice as he could fake. "Why do you deserve any of it?"

"Because I had Richard killed and did you a favor. Somebody needed to get rid of that bastard."

"A favor?"

"You heard me."

Jerry leaned back into the bookkeeper's chair, as if that would buy him any protection.

"I don't have seventy-five thousand dollars. The money's frozen. Richard's mom filed a claim."

"I don't care," Howard said.

"But it's up to the insurance company. You know how slow they can be."

"Jerry, you can stop right there, okay? No more buts. The days of you feeding me horseshit excuses are over. If the money is frozen, talk to Tammy's family. They're loaded. Ask her dad for it."

"I can't do that."

"You better—unless Tammy's dad wants to see his grandson hurt. I'll call myself if you're too much of a pussy. And you can forget about going to the cops. You want to know why?"

"I guess."

"Because I have a contract on you ready to go if you do anything I don't like. You're bought and paid for, and I'm the only one who can call it off. Got that? The only one! They can send me to prison and throw me in a hole. It won't stop the hit on you. That, I promise."

Jerry tried not crapping himself. He wasn't entirely sure this was real, a recurring theme since childhood.

"Why are you being like this, Howard? I don't get it. I never stole anything from you. I tried treating you well."

"I told you. I've had enough fucking around with all this money I'm owed. The whole business has caused me more hell than you could ever dream. I have creditors badgering me night and day because of what *you* two did. Not a good way to live, Jerry. Not at all."

"Your lawyers filed liens against us. This doesn't make sense."

"Oh, screw the lawyers. And screw more talking about talking. You have a week to get me the seventy-five thousand. I want it in two parts. Maybe you should write this down on one of your fancy pads. I want a twenty-five-thousand-dollar cashier's check, and a fifty-thousand-dollar check written out to me. Two parts. Understand?"

"Yes. But how do I know what you're saying is true, that this isn't some trick? You realize what you're saying. You must."

"Oh, doubting Jerry. I want you to play a little game with me. You call Paige and ask her about the caliber of the bullet they found at Richard's house and write down what she says on a sheet of paper. I'll write out my answer and we'll compare. Then you'll know I arranged it. Go ahead and call her. I've got time."

"I'm not going to do that."

"You're in dangerous waters, my friend. I've killed before Richard and gotten away with it. And I'll do it again—with you."

"Before Richard? What are you talking about? This is total insanity."

"Don't you remember that trial in San Bernardino? What do you think it was about, huh? A code violation? It was a murder charge."

"Murder? Nobody ever told me anything about murder," Jerry said, his voice rising an octave while wishing he were in Michigan. "You're trying to frighten me. You were a witness in some minor case that delayed when you could start work for us. That's how Richard described it."

"Let me clear things up, then, once and for all. I was the one on trial. Me. And like I told you, I got away with it once without being convicted and will do it again."

"Howard, c'mon."

"I made it as simple as I can. Call me when you have the money."

Howard, the man in blue, exited calmly after a handful of minutes, no doors slammed, as if he had already pocketed a five-figure check.

CHAPTER TWELVE
THE HOUSEGUEST

A YEAR AND A half earlier, there were two ways to travel in the El Camino: in the cab next to its driver, or feet first in the steel-blue cargo bay.

Glenn Colley's unsought education on the point would always torment him, all of it exploding from one benevolent act: his effort to line up accommodations for a hard-luck friend.

The lodging was in a shadow-strewn house on Coronado Drive in Arcadia, Pasadena's lily-white neighbor to the southeast, in a neighborhood radiating attractions. Santa Anita Park, the famed horseracing track, and the peacock-pecking gardens at the Los Angeles County Arboretum lay minutes away. A titanic indoor mall where something was always on sale—a duck-down vest, a Swedish loofah—gleamed across the boulevard.

If Tim Dwight longed for shopping or playing the ponies like any normal person, he must've realized it'd have to wait. Because he wasn't normal now: he was in an hour-by-hour battle to remain sober. He entered the two-bedroom residence on Coronado writhing to shake a heroin addiction after a state-run rehab freed him. Who better, Glenn calculated, to get Tim right than a straight-shooting, pull-your-weight taskmaster who took no guff?

Late summer 1977 was a time where you needed someone strong, what with the US and Soviet Union testing nuclear weapons like they were going out of style, the economy a dumpster fire, Elvis gone, and serial killers prowling the land. One of them, New York's David Berkowitz, a.k.a. "Son of Sam," contended that demons and a neighbor's dog whispered him to murder.

Howard Garrett, who dealt in reality, never let anyone besides a paying employer tell him what to do. And he didn't own a dog.

From the sidewalk, nothing much about his stucco, gold-painted house blinked warning signs that you better tread carefully. The red porch and double front doors appeared to signal open arms for anyone to knock. The property's single dash of flamboyance—a gabled decorative window in the center of the roof—conjured the illusion of hovering at night. Howard had extra room here for his new houseguest since Carol, his wife of eight years, moved out. She now yearned to patch things up, and he gave her the impression it was mutual by performing handyman chores for her. Lingering affection? How about healthcare; he wanted her Thrifty Drug employee insurance to fund his spinal surgery.

At twenty-six, Tim was young enough to be Howard's son, but his junkie lifestyle supplanted any youthful spark in him with a notable dullness. His gaunt frame, shaved head, and faraway eyes made manifest what the powdered opium stole from him: the best years of his life.

His addiction was so all-consuming, in fact, that he'd scored drugs mere hours after Riverside County's California Rehabilitation Center released him. His need for a dopamine rush even sent him out for narcotics a few days after unpacking his stuff at the makeshift halfway house that Howard created (for reasons only Howard knew). His mode of transport was the most hazardous object he could've picked. He took the El Camino—without permission.

Up in Oxnard, a sleepy farming and oil town north of Los Angeles, Tim bought an ounce of heroin from a local connection. Baggy in hand, he went to a drug buddy's nearby apartment, eager to get loaded. What he got wasn't a buzz but Miranda Rights after police busted down the door and threw him and his fellow users in jail. He did make one savvy decision on an otherwise rash trip. He gave authorities a fake name to prevent them from learning about his recent incarceration.

One shrewd act does not a gate close, even so. In gallivanting off in the Chevy, Tim provoked the inner crocodile off its owner to crawl out of its marshy lair for good. Any morsel of decency for others, any endowed compassion Howard retained through his miserable existence, evaporated. Why pretend you have fingernails when they're claws? He cherished that car, down to its silhouette resembling a hammerhead shark and the secrets he acted like were welded into the side panels. Unlike humans, the vehicle was powerful, loyal, and utilitarian. Worth the kinship.

Attached as he was, Howard would have consigned it to junkyard scrap metal to deter assholes with badges sniffing around it. Now an addict had stomped on his hospitality by keeping it a week. It was suicidal.

To smoke out Tim's whereabouts, Howard threw nuance to the wind. He pressured Glenn, Tim's sponsor, and another acquaintance nicknamed "Caveman" to accompany him to the residence of a Pomona couple who knew him. Howard, once inside, presented Mr. and Mrs. Robertson with an ultimatum: either they disclosed Tim's whereabouts, or he would make them sorry. When neither confessed any useful information, Howard and Caveman tied up the couple and their two children.

Showtime! Howard rammed the barrel of his pistol into the woman's mouth. Next, he fired his gun next to her husband's ear, smacking him for good measure. Anyone doubt his seriousness? Before leaving, he gave the Robertsons twenty-four hours to tell him what they weren't saying. Unless they wanted him to return, presumably to get medieval.

Tim, oblivious to the downstream effects of his absence, phoned Howard forty-eight or so hours later to say he was out of jail. No harm, no foul; the car was fine. Howard ordered him to stay where he was while he got someone to take him to Oxnard. There, he drove the misfit back to Coronado Avenue in the El Camino. Howard, who loved his recreational drugs as much as any grizzled, middle-age diabetic with nothing to lose could, decided the misadventures had to stop.

But first there would be drinks!

At dusk on Monday, September 13, 1977, Howard poured Tim a Greyhound from his carpeted home den. He mixed a cocktail for himself too and shook out painkillers for his wrenched back. Glenn, beckoned here to discuss the living arrangement with Tim, soon walked in, saying he would join them after he relieved himself. Tim bobbed his head at his friend, lounging in a chair next to Howard's desk, legs casually crossed. He was buzzed, and it didn't seem as if it were just his host's vodka doing it.

Glenn was zipping up his pants when he heard the noise that would be grooved into his memory banks. *Thunk.* It sounded like someone clubbed a watermelon with a Louisville Slugger. He jogged into the study to determine where that stomach-churning thwack originated, and he wouldn't relish the answer. Tim was no longer reclining in a chair, looking high. He was face up on the ground with a couple of bloody gashes indented on the side of his skull—gashes from where Howard clocked him with the unforgiving butt of a rifle.

Howard loomed over him, clutching the rifle. Glenn looked on, mouth agape.

"Why, Howard?" Tim asked in a whimper. "What did I do?"

Unblinking in one of his trances, Howard offered no reply. He bludgeoned Tim again with the wooden stock, this time so viciously that it split the butt in two. Tim was no longer verbal after that. The only action was blood pumping out of his head and onto Howard's yellow shag.

Before Glenn could raise an objection, Howard, out of his spell, aimed the rifle at him.

"You're involved in this too," he said in a stony voice. "So help me"

At that instant, Glenn realized that Howard had tricked him into being an accomplice to a premediated, first-degree murder. Then Howard was yelling, yelling that he couldn't have blood splashed all over his house, making Glenn grab towels from the master bedroom to tamp up the mess before it set in. While Glenn did, Howard cracked

Tim once more. He kneeled down next to him afterward, putting his ear to his chest.

"I don't hear anything," Howard said in a tone returning to normal.

Standing up, he noticed Glenn's dismay, and tried candy-coating his ambush as self-defense.

"I'm tired," he said with a sigh, "of having to sleep with a gun under my pillow."

It was body-disposal time as a result.

The two rolled Tim into a tan, fuzzy blanket and another covering, turning somebody's son into a human taquito. They carried their freight outside in the fading light, shoving it into the El Camino's cargo hold. For additional concealment, they draped a white painter's drop cloth over it. Howard tasked Glenn with another assignment before they did anything else. He needed him to rent a rug cleaner from the corner market to remove the bloodstains from the carpeting. Once it was steam cleaned, the three of them—Howard and Glenn up front, a limp body in the rear—exited peaceful Arcadia.

They drove east toward the sagebrush desert, stopping briefly at Glenn's parent's home in Covina in the central San Gabriel Valley so Glenn could borrow an empty gasoline container. Back on the San Bernardino Freeway they went. At the interchange with the highway you took to Las Vegas, Howard swerved to the right. Glenn, on Howard's word, started discarding evidence from the car window, just as Johnny later would in another Howard-orchestrated killing. First, Glenn jettisoned the brown paper bag containing the bloody towels, then another holding the dismantled rifle. Some of it rolled into a flood control wash.

Howard turned off the freeway at 10:30 p.m. in Redlands, a small, dusty San Bernardino town home to wild roses and military families associated with an Air Force base. At a Union 76 service station there, Glenn filled up the five-gallon metal gas container. They jumped back on the road, continuing east for another sixteen miles until they arrived at Live Oak Road in Yucaipa, another dot on the map, this one best known as the headquarters of the Stater Bros. supermarket chain.

They were in the boonies now, closer to Palm Springs than to LA, in rattlesnake-infested hills that few disinclined to mischief stumbled around at night. After stopping in the remotest place there he could find, Howard and his duped abettor hefted the carpet-wrapped body from the rear and set it down on the soil. Quietly, one of them drenched it with gasoline from the red-and-gold can. A trail of fuel was then poured to a distance away. Howard, in a blue parka and tennis shoes, did the rest. A match strike; a flick of the wrist; a little orange spark. Their cargo was engulfed in flames instantaneously. There was no eulogy, not even a brief consideration that Tim could be unconscious but still alive, leaving him to burn to a crisp under the cold evening stars.

On the late-night drive home, Howard explained to Glenn why he chose here rather than off Angeles Crest Highway, in the San Gabriel Mountains northwest of Pasadena. It was deception. When police identified the charred body, they would probably suspect it was a local drug-deal-gone-wrong and pin the murder on Tim's heroin connection in that area.

Tim's corpse was still smoldering when San Bernardino County Sheriffs discovered it the following day. It was so grotesquely seared that police were forced to send dental records to Loma Linda University to pinpoint whom it was. Leads to solve the murder were thin. So thin it took detectives thirty-two days to link Glenn to it.

Despite being terrified about the revenge Howard would exact if he knew he was squealing, Glenn squealed plenty. He described Tim's fatal error in using the El Camino, and the takeover invasion at the Robertson's. He painted the scene of how Howard lured him to his home and the funeral pyre in Yucaipa to blur his tracks. The police still wanted more, leaning on Glenn to cough up "Caveman's" real name for a chilling reason. They believed he knew about Howard's involvement in something unrelated—a bloody, unsolved crime that occurred a year earlier. Nothing tangible came from this thread of the investigation, putting the focus back on the remains that Howard burned into the desert floor.

Questioned about what Howard had been doing since, Glenn reported staying busy to keep himself out of a cellblock. He was weighing bolting to Mexico, something he'd long toyed with, in concert with a whimsical notion about buying an interest in a small hotel there—as if any tourist would want him as their concierge. Whether or not he intended to fly south ahead of a murder rap, Glenn noted Howard was ensuring his El Camino didn't betray him in the courtroom. Right after the killing, he replaced all four tires and got the car washed.

Yucaipa? Howard could now say. *He* wasn't in Yucaipa. He could scarcely pronounce the town's name.

Police arrested him days after hearing the entirety of Glenn's account, even so. San Bernardino County prosecutors, adamant that Howard was a risk to flee if out on his own recognizance, motioned the judge not to set bail. The judge did it anyway, pegging the amount at a then-astronomical $150,000. On December 30, Howard fooled them all by posting it through a bail bondsman—with his mother's financial aid. He plead not guilty.

Court proceedings in the People of the state of California versus Howard Landis Garrett Jr. commenced in late March 1978 in San Bernardino, an area subsumed today in the fashionably rebranded "Inland Empire." The timing was both sinister and karmic. The gavel banged weeks *after* Richard and Jerry hired him to oversee construction, much of it tied to remodeling luxury homes, a field the two had no reason dipping their toes into except naked ambition.

Marc Frenkel, one of the two attorneys that Howard would later sic on Jerry, represented the defendant in a trial rooted on shaky forensics. No murder weapon; one eyewitness; a carbonized body missing the killer's fingerprints. Frenkel attacked those weaknesses, courtroom brawler he was. He cited technical objections about admissible evidence. Raised doubts putting Howard at the scene of the crime. Disputed as prejudicial for the jury to hear about his client's previous legal scrapes. Howard, unconcerned about incriminating himself, testified on his own behalf, as did Carol, his estranged wife.

Prosecutors believed their circumstantial case would doom him, anyway. They had Glenn's blow-by-blow story. They had Howard's *one-way* airline ticket to Mazatlán, Mexico, a suspicious purchase for a supposedly innocent person to make weeks after a murder. They had tales of the El Camino being sterilized of mud and fibers.

Opposing sides presented their closing arguments in early May. The judge granted Howard, then employed at Space Matters a county away, permission to be absent during jury instructions, no explanation given. It was up to the citizens in the jury—folks named Norma, Julie, Benny, and William—afterward to decide if Howard was responsible.

They deliberated, if you could call it that, for all of sixty-five minutes. They found Howard not guilty on every count. The life he took of his shiftless houseguest would cost him nothing.

With that, the judge thanked the jurors for their service and erased Howard's bond. The defense lawyers packed up their briefcases. Their client was free to do as he wished. Namely seek out the meek.

•••

WHEN IT CAME TO life's most essential nutrient, Howard found himself a malnourished soul. He was either starved for it in his formative years or discovered an emotional incapacity to ladle it out to anyone before it spoiled. The love he stocked in his cupboards was mainly for himself, a love that justified him squashing anything he chose.

Howard was a Depression-era baby born in 1932 in Mount Vernon, Missouri, near the Missouri-Arkansas border. His parents divorced when he was four, and it was his Baptist-practicing mother who reared him. After Mabel remarried, the family relocated to the San Gabriel Valley. Howard wanted out too. Upon graduation from Mark Keppel High School in Alhambra, an asphalt-y, blue-collar city below South Pasadena, he blew town for the Bay Area, where his biological father, Howard Sr., resided. His first job out of school was an apprentice carpenter. It armed him with a union card and a decent upside.

Beneath that potential, a rabble-rousing strain that same year leached from him. During Christmastime 1949, police charged him with shoplifting from a drugstore on the Fort Ord Army base near Monterrey. Weeks later he was cuffed again, this time for swiping a car; no one in his family remembered anyone being arrested before. Yet five years passed without incident, suggesting Howard's troublemaking was a phase he shook off. That it'd been rebelliousness, not persona. It wasn't. Back in Southern California, it was a return to prior impulses. He became a one-man crime spree, smudging his rap sheet during one span with a reckless driving charge in LA, petty theft in Culver City, possession of a phony draft card, and burglary.

Just like before, Howard's run-ins with police halted without explanation, except this time it was for eighteen years. Was it the pride of wearing a tool belt to build something, like a respectable legacy? There were no more sirens, no more jail food, no more people anxious that he was a bad seed. In 1959, he married a woman named Alpha Hart. They remained wed for six years before divorcing over irreconcilable differences. Single, Howard continued hoeing his path to legitimacy by earning a contractor's license. To that he added an AA business degree from Pasadena Junior College, a real estate license from the state, and he pondered applying to law school.

At the end of the sixties, he married Carol, a kindhearted woman who wore heavy makeup, stacked her hair poufy style, and maintained an hourglass figure; she reminded some of an aging Vegas cocktail waitress, a fleshpot with road mileage. They first lived in Monrovia, then Arcadia for seven years. In that period Howard's only official crimes were for booze: DUIs in California and Arizona. By the time of his San Bernardino murder trial, the couple planned to divorce, or were tilting that way. When they reconciled, perhaps for different motivations, they downsized into a Pasadena apartment too small to warehouse Howard's impressive array of tools.

The shift was a humiliating contraction for someone who'd once made $25,000 (about $110,000 today) a year, and double that in his peak year. Someone who'd boasted that gabled property in Arcadia, several cars, and a pair of short-lived small businesses. His exoneration in the Tim Dwight murder should've given him runway to recover. To atone. Richard's abuse of his credit lines and related factors pancaked that, hastening his status change from middle class to just hanging on.

Howard's cynical, grievance-pimpled outlook now colored his world, a world where greedy executives, former bosses, ex-compatriots, and others abused him for their own selfish purposes. Their system continually bent him over his bandsaw to give him the shaft and had the audacity to tab it a free, capitalistic living. If he looked in the mirror to see a scaly complexion staring back, he blamed real-estate users for his mutation. *They* were the space monsters, not him.

He could've slapped down a few bucks at the box office to appreciate the simmering indignation in him was a national contagion. None of the characters in the *The Deer Hunter* or *Taxi Driver* were humming about sweet lands of liberty. The social commentary bellowed by the TV anchor in *Network*—about the tyranny of corporations over the little guy's interest, where everything (terrorism, cults, political sedition) was gristle for the entertainment sausage machine—must've resonated as nonfiction. In late seventies America, you were either in on the scam, or you were its patsies. As Howard Beale ranted in his polemic:

"I don't have to tell you things are bad...Everybody's out of work or scared of losing their job. The dollar buys a nickel's worth. Banks are going bust. Shopkeepers keep a gun under the counter. Punks are running wild in the street and there's nobody anywhere who seems to know what to do...We know the air is unfit to breathe and our food is unfit to eat...It's like everything everywhere is going crazy...All we say is: 'please...let me have my toaster and my TV and my steel-belted radials and I won't say anything...I don't want you to protest...I want you to riot....You've got to say: 'I'm a human being, god-dammit!...I want you to get up right now and go to the window. Open it, and stick your head out, and yell: I'm mad as hell and I'm not gonna take it anymore.'"

The Howard from Space Matters' world wasn't.

CHAPTER THIRTEEN
THE TOMBSTONE SUMMIT

WHEREVER HE WENT, JERRY seemed to weave among the dead. Richard. The shiva. His own innocence. Now a Mr. Murder with stringy hair and tinted blue sunglasses.

He skipped alerting the LAPD after Howard strolled out of the mansion, deciding to phone his answer man to spearhead his response to the abominable phraseology that Jerry next expected to hear in a hundred lifetimes. Since the discovery of Richard's devious ways, Benjamin Wynn had sprung papers on him at the Polo Lounge, then dueled with Howard's pugnacious lawyers during settlement negotiations. The day of the killing in Van Nuys, he drew homicide detectives to his Westwood office to hear his client tell what he knew.

Benjamin, with his mutton chops and wisdom beyond his years, was his usual accessible self.

"Come over right now," he told Jerry. "We need to take a walk."

Ordinarily a talk-radio-listening, slow-poke driver, he sped out from Hancock Park, replaying the soul-shaking words that had rolled like dice off Howard's tongue.

"You fucking Jews—you're all alike."

Funny thing about perspective; he would've given anything if an unscrupulous associate who stole the company blind constituted an emergency.

"I got away with it once without being convicted and will do it again."

Upstairs in his suite, Benjamin crooked his arm around Jerry's shoulder, patting him like a consoling uncle. Jerry, with a pallor comparable to a plate of uncooked shrimp, kept an eye on the garbage can because it was fifty-fifty that he'd have to sprint over to hurl into it.

"You're bought and paid for, and I'm the only one who can call it off. Got that?"

Benjamin's small law office was cloistered inside a modest high-rise filled with other professionals like him, on the western edge of Wilshire Boulevard. Blink and you'd miss it among the larger office towers, some with helipads and luxury apartments, flanking it. Many of West LA's landmark structures—the sprawling UCLA campus, the formidable Federal Building out of which the FBI worked, the rebuilt Veterans Administration's medical center, the Hillside Country Club—lay within walking distance.

For his tête-à-tête with Jerry, Benjamin rejected those spots for a quieter space directly behind his building. Where better to counsel someone how to stay alive than in a graveyard? The Westwood Village Memorial Park, now renamed the Pierce Brothers Westwood Village Memorial Park & Mortuary, was one of the tiniest cemeteries in the Southland. The grassy, urban expanse lacked the chapels and marble mausoleums of other death-industrial-complex outposts. But what the park missed in frills it compensated for in personalities from the stage and screen, this being the final resting place for the likes of Marilyn Monroe, Dean Martin, Roy Orbison, Natalie Wood, Jack Lemmon, Walter Matthau, Burt Lancaster, Bob Crane, and Truman Capote.

Zigzagging around the tombstones of some of them, Jerry had no time to be starstruck. He thrashed inside, trying to fathom what was real from surreal.

Five minutes in, Benjamin said he was ready to dispense his advice. It was sensitive—hence their cadaverous meeting site—and conditional.

"Before I say a word, you need to know something," he said.

Jerry, with his weak knees and nausea, looked up from his shoes.

"What?"

"If you ever tell a single soul about this conversation, I'll deny it. Categorically. Agreed?"

Jerry gyrated his head to check if anyone else was in the graveyard. No one was.

"This is going to be heavy, isn't it?"

"But do you agree?" Benjamin said, pressing. "I won't say a thing unless you do."

"Yeah, sure. I agree. Can we get on with it?"

"Good. I'll draw the lines of possibility."

Jerry, a natural at geometry, thought he could follow. Then he heard where Benjamin's lines ranged.

"As far as I can tell, you have three choices. Be forewarned: none of them are pleasant."

"None? What do you mean?"

"You can pay Howard. You can go to the police. Or, you can kill him. If it were me, I'd do the latter."

Jerry wasn't sure whether he'd heard Benjamin clearly or was about to bolt up in bed in sweat-knotted sheets.

"You recommend I do *what*?"

"I just outlined it."

"Tell me you have a rotten sense of humor. You're an officer of the court, for God's sake. You must be kidding."

"I'm not. You solicited me for advice, so I'm laying out alternatives. You have to decide whether to pick one."

"Not what you're suggesting."

"Ask yourself who Howard is. What he's capable of doing. From everything I know, and what you told me upstairs about your conversation with him, the man's an animal. And animals come back for more if you feed them. Once he decides you're a threat, or you get tired of paying him, he'll dispose of you and he'll walk away untouched."

"I don't know, Benjamin. I barely know my name, to be honest with you."

"You better start facing up to the facts. He's already confessed to killing two people. That's incredibly dangerous information for you to have. You realize that?"

"And this is what you're saying? I rush to you for legal advice, and the best you can do is tell me to kill the killer. What kind of attorney does that?"

"A damn realistic one, Jerry. Play out the string. You call the police to tell them that Howard has threatened to wipe out you and your family unless you pay him seventy-five thousand dollars. He goes to prison and then what?"

"He said he would contract my murder from there. But he was probably bluffing."

"You want to risk that? What happens if he gets released from prison without forgetting about who put him in there? You want to live the rest of your years looking in the rearview mirror? You'll be downing tranquilizers by the handful."

"Of course, I don't want that to happen. If he went to jail and got out, then maybe I'd take you up. But I have a family to worry about now—a son, a pregnant wife. What about them?"

"You don't believe Howard has other secrets? He just warned you he skated away from one murder charge."

"Don't bother reminding me how scary he is. It was like he came through the walls today."

"And here I assumed he was only a resentful hardass. Obviously it runs a lot deeper."

"You think?"

"Look. The police are investigating. That should make you feel better. It could well end up you won't have to take anything into your own hands."

"Good. Because I've never held a gun in them before."

"I'm no criminal lawyer, but I'll bet the LAPD already circled him as a suspect. It's nothing for them to check rap sheets."

"Shame we weren't more cautious before we hired him."

"I keep forgetting to ask you about that. How did you come to employ someone like him?"

"Richard brought him onboard after he answered our ad in the *LA Times*. Howard got a good recommendation from his last boss."

"A good recommendation, for him? That's fishy."

"As I've learned."

"Some people, I guess, know how to blend in until they see an opportunity, or get angry. Then they show what's really inside of them."

"I know what's inside of me, and I'm not killing anyone. Not even a Nazi sympathizer. With my luck, I'd be the one they sent to prison."

"You positive you don't want to think this over for twenty-four hours? This is a major decision we're talking about."

"Yeah, I'm sure."

"'Kay. Let's get back to my office then and bring those detectives back here. You have quite the story to tell."

"I wish that's all it was too—a story, not my life. I'm in a fog."

"Don't lose yourself in it."

"Easy for you to say. I just spent the morning staring into a blue abyss."

•••

LONG LIVE THE *LAPD! Three Cheers for Chief Daryl Gates*. Jerry could have sung those lines falsetto, a la Freddie Mercury, as detectives Richard Jamieson and Howard Landgren cloistered again with him in Benjamin's conference room. Their mastery of the situation made you gratified you paid taxes. Benjamin's hunch was right: Howard *was* the department's top suspect by day two. He had the motive. The skills. The background. It's why the detectives arrived with two binders packed with information about him.

Yet the more Jerry listened, the more he realized the police were still searching for definitive evidence tying him to Richard's balcony that night. Not only that, they said they'd require time to chase down leads implicating him as the impresario of other nefarious activities that Jerry knew nothing about. In other words, it was unlikely Howard would be sitting for his mugshot anytime soon, when Jerry would have preferred it to be today.

Jamieson, a long-legged, amiable man, and Landgren, a shorter, no-nonsense type, bombarded him with questions. As they did, Jerry marveled at the odds that the detectives assigned to this case shared first names with the two principals inciting it: Richard and Howard. It could make even an agnostic like Jerry believe God was a comedian.

They asked him to describe the sort of person this Garrett character was. Did Jerry every witness his temper? Could he catalog Howard's dealings with Richard? Had his ex-partner done anything to provoke him? Was Jerry aware of Howard's earlier jobs, his home life, his backstory? Any direct beefs between the two of them? Lastly, *why* did Howard quit Space Matters?

The detectives filled up an empty notepad with his responses, some of which were more complete than others. Relax, they told him as he caught his breath. As long as Howard assumed that he could strongarm him for the seventy-five thousand, he was safe. To help him sleep sounder, they would send a patrol car periodically by his Northridge home. And he could contact them night or day.

After they collected their binders and left, Jerry reflected on his head-spinning day. He was tremendously relieved the LAPD was onto Howard and simultaneously dispirited that there was no timetable for arresting him. While they investigated him—and Benjamin withdrew his recommendation that Jerry do to Howard what Howard did to Richard—he squirmed with the unease of a rabbit out in the open woods. He thought about his window-filled house, and about how well Howard knew the office layout. If he were to maintain a balancing act that kept his head down and his company afloat, he had no choice whom to phone next. They shared a last name.

From Benjamin's office, he called his sister, his only sibling, then a law student at Loyola University, a small, Jesuit-run college in downtown LA. After Jerry relayed his anxieties to her, she reached out to her dean, Father Richard Matthew Vashon. He recommended that she connect Jerry with a sharp criminal law professor who taught there. Michael Lightfoot didn't speak to Jerry from any academic ivory tower. He spoke pragmatically, explaining that because no one could divine how long the LAPD would need to construct a winnable case against such a wily adversary, he should build a team around *him*. Hiring his own private eyes would serve two purposes: it would bulk up his protection while making it simpler to keep tabs on the investigation's progress. It was the knowledge-equals-power correlation. Lightfoot never asked a dime for his services.

The professionals that Jerry hired that day from Benjamin's office made his former security guards seem like longhair mall cops. They had both enjoyed long careers—one high up in internal affairs at the LAPD, the other at the LA County Sheriff's Department—before retiring early. The older of the two was a friendly Irish American with a moon-shaped face and close-cropped red hair gone gray at the temples. He projected a fatherly, seen-it-all vibe. His colleague was a swarthier, gruffer man with Italian in his bloodline and a compact fearlessness about him. DeGernaye and Helder were their names. Their just-the-facts demeanor was reminiscent of the detectives from one of the few television shows that Jerry watched as a kid: *Dragnet*.

Benjamin, the original member of Jerry's protection team, refused to allow his client to return to Space Matters or his empty house in the foothills as the sun blazed into the Pacific. The last thing Jerry needed was isolation in the shadows. So Barry dragged him to his own West LA house, feeding him and sheltering him in the guest room. The following day, Jerry was back in his old routine, though webbed into a new reality.

How he'd adapt to it led him into an immediate flashpoint with his PIs. They were staunchly opposed to him driving any distance solo, including his regular space-planning sessions with Paul Fegen. When Jerry bristled, they reiterated that he was paying them to keep him safe, not be complacent while he made himself a sitting duck. He insisted that they didn't get it: Fegen was Space Matters's money client, the one they could ill afford to lose if the company was to survive. After some squabbling, they crafted a compromise. Jerry would meet with Fegen only late at night inside his well-fortified office building. And only if his hardnosed PIs chauffered him there.

They constituted one brick in his fortress. Still, it couldn't hurt to mortar in more. Jerry didn't even have to invite his rough-hewn friend to join the security detail that he'd cobbled together. Ari Allon, who stood out among Space Matters's trendy designers and drafters like a wrestler at a ballet, ached for the chance.

Ari, unlike other people in Jerry's world, wasn't a child of California, or a New York transplant with property holdings; wasn't a spoiled Westside brat like Richard, or a showboat like Fegen. He was a husky immigrant who'd grown up in Morocco's French Quarter, racing camels for thrills. When wars broke out in the Middle East, Ari abided his taste for adventure and heard the call of his Jewish brethren. He departed northern Africa to do his part, enlisting as a commando in the Israeli military. During his era fighting the Arabs, he had witnessed ghastly things on scorching sands bloodied with detached limbs and dead bodies, experiences that today rendered him at once world weary and fearsome. Ari, sick of combat, immigrated to LA to follow the archetype. He reinvented himself for a second act, in his instance trading in a helmet for a hard hat.

He launched a demolition business that put him on bulldozers, earthmovers, and other heavy machinery leveling space for contractors. For a change of pace, he sometimes hung out at Space Matters, doing odd jobs for Jerry, whose nerdy pluckiness he found delightful. Physically, Ari was an outlier, hairy as an ape, strong as an ox, with a pitted complexion and black hair trimmed pageboy style. To party, he favored tight silk shirts unbuttoned at the top, thick, gold disco chains, and cocaine. Though a native African, the man's spirit animal was a German shepherd who snapped at foreign dangers and slobbered over those he loved.

And if a friend needed his particular skill set, you didn't have to ask twice. Jerry, in once tangling with a Pico Boulevard landlord stiffing him for some $20,000 in planning work, barely needed to ask Ari once. The bill, accrued long before Richard was killed, was too much to ignore and yet not enough to sue over, leaving Jerry on the fence about retaining a collection agency. Then he glanced at the specimen sitting across from him and felt a swell of an idea. Hearing it, Ari broke into a devilish grin.

At about 4:00 p.m., he planted himself in the lobby of the deadbeat property owner. Jerry had suggested Ari make himself a benign nuisance there by loitering around the Oxford-shirt-wearing tenants. Ari, however, deviated for a more personal approach, calling Jerry's client from the ground floor to request they speak downstairs. When the executive approached, he puckered. He noticed Ari's sneer, saw his mucky clothes, and smelled his pungent stink, the latter the result of bulldozing in the LA heat.

"You don't pay my friend Jerry, I make parking lot out of building," Ari said in his signature English. "I bring my bulldozer."

Half an hour later, the landlord phoned Jerry waving the white flag; he promised to settle his design bill by tomorrow if he never saw Ari again. Perhaps, Jerry thought, *they* should have gone into business together: one expert at flattening buildings with diesel-fueled brute, the other gifted at configuring office space with a mechanical pencil.

While too late for that, Ari was right on time for *this* moment, persuading Jerry that he'd be his muscle. He'd moonlight as his bodyguard and even escort him when he visited Tammy and Jude back in Michigan. Given his way, he'd confront the "mothafocker" causing this. Ari, having seen Howard from afar in the Space Matters building, wasn't afraid of a windburned ex-carpenter from Pasadena next to the Kalashnikov-armed foes he squared off against in the roasting Middle East.

Gung-ho as he was to keep Jerry safe during the worst spring of his life, Ari was just one man unaware of the dozen or more people spending anxious days in fear of the "mothafocker" rounding their block.

In San Francisco, Robert Freeman kept his eyes peeled for Howard's El Camino, probably unaware that Johnny had nearly executed him on the sidewalk with his boss' .357. Back in Ontario, Robert's sister and mother replaced the locks and hid whatever guns they kept inside of their now-marked homes. Glenn Colley, who testified how Tim Dwight was bashed and burned to death, lived head down, convinced Howard had put a fatwa on him.

On the west side of the Harbor Freeway in LA, meanwhile, any number of folks had trouble forgetting the manner in which Richard died. Glass no longer seemed much of a barrier, and large, unblocked windows were reckless to linger in front of after sunset. By drawing their curtains and yanking their blinds, they sacrificed panoramas for safekeeping. Lump in Dr. Marmet, the elderly physician who tried to recruit Richard and Howard for his San Bernardino subdivision, as one of the affected. Informed of what happened, he vomited. One C-suite real-estate titan, more acquainted with everybody's leading suspect than the doctor, wished he could slip Howard amnesia potion to make him forget he ever existed.

That was his superpower. He reanimated his scowl on the inside of your eyelids.

CHAPTER FOURTEEN
BAIT AND RECORD

O N THE MORNING HE agreed to pose as live bait, twenty-seven-year-old Jerry Schneiderman dressed himself an old man attending his granddaughter's piano recital. Checked sportscoat. Burgundy sweater. White shirt. Gray slacks. In his palm was a Styrofoam cup of sludgy police coffee that detectives at the LAPD's Venice Boulevard substation handed him for this 7:00 a.m. hour. Jerry sipped it, though he was plenty awake.

The day marked a week since Howard promised to exterminate him unless he coughed up half the life insurance payout catalyzed by the bullet Howard arranged to have pierce Richard's window. Yesterday, detective Jamieson asked Jerry if he could handle such a nail-biting assignment, and Jerry said yes, he was up to it. He answered reflexively, unusual for him, without spinning through the myriad ways the self-incrimination trap being set for Howard could go wrong. The prospect of reuniting with his family after weeks apart overrode fastidious logic for sheer emotion.

From sunrise on, everything was novel. Jerry had never been inside a police station before. This one, by the 405 Freeway, was as dingy as the fast-food joints and dilapidated storefronts bunched around it. And he definitely had never been fitted to wear a secret wire and bulletproof vest so the LAPD could record the conversation, hardware now causing the day's first major snafu.

173

That's why the technicians responsible for preparing it were staring at each other with flustered expressions. Even with the loose-fitting clothes they told Jerry in advance to wear, his skinny chest made it obvious he'd been fitted with a lead-lined garment for protection. As in blatantly obvious. They tried smoothing the rigid thing down under his jacket, repositioning it under his sweater, and the difference was marginal. When Jerry looked down at himself, he felt like the Michelin Man. And it wasn't as if the LAPD could swap it for a kiddy model.

By eight, the quandary was mushrooming. It would be chancy to have Jerry meet Howard in a bloated outfit all but certain to tip him off that his words were being taped. Then again, it would be a gamble—some might say a lethal one—sending Jerry into a nose-to-nose encounter at Space Matters with someone so cunning without any protection from bullets or knife blades. If things turned bloody, the PR blowback against the department would live in infamy.

After agreement coalesced between Detective Jamieson and others, Jerry himself assented. To hasten Howard's capture, he would sit within arm's length of Richard's executioner with nothing but wool and cotton between them. The only foreign object under his clothes would be a small microphone attached by wire to a Walkman-sized transmitter harnessed to the small of his back. Police would be listening and recording every syllable from an unmarked van parked nearby. With any luck, Howard would drop his guard and crow about his accomplishments, just as he did before, all the way into a pair of chrome handcuffs. Should he try to get physical, armed police hiding just outside Jerry's office would pounce.

The phone was the next piece of "equipment" in the room. Jerry needed to call Howard at his Pasadena apartment to request he drop by the place he asserted he hated with a passion. Yeah, nothing to it. After rehearsing his lines, he got Howard on the line, saying simply they had to talk. An unreadable Howard agreed to an 11:00 a.m. appointment.

On his drive from Venice Boulevard to his office on Fremont Place, Jerry shivered with his first cold sweat of that April day. The LAPD, he realized, wouldn't have devoted so much manpower in a time of record-shattering murders unless him sticking his head into the lion's mouth to extract prosecutable language risked decapitation. Still, this was what he consented to, whether rashly or not, and wimping out would blow up a boatload of preparations. So, he'd trust the choreography. Bank on the reinforcements. He was also heartened to find out the department was an old pro at foiling murder-hire schemes. Besides the case involving Howard, Detective Jamieson acknowledged that he was actively investigating three other professional hits involving business and insurance.

•••

AT 11:00 A.M. ON the dot, a familiar visitor poked his head through the front door of Space Matters' mansion, searching for Jerry. With no sign of him in his ground-floor office, he withdrew it to wait outside. What upside could there be manufacturing small talk with former workmates curious about what he was doing there?

Jerry saw the man as soon as he drove up in Tammy's Seville; he had lent Ari the Cadillac in exchange for future services. Between the hand-wringing over the lead vest and Wilshire Boulevard's glacial traffic, he had arrived late for the staged appointment that he set up.

As such, Jerry was already on his heels.

Howard must've gleaned that he was being duped, that this rendezvous was too easy, because he switched things up. In his stead he dispatched a gofer half his age, a thin, buff, surfer type named Michael Bailey, who did some demolition work and ran errands for Howard when he supervised CM-2.

"What are you doing here?" Jerry asked outside the car, clutching a briefcase with a grip that Michael noticed was shaking.

"About to tell you Howard's new conditions for meeting," said Michael, attired in a pair of tan corduroy pants. Michael told Jerry not to be irked at him. He was only the envoy for someone uncomfortable being in a building whose owners scammed his credit lines and milked his contractor's license.

"Not comfortable after he scrambled Richard's brains?" Jerry said, standing by the Seville in the event he needed to hide behind it. "Really?"

Michael sidestepped debate, spelling out what Howard charged him with doing. He was to drive Jerry in the El Camino to Tiny Naylor's coffee shop nearby. There, Jerry was to use the restaurant's public pay phone to call the one at the Beverly Hills Café, another area restaurant, where Howard was waiting. Jerry had said they needed to speak. This, Howard responded through his Jeff Spicoli-esque emissary, was *how*.

"No," Jerry snapped. "Absolutely not." He wasn't going to Tiny Naylor's, or anywhere. How gullible did Howard think he was?

Michael was now stuck on a two-man chessboard in which Jerry wouldn't leave and Howard wouldn't come. How, he posed, could he even vamp a solution when his boss forbade him from touching a company phone that he assumed was bugged?

"That's not my problem," Jerry said. "It's Howard's."

A minute elapsed, and Michael shopped a compromise. What if they went to the payphone down the street, where Jerry could contact Howard at the café for their conversation, or devise an alternative meeting spot? This way, no one would have to worry about being overheard or kidnapped. Jerry liked it, forgetting in the process the cardinal rule detectives drilled into him. Whatever he did, he was not to step off the property.

Howard's gofer began walking down Wilshire, arms swinging, construction boots on concrete, Jerry trailing ten feet behind. But they didn't go a block before the procession halted. Something alarming was outlined in Michael's back pocket, Jerry uncertain if it was a hairbrush, a carpet-pad scraper, or a weapon. He studied it further: the object bore the L-shape of a small caliber pistol.

When Michael glanced back, Jerry was no longer following him. Whatever Michael was carrying in his pocket had Jerry grimacing, as if he could either use a swig of Pepto-Bismol or a shot of Jose Cuervo.

"You alright, man?" Michael asked. "You look terrible."

He doubled back, wrapping his arm around Jerry's shoulder as Benjamin did during his graveyard advice session.

"I'm not feeling so well," Jerry said, riffing off Michael's concern. "I think I have a stomach bug from last night. I can't go with you. Have Howard call me."

They'd reverted to stalemate, and Michael wrenched his arm off of Jerry, curtly saying he would tell Howard what happened. He then marched off with that unidentified item silhouetted in his corduroys' pocket.

Jerry returned to the mansion, sat down at his desk, and sighed. It wasn't even noon, and he was bushed. Howard outfoxed everyone again, but at least the suspense was over.

What a hollow assumption.

Not ten minutes later, Space Matters erupted in a commotion you could've mistaken for a cattle stampede. A small battalion of officers in dark clothing, protective vests, and helmets, each brandishing automatic weapons and ammo belts, barged through the mansion's front door.

Among the numerous things that Jerry did not know that morning was that members of the Special Weapons and Tactics (SWAT) team, an elite, paramilitary-style force the department conceived after the 1965 Watts riots, was already in covert position outside the building when he drove up. But he knew now. Everyone there did. The officers hoofed around, splitting up to check every room and cranny, seal off entryways, and eyeball anything suspicious. Others barked orders or spoke rapid-fire into walkie-talkies.

Then the commander of the LAPD invasion hollered orders directly at Jerry's staff.

"*Down!* Everybody down on the floor now. Get your faces into it, people."

The entire workforce was soon prostrate, noses pressed into places where their quality shoes just were. A few of the dozen-plus

SWAT officers pinned their bodies along the sides of the windows, peering out from unblinking eyes.

After about five minutes of confusion and clatter, the SWAT team leader spoke again to the space designers and planners.

"All clear," he announced. "Everybody can get up."

His officers helped the crew to their feet, even if no one was steady on them. Except for the hissing walkie-talkies, a silence engulfed the ground floor. That all shifted as folks let their emotions out, staring around in disbelief. First there was whimpering, then mumbling, before a general tugging on officers' elbows in confusion what this was about. There were stiletto looks at Jerry, too.

Lillian, the French decorator, hugged a shaken colleague, Michael, who had forgotten all about the wallpaper he was agonizing over pre-takeover, and was now a crying wreck.

Before Jerry knew it, there formed a tidal wave of questions from them, questions he couldn't begrudge anyone for asking. Why did they need to cower? Was this tied to Richard? Was someone trying to gun them down? Were the police going to hang around in case the unknown threat returned? Finally, *why* did Jerry let this raid occur without briefing them—before the LAPD stormtroopers scared the living daylights out of them?

"Down! Everybody down on the floor now."

The geeky twenty-seven-year-old from North Hollywood stood to the side, absorbing their *how-could-you* glares, feeling the wretch in his no-win situation. No one had given him advance notice this would happen. On the contrary, detectives at the Venice substation admonished him to say as little as possible about why there were plainclothes cops outside. Either way, employees banking on him for leadership were now contemptuous he left them hanging in a war zone.

The guilt stacked up, and Jerry knew he would turn to stone if this invisible gag remained. He pulled the SWAT commander aside, arguing in a loud whisper that his people "deserved to know the basics." The commander, soaking up the tension in the high-ceilinged office, couldn't help but agree, and cleared his voice. The reason his men poured into the building, he announced, was because of Howard Garrett, *the* leading suspect in the murder of Richard Kasparov. He just cruised by the office, and the SWAT team needed to rush in to safeguard everyone in the event he took a shot. A ringing silence reverberated again. But soon came more staff muttering, more knotted brows.

Naturally, there'd been hallway gossip about who was responsible for what befell Richard, and the needle usually vibrated at Howard. Richard, ever urbane and slick, the theory went, bilked and embarrassed a cowboy who refused to walk away from a loss. Brie, Space Matters' office manager, intuited this scenario as true. When a man in a warm-up suit knocked a few days earlier, saying he was an old friend of Jerry's who wanted to say hello, she told him to take off and tried flinging the door closed. Neither she nor the stranger backed down until Jerry hurried over to say he was safe to enter.

"Who is he?" Brie demanded to know. A plainclothes detective working Richard's homicide, Jerry quietly told her.

As to why Howard would want to kill the man he was pressuring for money, Jerry was lost. The commander, now joined by detectives, told him there was no charting the mechanisms of some extortion plots; maybe Howard was contemplating a warning shot to broadcast his unpredictability—something they'd already accounted for with the police helicopter tracking his movements all morning. They couldn't alert Jerry to any of that in the interest of secrecy, just as the SWAT team couldn't risk Howard squeezing off a bullet, no matter the momentary panic it stirred.

The commander, before ordering his men to leave, reassured Jerry's staff that any immediate hazard had passed and the situation was under control. He advised them to immediately notify him if they noticed Howard or his associates loitering.

•••

ON HIS END OF that Wednesday, Howard would've rejoiced about the pandemonium he triggered without trying had he known. But he was a preoccupied individual with a windfall to produce. After Michael picked him up at the café, describing Jerry's refusal to go with him, Howard made Michael roll him by Space Matters for intel-collection. He'd never squeeze off a shot without his .357 anyway.

An hour later, back at his apartment, Howard discovered a blinking answering machine. Just as expected, it was from Jerry requesting he call him back to reschedule the meeting. Howard made Michael dial the number while he enjoyed a cocktail, snatching the receiver when Jerry's nasally voice came on. The dialogue was curt and arctic. Jerry, having received fresh instructions from the detectives, said he would be waiting for him on a bench in front of the Los Angeles County Museum of Art. It was adjacent to Southern California's eeriest tourist attraction, the La Brea Tar Pits. Howard said he knew the place well.

This was the second biggest day in the short history of his niche business. Before Richard's murder, he put his core set of employees through training—target assessment, surveillance, evidence-free crime scenes—tailored to each's aptitude. Stipends were dictated by everyone's organizational importance. As assistant manager/lead assassin, Johnny earned the most, though the weirdo was being a complainer, nagging Howard to pay him for fulfilling his end of the contract. His colleagues, a poverty-scraping band of low-level offenders and junkies, all of whom Howard had positioned to scapegoat if required, included Crazy Eddy, cross-dressing Jamie, Chaser, and revolving part-timers like Michael. IBM wasn't built overnight, either. Personnel took time. As he impressed on his staff, he was evaluating everyone's performance in pursuit of that seventy-five thousand.

•••

AS JERRY UNDERSTOOD IT, the LAPD's revised plan involved new moving parts and old hazards. Facing Howard out in the open was more complex than it would have been in an enclosed office. Outside, the x-factors were endless, what with tourists milling about and the unexpected possible. Wardrobe-wise, it was the same as before. Jerry, as he had since the early morning eons ago, would continue wearing the recording device with no bulletproof vest.

He wished he could climb under a rock. Throughout his entire life, he never felt this pecked apart, resented by his staff while muscled by a predator adept at thinking two steps ahead.

But detectives still played the we-have-it-covered card. While they changed the venue for the meetup, they said, nothing else had. They would be monitoring every step from multiple positions and recording every word from an undercover van parked along Wilshire. As for firepower, they arranged that in spades. Across the boulevard, on the roof of the Mutual Benefit Life skyscraper opposite the museum, SWAT team sharpshooters would have high-powered rifles trained on Howard. Police marksmen would also be on his north, crouching on the roofs of the museum's three structures.

Here, they emphasized, was what Jerry needed to remember once Howard appeared. Should he flash a gun or a knife, Jerry was to slowly backpedal to avoid being struck in crossfire if the sharpshooters took preemptive action. Alternatively, if Howard grabbed him and marched him toward his car, Jerry was given two options to avoid flying bullets: either dip below the vehicle's roofline or dive into an open door. That's all!

Same as before, detectives assigned Jerry a harrowing task: getting a butcher to act carelessly when he was already on guard. Specifically, they wanted him to prod Howard to amplify on Richard's murder: the means, the motive, the ballistics, the accomplices. On top of that, he needed to coax Howard to repeat the mayhem he planned for him like someone seeking details about his own slaughter.

Jerry departed for his most dreaded meeting ever about 1:20 p.m., his mind teeming with fear, anticipation, and LAPD pointers on unleashing Howard's criminal bravado. The rest of him was either too numb or prickled by goosebumps to register much.

He headed west on Wilshire, letting his eyes trace the sweeping architecture—the regal Gothic churches, the black steel towers—that so intoxicated him before. The faster he drove, the more the boulevard skyline spliced sunlight into repeating sequences of light and dark, a photographic negative effect on a day of technicolor surrealism. In ordinary circumstances, he could have gawked for hours at the signature structures, intrigued by their history. What did ionic columns matter now?

He turned off Wilshire onto Curson Avenue east of the museum and parked the Seville. His rubbery legs then took him toward the largest of the fence-encircled tar pits. The viscous black pools hemmed inside were forty thousand years old, filled with organically occurring asphaltum. School kids, natural-history buffs, and out-of-towners had been fascinated by this shimmering goop since World War II.

Yet with all its choices in America's second-largest metropolis, the LAPD selected a bench here, a bench near the opaque ponds where recreated prehistoric critters indigenous to the region—bison, ground sloths, saber-toothed cats, mammoths—were trapped in inescapable muck, fated to die a petroleum death? Honestly: some restaurant patio wouldn't suffice? The pungent sulfur wafting off the tar pits' surfaces already made Jerry's eyes tear. Space planners like him, a sissy profession to most Americans in the bell curve, shouldn't tumble into a warped plot from a crime novel that Joseph Wambaugh's agent would've laughed out of his office.

He still put one foot in front of the other, edging closer to the bench while searching for the face that could slice right through you. He reminded himself not to gape up, just as the detectives cautioned, but he did anyway for comfort he wasn't alone on the plaza. He wasn't. Helmets of SWAT sharpshooters created a parapet of little black dots on the penthouse roof of the Mutual Benefit Life building across Wilshire. When he reached his meet-up point, he knew more guns were trained from behind. Somewhere overhead, he could hear the rhythmic thump from the blades of the LAPD helicopter, which was using the high-rises as cover.

Despite that armada, Jerry's gut was stretched over the proverbial rack. That Howard could be the same person who nearly welled up seeing Jerry bedside after his booze-fueled diabetic coma made you wonder how much you could know anybody.

"How about a hug, man?" Howard requested that day.

Jerry gazed back at the tar pit with the replica mammoth caught in the dark slurry, snout pointed skyward, braying at its fuckup meandering here. He could relate.

At 2:03 p.m., the El Camino deposited Howard onto the museum steps along the boulevard. As before, he was garbed in blue, a fashion reminder to Jerry about who was in control. They didn't shake hands.

Howard casually leaned against the rail in his tinted sunglasses, weathered fingers pinching a Kool. Feet away on the bench, Jerry gargled saliva.

"You alone?" Howard asked.

"Yes," Jerry lied.

"Oh, hell, I bet you're wired," Howard said dryly.

"Then you bet wrong."

"Yeah, whatever. Say, how's the wife and kid?"

"Fine. They're fine."

"So, do you have anything for me?"

"Like what?"

"Let's not play games again."

"This isn't a game. Not to me."

Jerry urged himself to avoid peering up. Or running.

"Then do you have my money? It's been a week."

"No. No, I don't. Nothing's changed from the last time we spoke. Richard's mom still has the insurance claim tied up. She says her family deserves all of it. There's nothing I can do."

"That's not true. You could've hit up Tammy's parents. We covered that before. Remember?"

"Yes—when you threatened me and my family. But I've thought about it since then, and I can't bring myself to ask Tammy's dad to wipe out his bank account. Seventy-five thousand dollars would break him."

"I see."

So many were monitoring this scene: two teams of sharpshooters, the people onboard the LAPD helicopter, the cops in the unmarked van. Howard had only a single supporting cast. Michael, after parking the El Camino, scurried over to hide in the bushes with a pair of binoculars and whatever it was in his back pocket. Nobody else from the team was there, especially the two who'd been with him on Richard's landing. They needed to mind their Ps and Qs, and prep with the others for their next target. Dr. Marmet or that one-percenter in Santa Barbara was now the hottest candidate.

"If you'd just give me a little more time," Jerry continued. "I can't close my eyes and make the money appear. I can't be responsible for what an insurance company does. Maybe you'd consider taking less than you asked for before. I just went through this thing with Richard. I had to pay lawyers, partly to deal with your claims. I'm strapped."

"There you go again with your poor-me routine," Howard said, then switching to dripping singsong. "*I can't, I can't, I can't...*"

"I don't know why you don't believe me," Jerry said, interrupting.

"You don't, huh? Well, I once believed Richard, and see where that got me? All I'm hearing now is what I heard before. You're useless. You truly are."

"But I'm not Richard! He screwed me just like you. The whole company might go under because of it."

"That's not my concern anymore."

"Obviously."

"Hey, don't get flip."

"I'm not. I'm trying to make you appreciate my situation."

The dialogue circled around this same argument until Howard heard enough. He was adjourning the meeting.

"Jerry, all I have to say is this: you've made your choice and I've made mine. See ya around."

He stubbed out his second cigarette and threw Jerry a smirk. Leisurely, he walked diagonally down the museum steps, to the west, where his shadow dissolved into LA's elephant-colored airshed.

Jerry let a minute elapse, then stomped his toes on the concrete steps to get blood circulating. By then, the sharpshooters on the penthouse of the Mutual Life building were gone, as was the LAPD's mobile-recording van. The showdown was over.

Jerry retraced his steps, past the make-believe mammoth, toward the parking lot. By the time he was driving to meet detectives back at the Venice Boulevard station for the debriefing, he permitted himself a smile. Howard would be arrested within a day or two, strung up by his own hubris. While he stood for arraignment, Tammy could book return flights home and he could release his PIs only a week after retaining them. If that wasn't cause for celebration, for Jerry to get drunk—which he rarely did—what was? Historic architecture might even become germane again.

The debriefing took place in the same drab room where he was wired up and given a pep talk that morning. He was drained yet electric, poised on the borderland of what once was, like he'd just aced the test of his life. The eyes of Jamieson and other detectives carried no luster, however. They were lightless, even dodgy.

Why, Jerry asked, wasn't everybody high-fiving one another?

Because, they admitted in the flattest of voices, the trap they set for Howard backfired on *them*. Jerry clenched his chair's armrest when he heard why.

The recording of the pivotal conversation needed to establish probable cause was a static-filled disaster. Except for the beginning of the conversation, when Howard astutely guessed that Jerry was wired, the tape was completely inaudible! The technical malfunction meant that no one was being arrested. Not today, maybe not next week. The basis to do so would've been shoddy.

Flush-cheeked, Jerry asked how could this have happened after extensive preparations? Unforeseen acoustics, the LAPD technicians said. The cumbersome recording device that Jerry wore underneath his clothes had, in effect, too sharp a hearing. Where it was supposed to chronicle Howard admitting—in analog clarity—that he engineered Richard's murder to get his foot on Jerry's neck was hissing white noise from bustling Wilshire Boulevard. Engine revs, car horns, a distant ambulance, and, mostly, gear-shifting Southern California Rapid Transit District buses continually stopping and starting contaminated the recording by overrunning it.

From a future prosecution standpoint, the tape was inadmissible.

Jerry sunk into his chair, sticky under his clothing. The LAPD needed more time to assemble a case after its operational fumble. Howard, detectives now acknowledged, had committed grisly acts during the last few years, acts that went well beyond Richard and an earlier victim that they had an obligation to sift through. They envisioned a multi-count, omnibus indictment that would guarantee life in prison for him, if not the death penalty. Eventually. The fact that Michael was part of Howard's team signaled they needed to throw a wider net. But they had no idea when they'd scoop anyone up.

Jerry wanted to stomp out to scream at the sky. What he craved so desperately was being swallowed by the dark acts of someone outside this room.

Officers told him to remove the jacket, vest, and shirt he purposefully wore to cloak the microphone too sensitive for its own good. When they ripped off the tape affixing the device to his sternum and back, it inflamed reddened skin. Don't be morose, they said. Howard's days of pillaging at will had a fast-approaching expiration date.

Jerry smiled weakly at the encouragement. He still had faith in the LAPD, just a bushel less than he did at sunrise.

As the debriefing progressed, one of the side detectives let his tongue slip in a comment that gashed Jerry again. He remarked that if the SWAT men reading Jerry's lips through their telephoto binoculars saw him mouth the words "don't shoot" in response to something Howard did, all this would've been moot. Under rules of engagement, they would've had the legal authority to fire on him to protect an informant.

Jerry boiled at the absurdity. One utterance of a two-word clause could've ended the saga on the museum plaza. Just a "don't shoot." Why, he questioned his handlers in something between an accusation and a whimper, were they just saying this now? They claimed they weren't. They'd gone over the safe words when he was being prepped that morning. Jerry wracked his memory for a playback. He couldn't find anything.

Whether they'd neglected to give him the proper instructions or he forgot staring into Howard's sunglasses in that pressure cooker of a meeting, his imagination latched onto the fantasy where Howard was shot dead because of his boldness. What a headline it could've been: "LAPD Kills Accused Murderer Foiled by Space Planner."

Alas, it was not to be. The missed chance slapped another slice of bread of this shit-sandwich of a day. The truth was incontestable: Howard was winning.

CHAPTER FIFTEEN
CATERPILLAR MAN

FROM THAT DAY FORWARD, Jerry's new living quarters were a glorified birdbox high above Wilshire, a stretch of road nearly as mythologized as Sunset Boulevard and Mulholland Drive. For someone afraid of heights and resistant to shackles, it was the worst of both worlds. And Jerry needed to get cozy in it.

Before the debriefing session finished, he assumed the detectives would inform him that they would be blanketing him with round-the-clock protection. Howard was onto them, as obvious from his sly "I'll bet you're wired" comment. Jerry knew he was too exposed in the wide spaces of the city for him to live as he had. He was right about that, and wrong in believing he'd still be sleeping on his own pillow.

The good people at the Hyatt Hotel would be taking care of that.

While the police couldn't legally force him to hunker down there, detectives strongly recommended he did in a non-choice choice. The structure, now renamed the Radisson Wilshire Plaza Hotel, was nothing rococo, nothing on any architectural tour, but it was convenient, sitting between Miracle Mile and downtown LA. Jerry was assured he would be much safer here on the seventh floor, housed next to other threatened witnesses and informants under LAPD guard, than an unwalled, glass-strewn foothill residence whose address Howard undoubtedly checked off in his black book.

Much as he didn't want to, Jerry agreed with the irreducible logic despite the economic wounds it'd inflict. Taxpayers footed the room-and-board bills for his new neighbors, many of them waiting to testify for the prosecution in upcoming trials. Because Jerry lacked official standing like them, he would be paying the tab from his own shellacked finances.

But could he still work his normal week, ten to twelve hours a day Monday through Friday, at Space Matters? Sadly, no, the detectives answered. He could pop in there only on a limited basis, once a week at most.

He had no time to brood or howl, no slack to bury his face in self-pity. If he needed to gather any personal possessions for a hiatus of unknown duration, he needed to do it *that* day, under the care of his PIs. Never had Jerry packed suitcases faster; never had he opened a dark closet fearing the boogeyman. As he left suburbia, where the good life with Tammy and Jude flowered, he said goodbye, uncertain if he would ever return.

His living arrangement featured a stiff queen-size bed, a regularly sanitized toilet, blackout shades, and a sunset-blocked view, all of that wedged into three hundred and fifty square feet. The officers who rimmed the floor controlled everyone's movements. Informants, arrayed in rooms by the type of criminal activity that they snitched on, were barred from fraternizing with others. Protocol trumped liberties here. Detectives, for instance, banned Jerry from venturing outside the Hyatt without his PIs or Ari glued to his hip. If he did exit the hotel, he needed to apprise police of his schedule beforehand, always aware that Howard and his cronies wanted the drop on him.

That first evening there, he called Tammy in Ann Arbor to give her a rundown on his flaming wreckage of a day. Asked where he was staying, he told her the LAPD forbid him from saying in case Howard bugged his phone; the police were listening, too, as the staticky line made clear. Tammy, recognizing the gloom in her husband's voice, tried cheering him up. "You oughta hear the new words Jude is learning," she said. Or how he stacks LEGO blocks with your spatial-imagination gene. When he manufactured a giggle for her benefit, she mentioned it would be only another week before he was in Michigan for a visit. There'd be nookie time then.

"Can't it be tomorrow?" Jerry said, downcast. "Really."

After she hung up, Tammy couldn't blunt the particulars of what transpired twenty-three hundred miles away. The debacle with the bulletproof vest; how the SWAT guys thundered in after a false alarm; the toady that tried to lure Jerry into a car; Howard's wicked smirk on the museum steps; the maddeningly inaudible tape. She was so unnerved that she went to her father, a pragmatic businessman in Michigan's automobile trade. Jerry, she told him, wasn't on the periphery of something heinous. He was in the epicenter of it.

Her father saw the anguish in his daughter's face, and, on his own volition, wasted little time contacting the LAPD case detectives long distance. He said that if the maniac just wanted money, he was prepared to wire the $75,000 from his personal bank account.

What a magnanimous offer, detectives responded. Now, forget it!

Once Howard obtained his cash, they said, he would have little incentive to keep Jerry (and what he knew) around. Paying that money could be signing his son-in-law's death sentence. The game plan was to continue fooling Howard that his windfall was coming while they burned through shoe leather investigating him. Tammy's father set the phone down, chastened and concerned.

In California, Jerry reclined on the bed in his cookie-cutter room, oblivious of these efforts and already feeling claustrophobic. He'd gut it out, nonetheless, keep his nerves better hidden next time. He ordered from room service, chewing what passed for a cheeseburger. He took a shower next, then tried losing himself in a sitcom. Before he drifted off as an agnostic who recited no prayers toward the heavens, the late-night news flickered on. The stories: Billy Carter, the president's redneck, beer-guzzling brother, was swearing never to drink again. There was also something about political bedlam in Iran, but Jerry's fuzzy head gave it no import.

•••

HOWARD SPENT THE REST of that day planting seeds, never taking cover a day in his life. From the museum/tar pits, he and Michael drove to inspect a building whose owner was soliciting remodeling bids. Murder for profit teased big money, but it was an inconsistent trade. For that reason, he hedged his bets by staying in the field that never made him rich.

While Jerry tucked in for the first time at the Hyatt, Howard also sampled the mood around his quarry's world. He phoned Bert, the Space Matters draftsman that he hadn't seen since the Langer's lunch—a lunch that Howard designed as his Trojan horse to learn what everybody knew that he didn't. Again, he cloaked himself in his blue-collar persona, acting the stressed-out contractor talking shop with a simpatico chum. Bert, a hardworking, chubby Filipino with a tender smile, was stupefied. Just hours earlier, the SWAT team bull-rushed into Space Matters, ordering everyone down in case the character on the other end of the line now uncorked a bullet.

Bert knew the best tactic was a potentially life-preserving one. Say as little as possible.

Howard tried cracking Bert's silence by kindling rapport and spewing grievances. You know that renovation job downtown I was working on? he said. I quit it; wasn't worth the time or bucks. Know that suite buildout that he and Jerry were supposed to be collaborating on, since it was okayed months back for CM-2? The clown in charge forgot to string the blinds or stretch the carpets.

Trying to groom this back channel, Howard said with creepy sweetness that his life would sure be easier if Jerry lived up to his responsibilities, wink-wink. Any chance you could nudge him to pay what he should?

Bert fibbed that he'd try.

"I still like him," Howard said of Jerry.

Gulping quietly, Bert replied he did too.

"I just called to see how you are," Howard said with a coo. "We're not enemies. I hope we remain friends for the rest of our lives."

···

BY HIS THIRD DAY confined at the Hyatt, Jerry was already a clairvoyant. A few weeks of this and he predicted he'd be wild-eyed with cabin fever. Much more of that, and he'd be batty.

On their visit to his room, his PIs discerned he was antsy, rubbing his palms and having trouble standing still. They excused themselves to speak out of his presence and walked back in after a few minutes with an idea. They said he could move around feeling relatively secure—if he was amenable to an identity makeover.

What did they mean? Jerry inquired. Fake being handicapped? Impersonate a punk-rocker with a mohawk and clothes-pinned nostril?

Nothing that extreme, they answered. But, also, nothing mild.

The next day, when Jerry stepped out onto Wilshire, he was in secondhand clothes that Ari brought over. Jerry cared not to know where Ari found them in production of the new him.

Instead of a Givenchy suit, Italian silk tie, and razor-shaved face, transformed Jerry was a reverse-image of his old self. This one wore a bumblebee yellow Caterpillar Construction T-shirt, matching baseball cap or denim beanie, and a five o'clock shadow. Khaki slacks he'd favored since childhood were replaced by button-fly Levi Strauss blue jeans. The overall impression fell in the couture wavelength between freelance laborer and pool-hall hustler.

He clad himself this way on his first visit to Space Matters since the SWAT team fiasco, a sight that elicited double takes from the general staff and light needling from friends. Any levity was short-lived. The PIs accompanying him were none too pleased that he'd demanded on being here. They wanted his office time whittled to an absolute minimum. To them, Jerry's disguise was a stopgap, not a panacea, one that might raise questions among his crew that the LAPD wasn't prepared to discuss. Another concern: even harmless water-cooler gossip about his new appearance could trickle to Howard and his gift for learning what you least wanted him to know.

In those first weeks of forced exile, Jerry slogged to keep his chin up, lethargy that spilled onto lackluster sketches he was forced to draw at his Hyatt in-room desk. Each time he picked up the phone, the annoying hiss reminded him his LAPD minders could be listening. When he instinctively flexed at day's end, it stabbed him remembering the home he'd deserted. Thinking about the company—a company flourishing a year ago, before Richard's gambit with luxury-home remodels—was no better. With revenue falling, he needed to gin up fresh clients at the same time he tried to restart job sites frozen by Howard's lawyers. If not for Paul Fegen's business, he'd be furloughing people.

"Things going wrongly or haphazard" he scribbled in a note to himself. "No direction."

Jamieson and Landgren, the LAPD detectives, could've written the same thing. They knew definitively that Howard was tied to Richard's murder, yet had virtually nothing besides what Jerry told them as evidence. Even with the binder of info about him, including his barbarism against poor Tim Dwight, they hadn't begun to penetrate the surface of the serrated triangle he and Richard had angled against Jerry.

CHAPTER SIXTEEN
THE OPPOSITE TEST

THROUGHOUT A PECULIAR BOYHOOD, Jerry rarely heard about folks who behaved animalistically: clawed people who fell into murderous trances, pretty-scaled ones who slithered out of responsibilities. Filling his eardrums, instead, were his mother's trepidations about microscopic dangers of everyday life geared to kill them. He was subjected to her warnings so frequently that he concocted a game to distinguish whether her tales were true or the fruits of a paranoid mind.

After, for example, Vera Schneiderman pulled him and his sister from school the day of a big Soviet test to bunker in their home hallway, jittery that radiation was spreading, little Jerry used his patented "opposite test" to determine if the reverse was likelier: that his mother must be exaggerating, for no one on his North Hollywood block was dropping dead.

Deduction became his reality Geiger counter, for Vera always had hobgoblins to avoid.

Food-borne germs were a favorite. When dining out, she often made her family bring their own silverware, and she forbid Jerry from partaking in friends' birthday cakes. Neither he nor his sister were permitted to eat at his leukemia-stricken grandmother's out of fear that cancer could be contagious. After Vera once noticed a yellow truck with a hazard-symbol triangle tooling around, she ordered her children to strip off their clothes for a decontaminating shower. The TV set, like other isotope-spewing electronics, was no innocent, either.

Other days, the dainty woman's hyper-alertness lapsed into depression so suffocating that she was unable to pry herself from bed. She needed her ten-year-old boy to help pick out her clothes, fix her coffee, and do grown-up chores. Most tragic of all? Vera's general aversion to taking the medication that would've regulated her angsts.

Her husband, Art, who'd elevated himself from an elementary school teacher to public school principal, was the family rock, its upbeat personality. Never much interested in striking it rich, he parlayed his law degree to serve pro-bono clients in his off time while co-running a kids' day camp during the summer. Peter Pan might've been his avatar. At toy stores, Art was the twinkle-eyed one on the floor playing with the latest models while his son stood guard for salesclerks. Many of the other dads on the Schneiderman's street northeast of downtown were factory men at defense contractor Lockheed Corporation in adjacent Burbank. Weekends for them revolved around beer consumption and car tinkering. Not Art, an athletic guy with brown hair, an accordion, and a Harley-Davidson. Fanciful, sure, but he was Jerry's conduit to the flourishes of innocence: hanging on monkey bars, ski trips to the High Sierras.

His wife, an art teacher, was still the dominant figure, ruling the family with a neurotic gyroscope that she herself yearned to stop. She was a bright and inquisitive woman, but also suspicious, manipulative, and challenging to understand, right down to her revulsion for lawyers, doctors, and the rich. Jerry was an unintended casualty of her warped views, confounded by her fearmongering while fascinated by its roots.

After the explosion of December 14, 1962, when he was eleven, he learned not all dangers were environmental. Sometimes they veered out of nowhere.

On that evening, a silvery cargo plane pitched out of a wet fog and toward the earth, propellers rotating at full speed. The Flying Tiger "Super H" Constellation, loaded with 40,000 pounds of freight and sloshing with jet fuel, was not going to make it to Burbank airport a mile-plus away. Vera realized this before anyone, just from the roar of the wounded aircraft. It fluttered so low it snapped the electrical lines.

"Arty, Arty," she shrieked through the house. "It's going to crash!"

The woman knew her calamities. The plane, with a wingspan half the length of a football field, cratered into Bellingham Avenue around 10:00 p.m., detonating like a bomb. The violence from it could be felt on sidewalks miles away, its hundred-foot-high fireball visible for miles. All five people aboard perished instantly, with three more dead on the ground. Among the destruction were six homes, two small businesses, and the locals' sense of tranquility. The nose cone that sheared off from the fuselage and the dislodged propeller that slashed a billboard were footnotes of obliteration.

Experiencing a night of explosions, wailing sirens, and death can rattle the psyche of an impressionable boy, and Jerry was never the same. In the future, he knew he'd need more than his reductionist opposite test to differentiate the implausible from the possible. Not that there's a way to forestall the sorrow its effect can bring. Across his street, one of the homes slammed into rubble was where his sister's best friend lived. Cathleen was a cute sixteen-year-old girl readying for a late date when the plane that should've been thousands of feet above canceled her future. The Schneiderman's were fortunate theirs wasn't too.

Jerry's personal gauntlet awaited inside the walls of public school. He was that pudgy, smart kid whom the teachers judged as unmotivated and prone to daydreaming. He earned Bs on half effort and was skipped ahead a year, but his proclivity to dress like an adult earned him not admiration for his individualism but cruelty that he wasn't conforming. While his peers donned Levi's, he wore dress slacks to keep his chubby thighs from swishing when he walked; while everyone carried bookbags, he toted a briefcase like a pre-Alex P. Keaton of the sitcom Family Ties. He couldn't have been a choicer target for the bullies if he tried. They bloodied his nose and stole his lunch, then ridiculed him as a loser, a whale, and a Jew. They dared him to punch back, which Jerry refrained from doing—until he learned to let them throw haymakers to get them off balance.

Drawing and artwork was where Jerry sparkled above the crowd, shapes and dimensions ballooning off his pencil. A Barnsdale Park exhibit even showcased his grade-school work. Engineer, architect: Jerry's talented left hand could draw his tomorrow.

Nobody could've expected that a tubby, self-conscious child like him could swim like a fish, either. In races at his father's camp near Laurel Canyon, Jerry's butterball body cut through the water, usually ahead of lither competition. Sometimes he didn't bother with one stroke, combining wind-milling arms and hectic leg chops. The pool was his habitat. At ten, he jumped into one at a birthday party to save a drowning little girl. He became a junior lifeguard the next year.

His Bellingham Avenue was populated with lower- and middle-class Angelenos in ranch and post-modern houses. It was by the Hollywood Freeway and yet a million miles from red-carpet Hollywood. By the early 1960s, more Jewish families like Jerry's moved in and older cracker types packed up for outlying towns. Even for its small, nondescript block, the Schneiderman's house was cramped; to Jerry it was 1,100 square feet of small spaces and original appliances. He shared a room with his sister until near puberty, when he relocated into the den. Typical teenage decorations—posters of all-star shortstops or NASA rockets or British guitarists—were absent.

Jerry had no ardent notions of what he would be in life, believing he'd pollinate that later. He merely wanted an exciting future, untethered from conspiracy theories about nuclear war, birthday cake, and microbes. To speed his freedom, he began saving for a car. Soon he took a part-time job drafting for a real-estate appraiser. Jerry's picaresque streak also emerged in these peach-fuzz years, him once trying to convince an uptight, right-wing teacher that he was a communist; another telling his mother, ever fond of quipping that God would punish him for not being nicer to her, that he could incite an earthquake. Moments later, a small temblor shook.

When he wasn't socializing with his small knot of school friends, Jerry hung out with local rabbis who saw something uniquely mature (and damaged) about him. They slipped him advice about making it, and sometimes whiskey. Jerry about then also decided to tackle his weight program by challenging himself. No more self-loathing about extra blubber that warded off the girls. Unassisted, he put himself on a strict protein diet, eating one meal a day, and then only meat and lettuce. There'd be no ice cream or slipups. Five months later he was a remarkable fifty pounds lighter.

For college, Jerry decided against a four-year university. Rather, he enrolled at the renowned Art Center of Design downtown, where his natural abilities were groomed in technical-school regimen. He just got "it," able to graduate a year and a half early in 1971, one day shy of his twentieth birthday. Diploma in hand, he fantasized about configuring skyscraper offices, of husbanding industrial psychology to colors and shapes, of employing light to stimulate drowsy workforces.

Swell dream. His formative jobs out of school in the tightly controlled, corporate space-planning circuit provided his real education. The Art Center standout was told to fill in other designer's plans or man the copy machine. Later, as his bosses sized up his skills—one describing him as the best young talent they'd ever seen—they assigned him more advanced projects. Then they invoiced clientele tens of thousands of dollars for schematics while rewarding him with janitor-level wages. Scrutinizing his paycheck one week, he tabulated he was earning twenty-four dollars a day.

Whether tasked with plotting space at vanilla city halls, libraries, or prisons, or assisting with cloud-poking high rises, the result was the circular. He was pricing his God-given creativity for pennies on the dollar.

When a rival poached him from an employer that'd shipped him off to Chicago, offering him an LA job, Jerry reckoned this was his big break. In truth, the only thing it broke was his trust in the system. Management was so jumpy about eager beavers like him stealing clients for other gigs that they barred him from interacting with them until his five-year anniversary of employment. Jerry lasted three subjugated months at the firm before leapfrogging himself to another.

Now he was only slightly less dejected at his career choice. In alphabetical order, Jerry passed through industry blue bloods and stalwarts—places like Carnelly Seleine, ERD, Heitschmidt Mounce Associates, Richmond, Manhoff & March, and SLS Environetics.

But Jerry's future was in his present, for it was at this last employer where he crossed paths with Richard Kasparov, a gifted planner and even better salesman whom management also underutilized. Jerry, no longer able to withstand the corporate turnbuckles, suggested to him that they quit to become their own bosses. Capitalize on their know-how. Turn the tables on mistreatment.

Richard asked where he should sign.

They set up camp on Pico Boulevard, with Jerry knowing little about Richard's background: his tempests and roguish behavior during his first marriage, the whirlwind trysts and irate ex-lovers that ensued. Richard's dabbles in pop psychology was another subject he tucked close to the vest. This included several treks to Esalen, a legendary retreat on California's central coast that synthesized Eastern mysticism with sex, "gestalt therapy," yoga, and other New Age self-enlightenment. Another twist Jerry didn't know: a few jobs back, Richard's womanizing and roving depression torpedoed his prospects with an earlier space-planning startup. Deep down, Jerry preferred not to delve into others' histories, for his own was often painful to revisit.

Tammy's entrance heralded a more normal existence where he could retire his opposite test.

They met in 1973 at the new ABC Entertainment Center in Century City, West Coast headquarters for the network behind *Happy Days* and other primetime hits. Jerry then was a shy, underpaid space planner back in his hometown; she was a former daddy's girl and whip-smart secretary who attended the snowy, partying University of Wisconsin.

One glance at Jerry and Tammy was smitten. One look at her, and Jerry was frozen. He was unaccustomed to cute women flirting with him, and unsure whether girlish Tammy was jailbait.

Jerry's then-boss sent him to the Entertainment Center to salvage bonehead space-planning leases that made little economic sense. Before he researched them, he couldn't fathom why ABC agreed to them. Then he did: these weren't deals negotiated by real-estate professionals. This was the amateur work of former Nixon administration campaign operatives, which the network hired to curry favor with the White House. These men, Roger-Stone-esque, were a year removed from working on the soon-to-be-infamous Campaign to Reelect the President (aka CREEP). As political dirty tricksters, their role was to discredit George McGovern, Nixon's Democratic Party opponent, by creating embarrassing, wildly apocryphal support groups like Communists for McGovern.

Jerry, though a political novice, thought the tricksters sordid.

Tammy left her ABC job after the Watergate scandal, but she didn't forget about the kinky-haired planner from North Hollywood. She cajoled mutual acquaintances to encourage Jerry into asking her out. That fizzled, so *she* took the initiative, inviting him to the premiere of a sports bar. Good call: their chemistry registered on the periodic table. Convinced he was her Mr. Right from that first date, Tammy brought him to meet her parents, who were out in California on vacation. Later that night she phoned them to declare they were getting married. Jerry was soon living in the apartment of a woman who represented the only significant romance of his undersexed life.

Eighteen months later, on the same day he cofounded Space Matters at twenty-five, they wed at an elaborate Jewish temple ceremony in Michigan. (Richard tagged along for the festivities, bedding a promiscuous bridesmaid.) Tammy's prophecy that she and Jerry were meant to be culminated with wedding rings.

In their early years together, they scrimped and lived modestly. Tammy earned her teaching credentials while also working a job at

Cedars-Sinai Medical Center near Beverly Hills. On some weekends, the doe-eyed administrator who resembled one of Marcia Brady's girl-friends was responsible for signing papers for terminally ill patients. The couple then bugged-out to Northridge, a master-planned suburb where the blocks formed like clamshells and backyard barbecues were pervasive. This was frontier Los Angeles, nonetheless, the last of the countrified hills. It was ideal for young families and early adopters, with a recently built freeway (the 118), markets, and pharmacies sprouting. South of them was Chatsworth, fast becoming the pornography-filming hub of America. To the north swelled bedroom communities like Santa Clarita, where many LAPD officers resided for the cheaper housing, and Palmdale, where NASA's new space shuttle sometimes landed.

Even as Jerry cut his management teeth at Space Matters, his life with Tammy beat to a homey, circadian predictability missing from his Bellingham Avenue boyhood. Once every week was *Bunco Night*, an evening of competitive dice throwing lubricated with friends, finger foods, and snappy commentary. Or it was *Gourmet Night*, a dinner party potluck with culinary themes. These weren't only excuses to get tipsy on wine or gorge on carbohydrates during the workweek. Tammy organized this social life in service to the picket-fence lifestyle that she romanticized since her adolescence.

After their first son, Jude, was born, Tammy devoted herself to being a stay-at-home mom. She just wished Jerry, whom she occasionally phoned at work to inquire if he wanted peas or carrots for dinner, would spend more time in Northridge and less around Hancock Park. Many weekends, he was so fried he could scarcely peel himself off the couch, and she petitioned him to pare back the workaholism so they could attend a movie or a play.

Someday, Jerry told her, someday. He realized how good he had it with Tammy, the woman he lifted onto a pedestal, the dream-girl he doodled cartoon rabbits for when he needed to apologize for something.

"She's everything I ever wanted," he told friends.

No opposite tests were required to measure how much he loved her.

CHAPTER SEVENTEEN
FRIENDLY SKIES, COLD EARTH

MOORED INSIDE THE HYATT, Jerry could conjure no tricks of the trade to make his cubed living space any roomier. The furniture was either too bulky for him to reposition or bolted into the floor. Paltry human interaction was another downside, and his now revolved around his PIs bringing him coffee and doughnuts during their updates.

How long? he pushed them. How long can a murderer remain free and him in this joyless limbo, maintaining relationships by dial tone?

No longer than you can handle, they answered; a few days to an indeterminate number of weeks.

To give him hope, they sprinkled tidbits and platitudes from their LAPD contacts, telling him the investigation was steaming ahead with evidence collection and interviews. After a while, though, it sounded like boilerplate for nobody really knowing when this would conclude. Realizing that Jerry was turning more squirrely by the day, they omitted passing along to him some of the nastier asides they'd heard about Howard's past.

Jerry tried to persuade those he called that he'd adapted to living alone in a "non-specific" location, repeating the phrase the police told him. Quizzed where he was, he gave the programmed response: under LAPD protection at an "area hotel," next question. Nearly everyone accepted his vagueness without knowing much about the sacrifices they entailed.

His grandmother, who lived in Chicago, appreciated that Jerry wasn't as hardy as he projected. He was scared, so she told him a secret. Not only were cops keeping him safe but also a cosmic guardian. And how did she know such an unknowable? Upon hearing about his predicament, she said she immediately spoke to her favorite rabbi—a rabbi she believed maintained a personal communications channel to God—and made a donation to his temple. Supposedly, the Lord later assured this rabbi that Jerry would outlast his adversary. In case the holy man was wrong, she prayed constantly.

If there was one person who made Jerry contemplate unplugging his room phone, it was his mother. True to form, Vera was a one-woman tornado of hunches, recommendations, and conspiracy theories about the provenance of Howard's actions. When he could no longer take the speculation, he asked her what she wanted him to do. The wise thing, the practical thing, she said. Scour his contacts for anybody able to reach to West Coast members of the Israeli Mafia. Nobody took care of malevolent pests like them.

Jerry slapped his head. *The Israeli Mafia?* His mother was now the second person, after his state-bar-accredited attorney, to advocate preemptive murder.

Before Richard was killed, Vera liked Howard. When she visited Space Matters while he was construction boss, he poured on the charm. He complimented her and acted dismayed that Jerry, about whom he pried for inside information, wasn't more appreciative of her attentions.

"Your son isn't treating you right, Mrs. Schneiderman," he said. "I'm going to tell him he better because you deserve it. He should be buying you flowers every week."

Informed about Howard's true colors, Vera segued from once enjoying his company to brainstorming about what role he played in the criminal underworld. She settled on the notion he was a soldier in an international racket trafficking in murder, narcotics, and other contraband—subjects she was hesitant to mention over the phone in fear Howard could be snooping.

Then why say anything farfetched at all? Jerry asked.

Because she loved her son, she said. Because he should feel free to confess that he was in the clutches of a mysterious global drug cartel with friends in high places, a subject where she was deprived of any special insight except for what she consumed from the news. Their back and forth, a continuation of their sweet-and-sour squabbles since Jerry was a teenager, always circled back to Vera's same question.

"What did you do, Jerry?"

"Nothing," he would answer.

"It must've been something."

Richard and Howard, she posited, must've been in cahoots, cooking up something dark against him before they turned on each other. But it couldn't have been in a vacuum.

After hearing "what did you do, Jerry?" reprised over and over, he reached his limit.

"Enough, mother!" he said. "*Enough*. Stop. I didn't do anything."

She got him so lathered repeating herself that he usually changed the subject to keep from hanging up. Okay, she said. Maybe he'd let her return to Space Matters to tidy up his slovenly office? This brought out another "please stop." The last time she went in, she made the clutter worse, and then began calling his staff to see how they were faring in the crisis.

•••

THIS WAS NO PLEASURE flight. This was Jerry's jailbreak from the Hyatt, his prison with a Gideon's Bible.

The first plane trip to Michigan was fueled on hope. Back then, he subscribed to a progression where Richard's assassin was rounded up swiftly, and his own family reunited without lasting psychological lesions. Back then, when the jet out of Los Angeles International Airport soared above Hillside Memorial where Richard was interred, he felt differently about his ex-partner. Jerry wanted to shed a tear for him then. Today, dressed in a beanie-topped disguise, he could have denounced Richard for uncaging Howard for the sake of a quick buck.

At LAX, he boarded the jetliner that would ferry him to Tammy and Jude in Michigan. He took any good he could find, and hearing those plane doors shut was hermetically sealed music. Bringing Ari along for personal security was more complex. Comforting as it was to have a watchdog an armrest away, it also meant tolerating a voluble personality.

Just enjoy the clouds, he thought.

Halfway into the trip, probably somewhere over the Nebraska cornfields, the stewardesses began serving cocktails from the drink cart to their first-class passengers. While they fussed over people a couple rows ahead, Ari's impish grin returned. He lifted his stocky frame out of his chair, snuck up to the cart, and wheeled it away from them.

"Cocktails, cocktails," he said. "Sir, would you like a drink?"

The former mercenary pranced along the narrow aisle with a towel draped over one hairy arm and his derriere rotating side to side.

"What about you, madam?" he asked an older woman with a saccharine, English Moroccan inflection. "I mix you something strong. You forget trip."

Ari had the plane's front section in stitches within a couple minutes of his hambone bartending. The stewardesses thought he was so hilarious that when the passengers deboarded at Detroit International, they filled up Ari's duffel bag with dozens of mini liquor bottles. He was welcome anytime, they said, to impersonate them at thirty thousand feet.

On rethinking things, downcast Jerry was glad Ari was here, recognizing his swarthy friend did all this to make *him* laugh.

Meeting them in the terminal was his pregnant wife, son, and some of his in-laws. Jerry strode straight toward them off the ramp, yet they didn't wave or smile at him. Then again, why would they greet a hatted stranger they didn't recognize? After a few seconds, he came around behind Tammy, tapping her on the shoulder.

"Jerry!" she said, leaping into his arms while Jude clutched the pant leg of his Levi's.

Following a long kiss, she stepped back for a gander of a husband as she'd never seen, one in a jean jacket, yellow Caterpillar shirt and hat, and black and yellow Caterpillar boots. Adding to the new him was the shaggy hair he blow-dried every morning to rubber band into a ponytail.

At her parents' place in Ann Arbor, she and Jerry took a walk to catch up on the occurrences in their respective cities. She was alarmed at how gaunt Jerry looked. He was troubled that she was noticeably thinner, even with the baby bulge. Weight-loss, Jerry then learned, was eclipsed by something worse, something Tammy said she needed to come clean on. Her family, she acknowledged, was wrestling with his confounding situation in LA. They felt awful about his life in hiding but, like his mother, were unable to wrap their heads around how someone as gentle as him was entwined with an embezzler and a killer.

Anything more, he asked, slightly staggered. Only if he really wanted to know. He convinced himself he did, so she elaborated.

Before he'd landed, there'd been a fiery quarrel about him at the house. The dispute erupted when one of her two brothers, a collections attorney, predicted that Jerry's endangerment might become their danger. What, he wondered, was to prevent the killer threatening him from trailing him to Michigan and wiping out the lot of them if it served his purposes?

"And where do you want us to go?" Tammy barked at him. "Iowa?"

The recriminations flew until their father, Mr. Wilson, reprimanded his grown kids to cork it. Whatever they thought of Jerry, they all supported Tammy.

He departed after five days of walking on eggshells. Tammy, again, cried at the Detroit airport, wishing he didn't need to leave. Don't fret, he told her. When this was over, there'd be one helluva bunco night in Northridge.

CHAPTER EIGHTEEN
WHAT PASSED FOR SWEET

THE CAPTIVITY HE WAS told probably wouldn't last deep into April was now spilling into May, with no telling whether he'd still be cooped up here into summer. Every morning that he woke up at the Hyatt, his room seemed tinier, its bulk-purchased amenities less functional than laminated reminders they weren't his. Never did he pine for anything as much as checking out.

His PIs, as a result, often doubled as psychologists on their visits. They quoted Abraham Lincoln, saying "this, too, shall pass away" and repackaged clichés about the virtue of patience. Focus on his space planning and keeping up with family. Just stop looking at the calendar.

Jerry for the thousandth time said he would try. That he was grateful for the tireless detectives. That he realized hurrying an arrest to bust him out of here could boomerang if Howard's defense lawyers sniffed out mistakes that got him freed on a technicality.

"Don't get me wrong," he said. "But, for crying out loud, how much proof does it take?"

He was testier than ever, rubbing his hands tic-like more, and with his ponytail, facial scruff, and intense eyes, appearing regressive.

Was he prepared to hear more about Howard's past to understand why the LAPD was moving so deliberately, the PIs asked.

Yes, he answered, from the foot of the bed he was sick of being in.

It wasn't only Jerry's former partner and Tim Dwight that Howard had sent to their graves in the last eighteen months. A Monrovia family and their friends were fortunate they weren't dead after an armed takeover-robbery carried out by unidentified men working for Howard, this only days before Richard was murdered. Digging further, police suspected Howard's involvement in bloodshed in Pomona three years ago, as well as a suspicious break-in at the Roosevelt Building. Anyone who thought he harbored a soft spot for women should talk to the mistress he was seeing behind Carol's back. He'd resorted to his trademark stunt by jamming a pistol into her mouth, warning he'd make her eat a bullet if she spoke out of school.

The mosaic the PIs tiled was of a creature whose ferocity was matched by confidence it could intimidate the weak and outthink its many trappers. Jerry hadn't yet heard the names of the subordinates in Howard's undiscovered outfit. Like authorities, he was ignorant about the stumblebum campaign to assassinate Richard, or Johnny's aborted murder of his old friend in Haight-Ashbury. But he knew he shouldn't whine. Being alive and all. The trials he'd already survived in less than three decades—the bullies and Flying Tiger plane crash, corporate subjugation and entrepreneurial betrayal—were field tests for him to survive this.

He recommitted to interface by telephone jack afterward, accepting the cauliflower ear that came with holding the phone for hours on end trying to keep Space Matters afloat. At night, with no decompressing hobbies to escape into—weed, Scotch, prayer, calisthenics, books—the TV was his kin. He listened absent-mindedly to *M*A*S*H* and *That's Incredible*, to news about the receding panic at Three Mile Island and the surging interest in the mysterious drowning of Carroll Rosenbloom, the silver-haired owner of the NFL's Los Angeles Rams. Drifting off into another monotonous sleep was the best R&R he could expect.

The highlight of most days was talking to select family and friends, and even those conversations were regulated by police unsure just how much Howard knew about where Jerry was. Speaking with his mother, conversely, was an exercise in patience. She was someone whose concern for your well-being sometimes translated into a sanity check.

Vera, to her credit, stopped recommending that her son recruit the Israeli Mafia, and no longer editorialized about Howard's place as a cog in an international narcotics syndicate.

On this day, she raised something scarier: an LA talk radio segment. When Jerry inquired what left-field subject captured her fancy now, she said it was the KABC-AM show hosted by Dr. Toni Grant. The engaging female psychologist with a predominantly female audience augured future celebrity shrinks, people like Dr. Phil, who plumbed people's personal woes and fraying relationships in front of televised audiences. Vera was a regular Dr. Grant listener, making Jerry ask why someone in his current shoes should care.

Because, his mother explained, she just recalled an old segment about a particular woman who called in. She was the wife of a husband she suspected had killed two people. Now that he was about to be released from jail, she needed advice about how to avoid becoming number three.

"And your point, Mother?"

"I'll tell you if you stop being so skeptical. The woman was Carol. Carol Garrett. You know, Howard's wife!"

Jerry twisted the phone cord around his fingers. It was better than his neck.

"I don't believe you," he said. "You're mixing her up with someone else."

"I'm not," she said. "I know what I heard."

He questioned her when this was. She said a few years ago, like in fall 1977.

"But why would you wait so long to tell me?" Jerry said. "That's not like you."

"Because I put it out of my head. I assumed it was another Carol, until Howard did all these reprehensible things, and it rang a bell… Why aren't you saying anything?"

"What's left to say? It's just all a nightmare."

"Howard's sick, Jerry. Mentally sick. Who knows how he thinks? Watch yourself."

"Oh, my God. What do you think I'm doing?"

He slumped on his bed after their conversation, thinking hard about how he arrived here. His grating mother, of all people, made him confront what he'd tried packing his ears not to hear. The killer who'd masqueraded behind his tool belt and Richard, the hothouse Prince Charming, *had* been colluding together against him. The accounting books that he re-perused weren't wrong. He was just delusional before.

In hindsight, Richard had started fleecing him months back, beginning with a remodel at the Valley residence of tax attorney "Mikey" Krakow. Richard's company formally inked the deal, but it was CM-2, the spinoff that he pushed Jerry for them to charter, that Richard invoiced for the materials. This sleight of hand, which bedeviled their CPA for months, turned a honking profit for Richard. Mikey, likely given a discounted rate, never breathed a word. This was the same Mikey whom Jerry knew since they were North Hollywood teenagers, and the same Mikey who performed some minor legal work for Space Matters. It was also the same Mikey later indicted for his connection to a shady poultry franchise.

Months back, with Richard and Paige at the Universal Amphitheater for a Donna Summer concert, Mikey declared this about their con, "What Jerry doesn't know won't hurt him."

Not only was Mikey a shyster with a chic zip code, his prediction was as wrong as it could be.

Sometime during the remodeling at Mikey's place, Jerry surmised, Howard must've uncovered Richard's swindle and curled his finger at him. Howard, with his affection for extortion, probably demanded he receive some of these ill-gotten gains or he'd expose it. But Howard never imagined that Richard had the stones to defraud him by secretly running up tabs on his credit lines.

Richard wasn't like most people, though. Promises to him were discretionary, rules optional. None of his record of atrocious behavior—shoplifting, lying to a disappointed boss that he might be terminally ill, abusing women, serial infidelities, embezzlement—ever deterred him much from adding more. Not until he hornswoggled someone of Howard's wickedness.

Lying there on the sheets, with crumbs sprinkled about, Jerry's post-mortem drew around to an unflattering portrait of himself as a willing dupe. By letting himself be a party to Richard's hunger for money and status—whatever his subconscious quest to prove to his dead father that he was "successful"—Jerry might as well have strung a price around his own soul. It wasn't only what Richard never told him. It was what Jerry intentionally decided not to hear.

The two men who wrecked everything, in other words, never could have done it without Jerry's own baggage with self-worth and avarice.

•••

HOWARD, LIKE ALL ENTREPRENEURS, had to plan for the future while concentrating on the now. Before his next moneymaking venture, he needed to secure his windfall from the kill-Richard-strongarm-Jerry initiative. Seventy-five thousand dollars would extinguish his business debts, pay personal bills, and bankroll operations for a good year. He wasn't living in expensive Pasadena rent-free, after all. And the employees he chastized to keep legit until their next mission were dependent on his stipends. With so much at stake, he trained his eyes— eyes described by one associate as bee-bees for pupils and cracked plates for irises—on anyone who could jeopardize the probability of Jerry writing him those checks. It could leave a CEO busy.

The local family of Robert Freeman, the hitman who dared to resign, was a special worry about blabbing to police. Dissuasion was Howard's ticket to prevent that. Days after Richard's shooting, he and Johnny showed up uninvited at the Ontario home of Robert's sister, Janice, while she was at work. They tried to enter by smashing a door handle and removing screens over windows. Was it purely for intimidation, or also in search of Robert's Bay Area address to shut him up for good, maybe to steal a gun for the next plunder? Whatever the purpose, it gave Janice's eleven-year-old daughter, home sick from school that day, the fright of her life. Janice dashed home as soon as the girl phoned her that intruders were trying to break in, finding they'd left. That night, Johnny called Janice to calm her down. She told him not to bother and hung up. Days later, Janice's phone rang again.

"You are going to die tonight," a voice told her.

Fear of the unknown continued plaguing the Buonsanti family, as well. The night Howard's men muscled in was the last night their Monrovia home was homey. Even with a slap-dashed alarm system and Luis's new J.C. Penney shotgun. Even with family lore about how Sergio's fondness for *Laverne & Shirley* saved them, and Luis's later decision to hire an LAPD officer-turned-PI to protect what he couldn't.

Since that March evening, Luis had grown increasingly confident that he knew who had orchestrated it. To kick the tires on his theory, he contacted Manuel, Howard's stepfather, with whom he had cultivated a warm friendship. Manuel was a tall, gray-haired Latino man who smoked a pipe, knocked back hot chilis, and enjoyed his liquor.

What, Luis asked him diplomatically, was his opinion of his stepson?

Not much, Manuel said in a surprise. Howard had recently pushed his mother to give him a whopping $10,000, money Howard must've used as payroll for his killings-for-cash operation while spinning it as funds he needed to tide him over through a rash of lean months.

But was Howard capable of worse? Luis pressed on. Could somebody who'd been so generous to them, someone who'd thrown him work and dressed up as Saint Nick for his children, putrefy into someone so cruel that he'd send those blood-lusting little goons after him? Monrovia police had asked the same question.

Manuel, to Luis's double astonishment, responded that Howard was *more* than capable of intimate evil, for it dovetailed with his own long-held suspicions.

For years, Manuel lived (or squirmed) with a hunch: that Howard was involved in the demise of first wife, Alpha, in the early 1970s. Her official cause of death was ruled a drug overdose. Among those with additional details, though, her ex was *the* cause in an intricately planned, unprosecuted homicide. Manuel conjectured that materialism was the motive. Howard craved her San Gabriel Valley house and other possessions, things that would've been off limits in a divorce.

"I bet my life," Manuel told Luis, "that he killed her."

If so, Luis was closer to Alpha than he realized. When Howard and his mother donated clothes to Luis's family after they emigrated from Argentina, Howard added some of Alpha's wardrobe. Evidentiary laundering, you might call it.

Anything else he should know? Luis inquired.

Yeah, Manuel said.

"He thinks that murder-for-hire is sweet."

Suddenly, the pixels arranged themselves into the portrait of a beast who never gives up on its prey.

On a Friday three weeks after the invasion at his house, Luis was driving home in the used Cadillac that he had just purchased. Going northbound on Santa Anita Avenue, not far from Howard's old place in Arcadia, he punched through a yellow light. A sheriff deputy in a patrol car that witnessed it pulled him over. On the seat next to Luis was the .350 that his PI lent him for protection when he went out. Seeing the sheriff loom in his mirror, Luis panicked: he knocked the pistol to the floor, reckoning that no one would believe his explanation for carrying it.

True. The deputy and his partner drew their own guns and gave Luis the business.

Everything unraveled afterward. The officers hauled him to the station, denied him his phone call, strip-searched him, and held him overnight; his car's belongings were confiscated too. Now accused of possession of a concealed weapon, the car repair shop owner and part-time real-estate flipper needed to lawyer up. It required six months of headaches and money to resolve it.

At first, Luis blamed the incident on another stroke of bad luck and personal carelessness. But everything is not as it seems on first blush. He later remembered confiding to Howard that he'd bought a gun to defend his family after what occurred that surreal Wednesday evening. Howard, for a dime, could have made an anonymous call to the Sheriff's Department to alert them about an "immigrant" driving around with a firearm. Was this why they stopped and humiliated him for breezing through a yellow light? Because somebody whose own stepfather said "thinks that murder-for-hire is sweet" was emasculating him before a second attack.

Winding back the clock further, Howard, Luis recalled, once propositioned him about using his legal auto-repair shop as a front for people who wanted their perfectly good vehicles destroyed for illicit reasons. Luis immediately responded that he wanted no part of any such "dirty business" that slimed his conscience. Later, he discovered, Howard scrawled his name and phone number on one of *his* business cards. For a while, Luis persuaded himself that he must've misunderstood Howard's idea. Now he knew otherwise, with Howard's abundant spite as proof.

Paige, Richard's widow, could empathize about raw survival inside the coils of Howard's meat grinder. She didn't know for certain that he killed Richard, but he seemed to have carved his initials into their old house: the threatening phone calls there about Richard's debts; the kidnap attempt on Rebecca off the deck; the daylight burglary at the place where Howard sat leisurely during better times. Paige, as Luis, had also witnessed firsthand trailers of his coming attractions.

On that holiday weekend when, as new acquaintances, she, Richard, Howard, and Carol socialized in Palm Springs, there was a disturbing incident. Howard snorted coke, maybe not alone, and there were cocktails and conversation—once Howard and his better half arrived at Pal Joey's restaurant. When they did, they were two hours late, and Carol was wearing sunglasses to conceal a shiner that she tried to explain away as the result of a klutzy stumble into a doorknob (as opposed to its collision with Howard's fist).

After the couples parted, Paige elbowed Richard, questioning him about whether he considered a background check on his laconic, Hawaiian-shirt-wearing new colleague. Aside from whatever happened to Carol, there was something about how he stared at you that was as much carnivoran assessment as typical eye contact.

Richard told her she was misconstruing a person merely rough about the edges. And would Howard's former boss at esteemed Smythe & Hargill endorse a cretin? Still, she wasn't the only woman whose female instincts about him beeped dismay. Brie, Richard's ex-girlfriend and Space Matters' office manager, felt the skin crawl up her arms the first time that she glimpsed Howard from twenty feet across the mansion. False reading, Richard later pacified her.

For Paige, every day the what-ifs came and regrets deepened. So too did her puzzlement about why Richard did so little to insulate himself from a man he knew wanted him pushing up daisies. Even somebody afraid to fly like him could've booked a ticket on Amtrak or driven his Cougar for a month's stay in Yosemite. Could've rented a houseboat in San Diego.

Because he didn't attempt any of those things, Paige was now a recluse herself, exiled with her grief, unsure how to support her daughter and saddled with her in-law's hostility. She was suspicious, without any proof, that Jerry might've pressed Howard's buttons, though Jerry could've benefited if she'd warned him about Howard's early predations against her family.

Now she was down twenty pounds, a common symptom of Howard-itis, scraping by on an insurance payout on Richard unrelated to Space Matters. Even that wasn't sufficient to maintain Design Wise, the firm that Richard assisted her launch, so she folded it. She agonized how to safeguard baby Rebecca in the event someone got in, deciding on an interior lock and keypad. This was no small concern for someone prickled by the feeling that she was being constantly watched. When the sun went down, she generally went in, with plainclothes cops sometimes stationed outside her rental's door. One night, after Paige returned, an officer walked around her place with his gun out.

Her Richard may have once been a little king of LA, but Howard was reigning now, exerting influence as if whatever blocked him from being caught was made of law enforcement kryptonite. Then again, it was a city of costumes. Why exactly would the LAPD pop a journeyman supervisor trying to make ends meet after being ripped off by his last employer?

That May, Howard picked up a freelance construction gig with Carlos Villalvazo, a former Space Matters employee who'd briefly resigned to launch his own firm. The job off Vermont Avenue mid-city was at the offices of the California Association of Realtors, a well-known industry trade group created in 1905 to dispel perceptions of misconduct in the business. Its efforts got through the state legislature bellwether real-estate licensing laws that legitimized the profession.

Carlos, unaware that a man with fingerprints on multiple murders was on the premises of an organization promoting integrity, mentioned an obvious subject to Howard: Richard's murder.

Howard wasn't hesitant about sharing his unique knowledge.

"The bullet," he told Carlos, "went right down through the window and killed him."

Michael Bailey, who still worked for Howard despite mixed emotions about him, around then heard his boss cluck about the victim.

"Well," Howard said, "it couldn't have happened to a nicer guy."

CHAPTER NINETEEN
EARS AND DEEDS

FOR THE FIRST TIME in a chain of hamstrung weeks, Jerry could actually think space plans, not space invaders with high-powered rifles. He could sit behind his Space Matters desk with his staff to debate canned versus fluorescent lights for the next Fegen suite, or whether to sketch a radical open floor plan or traditional one for an insurance company. Stacked up behind those decisions were a dozen others begging for attention. Like general finances and office morale.

It was intoxicating to be surrounded by the prosaic again, even dressed up in construction boots, Levi's, and a beanie with his PIs beside him. On this rare visit to the office, Jerry was back in his environment, with blueprints unfurled and phones ringing. One call was patched directly to him.

"Pay up or you're going to die!" said a strange voice of Hispanic descent. "The contract's written."

Jerry was alerted this could happen. So he tried not to allow the chilling little message that Howard must've composed from derailing what the LAPD urged him to do: keep any suspicious call on the line long enough for them to trace its geographic source.

"I'm sorry," he responded. "Can you repeat that?"

In the seconds before the man hung up, Jerry heard a gargle-y splashing noise reminiscent of ocean waves, as if one of Howard's henchmen was phoning from the beach to taunt him. The technicians who bugged Jerry's office phones promised they would analyze the background acoustics. But there'd be no reverse engineering where the call emanated from because the messenger had been schooled not to dawdle on the line too long.

Because it would be too risky to keep him at Space Matters after that, Jerry's PIs whisked him back to the Hyatt. If Howard was bird-dogging his movements, as the timing of this verbal strongarming implied, then he could conceivably follow him elsewhere.

"How much longer?" Jerry badgered his PIs back in his room. "Can't they arrest him now and investigate the rest after he's in custody?"

Sorry, they said. No can do. Evidence collection was dictating the timetable, arguably more than the hazard level to him.

Besides, his PIs were now asking him more detailed questions about whether he knew this person or remembered that incident, feeding anything valuable he recalled to their contacts at LAPD's Parker Center headquarters across from city hall. Jerry, in return, was learning more about what detectives were unearthing. Howard fraternized with someone who'd been in prison gangs (Johnny) and someone else inducted into the Aryan Brotherhood (Robert). He had his mitts in this and his nose in that. It could make you want to muffle your ears.

Absent from detectives' notebooks was the sprawl and scope of Howard's ambition to monetize the death of as many as half a dozen Southern California real estate men in his boutique murder enterprise. Richard was only the first. Authorities could only guess who might be in the guillotine after Jerry.

Up in his room, where few incoming calls were permitted, he dialed Ari to vent about a purgatory defined by room-service food and navel gazing. Ari, hearing Jerry's latest bout of frustration after promising himself to suck it up, repeated what he had been saying. It was well past time for *him* to do to Howard what the Israeli military taught him.

"You don't worry, Jerry. Me kill that mothafocker. The police afraid. Me not."

Vera Schneiderman might have approved. Her son could not.

•••

HE WAS SOON HURTLING over America's flyover states for a third trip to Michigan since Richard met his fate. Beanie on, jean jacket buttoned, Jerry's disguise was starting to feel like old hat. Ari was next to him again, whispering encouragements. Reading the mood, Ari opted against reprising his boozy-stewardess comedy routine.

If Jerry thought the Midwest was frosty for springtime when he stepped outside, it was balmy compared with the house he strode into in Ann Arbor. As before, Tammy's mother and father remarked how good it was to see him and prepared him a post-flight snack and drink. Unlike the last trip, Jerry sensed aloofness in their manners and mistrust in their eyes.

Together in her old childhood room, Tammy admitted that the paranoia bug had spread outward from her brother. The opinion he voiced earlier—that the trouble stalking Jerry in LA could migrate to them—was becoming the Wilson's communal dread. At some point, they expected to peer out the window at the Michigan landscape to see armed strangers slinking toward their property.

"Was it that touchy?" Jerry asked.

And then some, Tammy replied. Someone in her family had already phoned the police after they mistook something outdoors for California killers.

Keeping true to the couple's no-secrets policy, she then told Jerry about how, on the day the LAPD botched recording Howard's self-incriminating remarks near the La Brea Tar Pits, her dad tried galloping in on the white horse. How he contacted detectives to offer to pay Howard off, valiance they lectured him would probably produce a dead son-in-law.

Weightless—that's how Tammy was in the aftermath. Weightless and powerless.

And Jerry wore this new crown of suspicion the way he had at Richard's wake: with ire that anyone had even considered sizing him for one. Where was the faith in the person that Tammy knew she was going to marry after their first date? Didn't anyone besides her father, the broad-shouldered patriarch, appreciate what he was under, camped in a claustrophobic hotel room, away from those he loved, to keep his company solvent and staff employed?

By the end of this trip, the pair saw the obvious in each other. Tammy was brittle, sobbing off and on, her usual spark reduced to an ember, looking, in clinical terms, like she was failing to thrive. She weighed only ninety pounds entering the baby's third trimester, her pregnant belly protruding further over her scrawny body. Jerry seemed to be imitating her, shedding pounds through a digestive tract frequently cramping. In LA, his room-service fare—sauce-smothered chicken, salty patty melts, sinful chocolate cake—regularly lay on its tray half-eaten outside his door.

Another commonality? Neither was sleeping well, so they couldn't even dream about a better day.

In waking hours, Tammy's head was stuck just where Jerry's was, hazy why the LAPD wasn't making more progress to drop the curtain on Howard. Jerry and Ari, who wisely stayed in the Wilson's basement most of the visit, left for California more submissive than when they arrived.

When Jerry phoned Tammy days later from the Hyatt, he never heard her so wrought, as she attempted to contain her internal floodwaters from breaking. Jerry begged her to get out whatever was punishing her; secrets can do that. A few heaves later, she elaborated about what her brother wanted her to contemplate undergoing.

"An abortion?" Jerry said, bleating into the receiver after she confessed. "He has no right to say that. That's between us! I don't tell him how to run his life."

Tammy tried explaining her brother's perspective, and that only deepened the hurt. He believed that preemptive action was needed to cushion his sister for the next foreseeable chapter in her life. A chapter in which Jerry was dead and she was on her own. One fatherless child would be rough. Two would be tragic.

"Nobody," her brother said of Jerry, "has problems like these" unless they were warranted to some degree.

Tammy sniffled on a call in which any eavesdropping LAPD techs were treated to about the most private conversation a husband and wife could have: whether to terminate an innocent life or keep it. Don't take any of this personally, Tammy said in a choked voice. It came from a protective sibling confused about an incomprehensible situation.

"But you're not really considering taking his advice, are you? Ending the pregnancy? We might not survive it."

"Of course not," Tammy answered through the static fizz. "I love you and Jude and what's inside me *more* than anything. I still just don't understand why this is happening. It's not normal."

•••

THERE WAS NO OTHER explanation, other than the faint possibility Howard had a mole inside Space Matters or some facility with the dark arts. He must've stationed one of his men outside the building with binoculars during business hours to notify him when Jerry was present. Stationed someone so nonchalant or obscured that he was invisible to the trained eye.

That's because *the* voice returned. The dialogue was identical from before, as was its breathy menace.

"Jerry?" the Hispanic-accented caller said.

"Yes."

"Pay up or you're going to die. The contract's written."

Click.

Some details, however, were filling in. The police who listened to the first threatening call surmised that the background noise could've been waves crashing on the shore. It was there again this time, yet when they analyzed it further, they determined it wasn't originating from a beach but a bowling alley—a bowling alley whose tumbling pins created that gurgle and whose clinking beer bottles accented it with hollow notes. Maddeningly, that represented the meat of their findings. Both times the caller hung up before anyone could nail down his coordinates.

Before his PIs rushed him back to the Hyatt, Jerry surveyed a staff doing their jobs in an ocean of uncertainty. A staff toiling for a twenty-seven-year-old boss forbidden from disclosing where he or the family they were used to seeing was staying—a boss costumed in Levi's and Caterpillar Construction garb because the murder investigation involving two people who worked there until a few months ago appeared to have stalled. A few employees, convinced Space Matters would inevitably go belly-up, had dusted off their résumés for openings at rival firms. Others kept the front door in their peripheral vision in the case a SWAT team massed for another floor-shaking performance.

Abysmal as morale was, at least nobody was recirculating the "ghost story" about how all of the mansions' previous owners perished before old age. Some obvious comparisons are better left unsaid.

What could Bert do to motivate everybody in Jerry's protracted absence? Preach that next year, in 1980, they would rebound like Magic Johnson in the NCAA title game? That by being here, they epitomized bravery and loyalty? You had to feel for Bert. Nine to six, it was double duty as draftsman and temporary boss. Then, during some midnights, he was a killer's conduit to scavenge for insights into Jerry's state of mind.

"Remind him that I really need to talk to him," Howard laced into his goodbyes.

Jerry was now down to one vestige from the old routine blown up by Johnny William's bullet. It was his regular meetings with Paul Fegen at his capacious office at the Glendale Federal building. The man's empire of far-flung, under-lease commercial buildings would be even more invaluable for Space Matters' cash flow after the crisis was over. Time around a creative eccentric like Fegen had another benefit: it was good exercise for Jerry's sidetracked mind. What differentiated it from before was the logistics: doing it late at night, sometimes up to 11:00 p.m., with Jerry's PIs driving him.

One evening when a gauzy coastal mist rolled in, something else burst out of the ordinary. Jerry's hired-gun detectives noticed it in the mirrors. When they switched lanes, a suspicious car hanging back in traffic switched lanes. When they sped up, the vehicle apparently tailing them kept up. The patchy fog made it impossible to see faces through the windshield, only the fact their car was still there. Even as traffic thinned out as they neared Fegen's headquarters, it remained.

The PIs in hurried voices debated possible escape routes and told Jerry to sink down into the rear seat. They changed lanes, watching for two circular slashes of yellowish light to follow, and caressed their holsters. These were some nervous blocks. Just before they arrived at Fegen's office garage, the stress broke when the sedan turned off Wilshire.

●●●

UNLIKE AFTER OTHER LATE nights with Fegen, Jerry didn't shower and then flip on TV to make himself doze off. Tonight, after the scare on eerie Wilshire, he emptied his briefcase. He rooted around into its side pocket, searching for a document that opened a lid into his nemesis' head. Out came the letter that Howard mailed to him and Tammy, the one demanding that his personal stuff be returned, debts repaid, and credit lines restored to good standing. Rereading it again, Jerry saw he probably misclassified it before as a burnout's diatribe. On second consideration, it was a declaration of independence against a prissy executive class that Howard perceived had been accumulating their pretty things on the backs of expendable rednecks like him.

Translate Howard's typed-up disgust, and you'd appreciate that what happened to him at Space Matters represented his last straw. One passage popped out to Jerry.

"I have more time in the pay line than you have in the chow line. And I will be damned and go to hell before I will stand like a tall dog and let you or other members of your firm screw us. That, my old friend, you can bet on."

He lay back on the mattress now imprinted with his body, studying every word. All things being equal, how far would Howard go, really go, not to get screwed by Jerry? Was that $75,000 and another corpse worth life in prison for him? A shootout with the LAPD? It was past midnight, and Jerry yawned. Maybe he was overthinking things? Perhaps this was only a mental Polaroid of a depraved person still capable of being rational. Howard was no evil genius. He was playing the odds like an inveterate gambler. When Jerry fell asleep, the letter was back in his briefcase.

The next day, after his PIs departed following the worst briefing to date, he would reread every word.

They came into his room this morning without doughnuts, coffee, or streetwise reassurances that all would be okay. Jerry asked if anyone was hurt; not yet, they answered. But the LAPD had just shared with them a piece of intel that he deserved to hear. And he better sit down.

In July 1973, while the Watergate scandal rippled and Vietnam still raged, kidnappers in Europe snatched the seventeen-year-old grandson of oil tycoon John Paul Getty. His captors, bandits from Italy's mountainous Calabria region, whisked him to the southern part of the boot-shaped country. They chained the boy in a cave, demanding a multimillion-dollar ransom. The Gettys, however, initially refused to pay it, doubting the abduction was genuine. They suggested it might've been a hoax or even a scheme by the grandson himself to dupe his moneybags grandfather into shelling out some of his fortune. When no payment arrived, the kidnappers wrote a second pay-up letter. Upon receiving it, John Paul Sr. took a stand. The man that *Forbes* magazine once deemed America's richest person decreed, in an echo of future US antiterrorism policy, that there'd be no negotiations with criminals!

The men shackling his grandson in response got out a blade. In November 1973, a newspaper in Rome received an envelope from them. Inside of it was a lock of the teenager's hair and one of his decomposing ears. They promised to lop off the other ear if no money arrived in ten days.

"In other words," they wrote, "he will arrive in little bits."

John Paul Sr. softened his position after the maiming. He bargained directly with the captors, whittling the payout down to about three million. Ransom paid, the kidnappers released his heir after six months of confinement.

Jerry was mystified about how this infamous, six-year-old incident connected to him.

You're about to find out, his PIs said.

Howard, the police recently learned, was such an enthusiast of that kidnapping pressure campaign that he *was* scheming to apply the same technique to Jerry's toddler son once they smoked out his whereabouts. While Howard was still actively searching for Jerry, abduction was his new priority, his fresh hunger. In case the family was back from hiding, Howard was regularly driving past the Schneiderman's place in Northridge. By slicing off the little boy's ear or finger, he would throttle his father to do what, so far, he'd refused: pay up.

Jerry awoke the next morning from a sleepless night dizzy and sweaty. He chugged a glass of water, and then another, to sate a ravenous thirst. Was it that salty room service burger or an SOS from a psyche on a self-preservation setting? Tammy, the previous night, chipped off another piece of him. She admitted that indeed she was vacillating about whether to continue the pregnancy—and wasn't sure she wanted to return to California if Howard was caught.

He sprawled back onto his bed afterward. Just him and a swell of unadulterated anger ripping through him like the onset of a jungle infection; Howard had no franchise on indignation. Since Richard's murder, Jerry had cycled through a broadband of emotions—spurts of depression, self-martyrdom, semi-denial, and quasi-rationalization. Now Howard plotted to disfigure his son, maybe kill everyone related to him, and burn down his house for supplemental amusement.

The was no Chicken Little overreaction. This was the oppression that only he could end if he hoped to stop caroming between reality and delusion.

"This doesn't happen to normal people," Tammy said.

"Hitler should have just killed all of you," Howard whispered.

"You can pay [him]. You can go to the police. Or you can kill him. If it were me, I'd do the latter," his lawyer advised him.

"Down! Everybody down on the floor now," the SWAT commander hollered.

"Me kill that mothafocker," Ari offered. *"The police afraid. Me not."*

"Pay up or you're going to die," the voice from the bowling alley murmured.

The most stabbing remark of all emanated from his mother.

"Jerry," she asked. *"What did you do?"*

When he cracked the door for his PIs on the day he arose parched, they greeted a different Jerry. A Jerry who struck them as a smidge unhinged with eyes wide and disheveled clothes; a Jerry acting from his own lizard ganglia to survive.

"You all right?" the older, red-haired one asked, stepping into a room so trashed with papers and clothes you couldn't see the carpeting. "Howard didn't call you here last night? If he did, we have problems."

"There wasn't any call, but we have a problem. Make that I have a problem."

The PIs stared at each other and entered.

"I can't take this anymore," he said, standing in front of the window he'd been repeatedly warned to avoid.

"Well, you have no choice. I know we must sound like broken records."

"But I do have a choice. I've done everything the LAPD asked. I was their bait on the museum plaza, and they couldn't hook anything. Then I later find out that the SWAT team would've killed Howard if they saw me say 'don't shoot!' That was, what, weeks ago?"

"We know it must seem unbearable, but you need to respect the process. Let the department build an ironclad case. If you want justice for Richard and all these other people that Howard hurt, you'll have to dig deeper. The LAPD can't take shortcuts because you're freaked out and miss your family."

"Stressed out? That's all you think I am?"

"This must be the last thing you want to hear after we told you about Howard's kidnapping idea. We sympathize."

Jerry circled the room. Then he returned to where he stood.

"You realize that if they continue dithering, it will bankrupt the company. My marriage may not last, either. Nobody's could under this weight. My in-laws in Michigan are seeing imaginary gunmen out their windows. It's too intense for everybody."

Small bubbles danced in the corners of Jerry's mouth; sweat beaded under his ponytail.

"Take it easy," the PI said, hoping that Jerry would sit down, his partner nodding in agreement. "You're probably a week or two away from getting out of here. The cold ones will be on us when we get the word."

"A week away. Oh, I don't think so."

"I don't see how we can speed things up. The investigation could be at some delicate juncture. Your best move is to continue doing what they're instructing."

Jerry no longer accepted that premise. He'd already resorted to his Old Reliable, opposite testing the LAPD's continual declaration (or lip service) that Howard teetered on the brink of apprehension. If the police had such a strong handle on his activities, with reams of evidence that could put him away for multiple murders and associated bloodshed, he would've been stewing by now inside a cellblock. If they had him dead to rights, the unnamed associates Jerry kept hearing about would be sharing a concrete bench with him. Yet none of that had occurred weeks after Richard was slid into that mausoleum.

"Actually, I'm the one who's going to give an order. To *you*! I want you to pick up that phone on my nightstand and call Detective Jamieson. You tell him that either they arrest Howard by tomorrow or I'm driving out to Pasadena to finish the job. I don't care if Jamieson has to pester [LAPD chief] Daryl Gates."

"Jerry. Please," the PI said. "Going out there would be the worst possible thing to do. You could blow the entire investigation. You want to live here another year? Or get shot?"

"I don't care, I honestly don't. If Howard shoots me, so be it. If they convict me for killing him, I'll accept it. He'll destroy everything if I don't end this."

The fatherly PI rubbed his temples and took a breath.

"You've hit a wall," he said. "Normal. You're not the first witness to go stir-crazy."

Jerry hadn't moved an inch.

"I'll repeat myself. You instruct the detectives to arrest him or I'm ringing his buzzer and seeing what happens. If I have a gun the LAPD will have to decide whom to kill."

"You'll do no such thing."

"Yes, I will. I'm done putting everyone—you, the LAPD, Ari—between him and me. Being passive. How many more people is Howard going to squash while protocol is being observed?"

"Give us a sec," said the PI who looked like he could've used an Irish whiskey.

They traipsed from the room to speak privately at the end of the hallway. Jerry stole a peek at them from the doorway with hot sweat on his back. The ginger PI who'd been trying to talk Jerry off the ledge stared down at his loafers while his colleague said his peace. Jerry thought he overheard that one saying, "You can't blame him."

They came back looking less authoritative. As former cops, they understood that should Jerry confront Howard on his home turf, one of the two might not survive it; chances were that it would be Jerry fitted with a toe tag. Even with the county morgue filled to its gills with corpses, the press would crucify LAPD brass after they discovered what they'd put Jerry through.

"How about this? We can't promise anything, but we'll deliver your message," the lead PI said. "You've done everything and more asked of you. Let's hope that makes a difference."

"Good," he answered, arms akimbo. "Somebody finally heard me."

"There are things about Howard you don't want to know," Richard said.

And Jerry's ultimatum—or half-bluff, or breakdown, or whatever it was—must've been what the police needed to hear. The next morning, May 11, 1979, at 7:20 a.m., the LAPD garrisoned around Howard's Del Mar Boulevard apartment, weapons ready. They marched up a flight, arraying themselves outside the Garretts's second-floor unit.

One of the officers pounded on his door. Carol answered it.

From the reek of marijuana, emptied booze bottles, and other paraphernalia strewn about, it was obvious that she and the estranged husband that she once called into the Dr. Toni Grant show about partied to dawn.

Where is *he,* they asked her?

Carol pointed.

They brushed by and threw open the bedroom door.

And there lay Howard Garrett on the mattress, naked and high, flabbergasted at outsiders tramping into the lair where he'd drummed fingers on his chin, deciding what next to devour.

"Oh, shit," he said loudly as the handcuffs clamped on.

He was photographed hours later for a mugshot wearing a short-sleeve floral shirt and a defeated glower.

•••

HE PHONED TAMMY AS soon as he heard that Howard was in lockup, delirious for the first time in forever. Book your flight home. Tammy said she would, crying happy tears this time.

After he hung up, Jerry flopped back on his hotel bed, thinking he might just bounce on it later, fist-pumping air for outwitting you-know-who.

It was bye, bye Hyatt. So long, salt burger.

Before he threw clothes into the suitcase that'd been hibernating in the back of the closet and checked out, his PIs swung by to congratulate him on his forbearance and, yes, his ballsy counterstroke. Jerry told them how eager he was to sleep in his own bed in Northridge. They disappointed him by saying he best not do that for a few days, for there remained mopping up to complete. The LAPD still hadn't identified, let alone rounded up, any of Howard's accomplices. There also was the possibility, faint as it was, that a persnickety judge could release Howard for either lack of probable cause or a loophole. Why take a grain of risk?

Jerry was about to protest when they recommended a surefire locale where he would be safe. He'd gone to these extremes, so what was a brief stopover after a monumental victory?

Within a few hours he was a houseguest at Ari's duplex off Melrose Avenue in West Hollywood. Some stopover. In hauling his traumatized self here, Jerry exited his sterile cube at the Hyatt for a post-marital demilitarized zone. After Ari and his wife split up, they'd decided for financial reasons to remain living in the bottom floor of the same derelict residence. To bring order to chaos, they allotted what rooms each could occupy using Ari's jury-rigged partitions and posted rules. Some of the walls were half-demolished, as only Ari could leave them. The unfinished nature of them reminded Jerry of one of Richard's luxury-home remodels.

Besides granting him sanctuary, Ari tried cajoling his friend into embracing other comforts. He recommended Jerry accompany him to the clubs, bars, or wherever LA's starry nightlife took them on a well-earned bender. They could do anything: cavort, drink, snort, laugh, disco. Spoof Howard. Ari also wanted Jerry to see him out of his building-demolition clothes and in his silk threads and gold chains.

Sorry, Jerry said. He was too fried to try to keep up as Ari's party wingman. He intended to sleep. And sleep he did, more soundly than he had since March 27.

After days in Ari's bifurcated domesticity, Jerry recited his lines of thanks to him. Where to even begin? The hospitality, the disguise, the travel to Michigan that cost Ari work, the jokes. Most vitally, for undying friendship by a man the LA construction world judged as a funny-looking savage on a bulldozer.

After they hugged, Jerry climbed into the Seville and steered west.

Driving up his old street, as the loamy foothills of Northridge filled his windshield, someone who rarely cried grew misty. The window-filled house that his family evacuated, afraid of hitmen outside, would be reinhabited again. A spruce-up was in order first for a property that looked like it'd slipped from temporary desertion into a squatters' hovel. Fliers were piled up in the entryway. Cobwebs embroidered the sidings. The shin-high grass could've hidden a coyote.

Jerry never glimpsed anything so picturesque before.

CHAPTER TWENTY
THE SUPREME COURT OF VAN NUYS

Downtown's Clara Shortridge Foltz Criminal Justice Center, the white, honeycombed behemoth piercing the sky next to Los Angeles's gangster-era city hall, has long been the intersection of celebrity and horror, B-roll and body bags. Inside these flag-draped walls, some of the West Coast's most notorious defendants—Charles Manson, Richard "The Night Stalker" Ramirez, O. J. Simpson, Phil Spector—have asserted their innocence, often with the paparazzi and media horde jockeying on the plaza outside for a quote and a photograph.

Far to the northwest, on the opposite side of the jurisprudence-glamor scale, sat the Van Nuys's Municipal Court, an architectural pipsqueak that blended into the valley's self-repeating patchwork of kebab shops, postwar subdivisions, horse ranches, and freeway tentacles stretching every direction. It was here, under fluorescent lighting and surrounded by the same wood paneling, where everybody sucked into the whirlpool of Richard's execution was drawn for the next few years.

Though bereft of much media coverage, tabloid or mainstream, the proceedings showcased a cast of characters from a madcap black comedy—a play in which the only heroes were antiheroes, and the colorful villains, except for Richard, hailed from a white-trash subculture of lush neglect that explained who they were. Courthouse geography couldn't have been cinematically on the button either, just two and a half miles from where the yellow crime scene tape was stretched.

Among those raising their right hand was Howard's now-warring ex-employees. People their ringleader thirsted to kill, extort, and intimidate—Jerry, Paige, the Buonsanti clan—swore oaths too, as did LAPD detectives Jamieson and Landgren, Howard's bulldog lawyers, and some of the tangentially involved.

Regularly taking them in was a gaggle of mostly white-haired old men, an informal club of legal groupies who flocked to the Van Nuys courthouse for the juiciest cases. The trial watchers now welcomed a new member with more vested interest than the usual docket rubbernecker. Art Schneiderman, Jerry's father, wouldn't be anyplace else.

Prosecutors with the LA County District Attorney's office, who'd been surprised by the dimensions of Howard's murder enterprise, had plenty to deconstruct for the jury. And they never would've gotten here without a bisexual, heroin-shooting, white-supremacist-joining career thief with a morsel of conscience! In May, just as Jerry's ultimatum accelerated Howard's capture, Robert Freeman initiated something arguably more potent. He exposed Howard's plans with the specifics only he knew.

Robert's attorney placed two conditions on his priceless testimony: immunity from being charged in Richard's murder, and protection from Howard, who he knew would love to peel his skin off. Demands met, he gave investigators the names of two ex-colleagues who could corroborate the tale he found it nearly impossible to make any noncriminal believe.

Using his tip, detectives traveled to San Francisco City Jail to interview Jamie Jones. He refused to speak until Robert's wife, Elena, was pressed into action to persuade him. After Jamie was Mirandized, he described an alternative cast of players. He claimed, likely in fear of Howard, that *he* drove Johnny to Richard's that night and stayed put in the El Camino while Johnny fired his shot; he said that neither Howard nor Chaser Villa was present.

Johnny's home in Ontario was the LAPD's next stop. Anticipating resistance, they entered with a search warrant and discovered the rifle stock of the M-1 murder weapon. Unlike the other components he threw out the El Camino's window near Magic Mountain, Johnny kept this part, maybe as a firearms souvenir. He shouldn't have. Authorities then went to Howard's Pasadena condo, scooping up documentation of his dealings with Richard and Jerry, and Luis Buonsanti's business card.

As it sifted through these threads, the DA's office needed one lodestar member of Howard's team to detail for the jury the type of person he was. Robert may have been the first to acknowledge his involvement in the sordid business of killing Richard. Still, it was his childhood pal, the man who'd tried taking him out with a .357, with the most explosive tale to share.

But getting Johnny to be honest was pulling mussels from a closed shell. Like Jamie, he initially lied through his teeth, contending that he was merely the driver that night, and that it was Howard who killed Richard alongside Chaser Villa on the sun deck. Johnny seemed to be slaloming between statutes in the California penal code that levied different punishments for killers and accomplices. Where Johnny was truthful was about his hatred for rats (though he would soon become one himself). During his formative discussions with police, he fingered Chaser—not Crazy Eddy Reyes—as being with him at the Buonsantis. Johnny assumed it was Chaser who finked on him to authorities about these crimes, and claimed Crazy Eddy was just as furious. So furious that the next time Chaser came to Crazy Eddy's basement to shoot up smack, Johnny said that Crazy Eddy intended to load his syringe with a fatal overdose. The DA's assessment: the staff Howard built with his management pyramid now resembled a viper pit.

Johnny required an incentive to tell the whole truth and nothing but, so prosecutors in June cudgeled him with an inducement. They charged him with first-degree murder with special circumstances, a count that made him eligible for the California death penalty. Johnny's attorney, deputy public defender Howard Waco, shopped a bargain to remove that from the table. His client would plead guilty to first-degree murder—so long as the special circumstance charge was rescinded.

Then he'd sing loudly what he knew about Howard. To underscore his willingness, Johnny agreed to a lie detector test.

Deputy district attorney Jeffrey Jonas, the case's chief prosecutor, had in Johnny a star witness tricky to pigeonhole. The man, he wrote, was a "strange" person who was "not bright, to say the least." Johnny's own father backed up that assessment, noting his son suffered from "brain damage," among other mental deficiencies. But don't read too much into it, Jonas said, for "he is very capable of killings; in fact, I would say he has an obsession about guns and killing [that Howard] Garrett has been able to exploit...To Williams, killing or hurting a human being has no more significance than eating a meal."

Nobody on record questioned if this collectively dim view of Johnny's IQ was the result of epilepsy, heroin addiction, or his unappreciated acting skills. Nobody in open court pondered if Johnny, given his photographic memory, tactical thinking, and nuanced understanding of California criminal law, was pretending to be a knuckle-dragging simpleton to protect his own interests. Johnny's true acuity was something neither he nor the DA wanted to drill down on too deep on because he didn't want to appear too bright, and the DA needed to present him as someone implicating a higher-functioning reptile who'd admitted nothing.

Howard, upon arrest, gloated to police that "they will never make any of it stick." He'd walked before, and he would again. Jonas characterized him as "vain and arrogant," with wanton notions about keeping people in line, punishing them when they crossed it, and extinguishing victims with impunity.

As Jonas described in a pretrial memo:

"Howard Landis Garrett...is a methodical, conniving, and scheming individual who has utilized and preyed upon the weaknesses of others to his advantage...Our evidence shows [he] has contracted for the deaths of at least four people, not including the Buonsantis. He also has no regard or value for life...I deem him to be far more dangerous than Williams because of his intelligence and sophistication. Regardless of whether he pulled the trigger, he

is the mastermind…All the witnesses and accomplices we have approached state that Garrett believes now [particularly because of his acquittal in San Bernardino County], that he is beyond the law; that he is untouchable…too smart to get caught."

Of everyone charged, Jonas concluded, Howard deserved the gas chamber that California voters just the year before reaffirmed they wanted after it'd been struck down as unconstitutional as cruel and unusual punishment. Howard, the DA said, was unlikely to ever be rehabilitated, and it would be in society's best interest for the state to execute him since that was an option again.

At his preliminary hearing in early August, observers noticed how different he looked except for the frown on his leathery face. Now that he swapped his blue jeans–Hawaiian shirt combo for a typical prisoner's jumpsuit, he appeared defanged, though no one was running up to the defendant's table to take a peek inside his mouth.

The next trial milestone was his arraignment on September 11, 1979. Howard, as expected, plead not guilty to a cargo hold full of charges. For Richard's execution, the DA's office charged him with murder with special circumstance, citing his premeditation and planning. In a nod to his killing-for-profit scheme, they tacked on conspiracy to commit murder and solicitation for it. Prosecutors also consolidated all his cruelty against Jerry into a single count: attempted extortion. For the Buonsanti incident, they slapped him with attempted robbery and five counts of attempted murder.

County prosecutors and the LAPD flailed in one element of the investigation that helped keep Jerry holed up in the Hyatt for so long. A lack of evidence prevented them from bundling their suspicions about Howard's links to other killings and bedlam into additional counts. Nothing, either, could be imposed on him in connection with the Tim Dwight murder, which he bragged to Jerry he was behind, because of the provision against double-jeopardy trials.

In October 1980, the main event commenced under the direction of LA County Superior Court Judge Leonard S. Wolf. One of Jonas's first questions to Johnny established the atmosphere. Asked how many people he murdered in his lifetime, he replied four, including Richard Kasparov, without a flinch of hesitation. Jonas used that response to depict him as someone not so much immoral but deprived of a conscience. The part of him that should've cared that his actions tore families asunder, cost two young children their father, and destroyed things that it took people years to accomplish was simply nonexistent from his neurology. Yes: he was the perfect killer.

And whatever you thought of how he spoke, Johnny was able to freely size up the bigger picture. He wasn't on trial here, having already plead guilty to first-degree murder for shooting Richard with the M-1 rifle that he pawned with the Cartier watch he swiped from Richard's bedroom. For the next twenty-five years, his address would be Soledad State Prison on California's central coast. He wouldn't be eligible for early release until the mid-1990s, so in effect he was testifying with house money as a repeat felon and friend of the DA.

Johnny still had his qualms too. If he'd remained in Howard's employ, he'd be filing a grievance with human resources. At the top of his complaint list was Howard's pigheaded refusal to pay him for whacking Richard, which Johnny had reminded him about on multiple occasions, as well as Howard's welching on other agreed-upon compensation. Altogether, he claimed he was owed $12,000, money he sorely could've used. To Johnny, the hypocrisy of being stiffed like this stunk to high heaven. Howard, who'd spouted his umbrage about deadbeats, was just as much one as the person he had Johnny slaughter.

His other beef: the home invasion robbery of the Buonsantis, which Luis's older son had foiled. Prosecutors earlier said the incident qualified as attempted mass murder, but Johnny carped that was an overreach, for he never would've executed Luis's children. He was cold-blooded, but he wasn't a butcher. If Howard narrowed his instructions to kill only Luis, Johnny said he would have complied, just as long as Luis's family was blocked from seeing the blood spray.

Karma always gets the last laugh, though. The $55,000 that motivated Howard to dispatch Johnny and Crazy Eddy there to retrieve was fantasy all along. Luis kept no cash in a floor safe, under a mattress, or beneath a floorboard. How could he? The amount represented the *equity* the entrepreneurial auto mechanic had accumulated in his Monrovia residence. When Luis in his choppy syntax voiced that he had money "in the house," Howard's rapacious ears misinterpreted it.

Johnny, asked to place Richard's murder in context, then educated the jury like a grizzled sociologist. What Howard commissioned, he explained, wasn't unusual, not in the underbelly of the city of Spago and the Fabulous Forum, where hitmen were always in demand. When folks read about unsolved murders attributed to domestic disputes or robberies gone wrong, many times they were reading about the handiwork of paid assassins. Just by himself, Johnny declared knowing of twenty-five contract killings in which no one was caught. In a 1984 *Los Angeles* magazine article on this subject, he depicted a vengeful metropolis where payback was as prevalent as silicone and cocaine. Killers searching for employment congregated like day laborers at pimp bars in South Central and at Valley watering holes. Back then, a hired gun would cost you less than a major transmission job. Five hundred dollars was the going rate.

Johnny, with his bushy hair and Charles Nelson Reilly glasses, was finally ready for his star turn to detail what no else would. In an impassive voice, he painted for the court a serene portrait of what he, Howard, and Chaser glimpsed through Richard's second-floor sliding-glass window. You could forget to breathe listening to his storytelling.

"Susan is reading...[what] looks like a book and she's sitting with her back up against the bed. [Richard] is laying kind of like [he's] got his hands under his head...He's got lights along the bottom of the wall up to the glass door that are facing the bed...It is dark out [on the landing]...He looked right at us [but] he couldn't see us...I shoot him...[I saw his] head drop forward. I knew I hit him. I have been shooting guns since I was nine years old...He jerked and relaxed. I figured he was dead."

BESIDES JOHNNY, ROBERT WAS the prosecutors' other ace witness. Much like Paige, he learned that once bad intentions get a headwind, they blow over backstops like they were made from papier-mâché. Robert nearly lost an eye to it. After he escaped to San Francisco in Howard's El Camino, he decided that he would rather take his chances there than risk his employer's wrath in LA. Next he did something stunning: he flexed moral backbone. His objective: halt the very murder that Howard was fanatical about him carrying out.

In March, a day or so after Johnny had tried executing him in San Francisco, Robert flew back for a court appointment right here in Van Nuys to face an old burglary charge. He might not have traveled down for the hearing except for the rapidly closing window that it provided him. Not only was foreknowledge of Richard's fate consuming him, he knew a heads-up might buy him immunity for his involvement while reducing his jail time for unrelated crimes.

His vessel for disruption was a woman named Susanne Green. It was an apt name for the court-appointed lawyer, who first represented him when he was in the San Bernardino jail during winter 1978 without enough cash to make bail—a situation Howard soon manipulated to groom a controllable assassin. At the time, Susanne's state bar license was dripping ink; she had been a member for only a month. Her uncle, Harry Weiss, an elegant, monocle-wearing character considered one of the deans of LA criminal defense lawyers, might've been better suited to the task.

Yet Susanne won a continuance on Robert's burglary charge, and the two afterward retired to a bench just beyond the door where they were now. That's when the iron-pumping ex-con unburdened himself of his incendiary secrets—Howard's kill list, starting with Richard, and his Svengali-like magic for knowing things and beating raps.

Robert's confession so unnerved Susanne that by the time he finished, she too anxiously scanned the hallway for signs of Howard despite being in a police-protected facility. Law school didn't cover this. For a moment, she was heartened spotting an assistant DA whom she knew. But when she approached him for guidance, he couldn't be bothered. He was leaving his post soon for another job.

The untested lawyer was boxed inside of a dilemma with no obvious daylight out. On one hand, anything Robert told her was covered under strict attorney-client privilege. Divulging their private dealings, no matter the reason, could be grounds for disbarment, effectively terminating her career before it achieved liftoff. Withholding the information wasn't much better. Someone could fashion the argument that by doing nothing to interrupt a premeditated homicide, pulp-novel-ish sounding as it was, she made herself an accomplice.

Advice from gray-haired mentors: that's what Susanne determined she needed.

She contacted her law school ethics professor, who told her that he never heard of such a pickle. Then she met in the chambers of Armand Arabian, a Superior Court judge long admired by police. He was of minimal help. As a sitting judge, he testified he was "not in the business of giving legal advice," even to skittish colleagues reqiring hand-holding. He also fretted about conflict-of-interest accusations should Susanne appear in his courtroom on future cases.

"So, not to be rude to her and knowing she's inexperienced to some degree, I let her blurt out whatever it was because she blurted it out anyway," Arabian explained. "I had no control over that. I selectively listened to what it was [and] instantly knew" the conversation had to cease.

Arabian's best counsel? For Suzanne to speak with a seasoned, criminal defense lawyer. Robert Shapiro, he added, might be able to ascertain whether her "problem" involved "ethical, legal, or moral" dimensions meriting intervention. Shapiro, when contacted, was blunt. The former prosecutor said he believed that Robert's account was almost certainly fabricated. Veteran defense attorneys, she said he told her, constantly hear whoppers from clients trying to worm into prosecutor's good graces.

Susanne's three legal elders left her confused about what do, meaning she had to decide. Break confidentiality? Wash her hands of it, hoping that blood didn't stain them later? She gave Robert's account a half-percent chance of authenticity. The rub: whether she could live with herself if that one in two hundred hit like some homicide slot machine.

She couldn't, so she drew inspiration not from the sandstone pillars of justice but from the legend of King Solomon: she'd place a lifesaving call from the citadel of anonymity. On the Saturday morning preceding the killing, she phoned Paige, exhorting her to grill Richard about *who* would want him dead and to do something to prevent it. In Susanne's estimation, her newsflash transcended the drawbacks that she communicated it without additional details or a name behind it. Her measured remedy went nowhere. The LAPD didn't take Paige's account seriously, saying the threat lacked a who, what, and when. Richard, prideful and delusional, himself accused her of fabricating the call in a child-support subterfuge.

Three days later, an M-1 bullet rocketed through his sliding-glass window.

Robert, now proved credible, told Susanne afterward that she might as well organize his funeral unless she protected him from Howard's pathological hunger for revenge. She postponed his next court date, and, about May 1, as the LAPD inquiry into Howard sputtered and stalled, with no smoking gun unearthed, contacted detectives working Richard's murder with the gift they never saw coming. Between Robert and Johnny, there went Howard's cloak as a wrongly accused, Chevy-driving everyman.

On the witness stand explaining her role, Robert's lawyer was hazy about what Arabian specifically advised. Shapiro did not appear to be in the court's incomplete trial record. When the general public later heard the names Arabian and Shapiro, it wasn't for the oddities of Richard Kasparov's murder.

In 1990, then-Governor George Deukmejian appointed the law-and-order Arabian to the California Supreme Court as part of a conservative majority replacing Rose Bird and two other liberal associates. The former Army paratrooper, who loved cats, was tough on rapists, quoted famous writers in his opinions, and could've been the bald-headed brother of actor Jeffrey Tambor, served until 1996.

Shapiro barged into the limelight as a member of O. J. Simpson's legal "Dream Team" during his double-murder trial in the mid-1990s. Articulate, dapper, and phlegmatic, he was the opposite of his more flamboyant colleague Johnny Cochran in their winning defense of the ex-football star/pitchman. Celebrities Darryl Strawberry, Johnny Carson, Linda Lovelace, Christian Brando, and Lindsay Lohan also received Shapiro's services. More recently, he was one of the founders of LegalZoom.com, the online site connecting small businesses to legal services. A 2018 *Bloomberg* story valued the entity at $2 billion.

•••

As HIS TRIAL ADVANCED, Howard displayed the bravado of someone confident he would strut out a free man, whatever the aspersions of his former acolytes. He'd done his homework *before* the LAPD yanked him naked out of his bedroom, lining up alibis, fall guys, and scare tactics. When he heard that Johnny intended to testify against him, there was no panic. With Johnny's prior arrests and spoken disregard for human life, why would jurors believe him over a state-certified contractor? And which of them was going to take the word of a shady, deal-cutting, unrepentant thief like Robert Freeman? A man only out to save himself.

Robert's sister's testimony suggested the jurors should listen. For months now, she'd lived continually with Howard's pounding fixation to track down her brother to keep him from snitching. In July 1979, as Howard sat in the clink, supposed police officers working Richard's homicide knocked at her Ontario home. They drove her to a restaurant in the southeastern San Gabriel Valley, where they leaned on her for a single slab of information: Robert's whereabouts. Janice, sensing something fishy about the men without IDs, told them her guess was as good as theirs.

Howard's other legal tactic: to make the victim's licentious past as an operator, playboy, and recreational drug enthusiast a conspirator. The same shadow of suspicion engulfing him needed to shine on others that Richard used, infuriated, and/or scammed. On this subject, Howard asked, *why* wasn't Robert Freeman's drug-dealing an investigative target? Someone even observed him selling Richard coke at a West LA restaurant, something that Howard knew all about because he'd puppeteered the transaction in case he needed to make Robert the fall guy. It sounded plausible enough in a powder-crazed city, even if Howard's red herring brought no independent corroboration.

During his bid for exoneration, he called laughable any references that he discussed four contract hits with some of the DA's prized witnesses. These scruffy characters, none of them exactly Mensa-caliber intellects, were too obtuse to recognize that his words were little more than beer-time bluster from someone demoralized at his economic plight. It was florid metaphor. Nothing literal. On reflection, he never should've vented to that crowd, most of them folks he recently met. His lawyers expanded on this, noting that Richard and Jerry were just two of many white-collar real-estate men who exploited their client through his career. None of the others were dead.

Over and over, Howard and his attorneys were boomerangs of denial in that courtroom, "never" their centerpiece term. Among the rebuttals: he *never* arranged any contract murder; *never* drove an assassin past Richard's tree-lined house on scouting expeditions; *never* sent men to ransack the Buonsanti's home; *never* squatted on Richard's sun deck with Johnny and Chaser; *never* authorized the bullet that made landing in Richard's brain; *never* threatened Jerry for seventy-five thousand or his life; *never* directed pay-up-or-die calls to him at Space Matters; and *never* scrawled names of future victims for his purported murder-for-money apparatus.

Howard did acknowledge one misdeed: that he worked for Richard's secretly minted company, Kasparov Design, which Richard created to embezzle materials and mine profits from CM-2, Space Matters's luxury-home-remodeling spinoff. He even justified that, saying this sort of underhanded practice was common in dog-eat-dog real estate, not some despicable conspiracy against naive Jerry. But that wasn't the extent of it. The prosecutors' theory that he used Richard's dishonesty to blackmail him—before Richard started bilking Howard's credit lines in a second flimflam—was, his lawyers argued, horse crap.

Another DA falsehood in its cockamamie case: that the letter that Howard mailed to Jerry and Tammy was a violence-portending shot across their bows. The correspondence, he said on the stand, was to "get [his] points across" about his determination to have the company honor its debts and reunite him with his stuff. This was about dignity.

Howard's wall of disavowals slowed with his admission that yes, he was aware of the $150,000 life insurance policy that Jerry and Richard bought in case one of them perished. That was irrelevant too, for knowledge did not equal motive. Broadly speaking, he wanted the fine ladies and gentlemen of the jury to know, he still harbored no long-term grudges against his former employers despite their machinations.

"I liked them both," Howard answered when questioned how he felt about them.

Wasn't that magnanimous of him?

As to his old protégé and friend Luis Buonsanti, the DA again was casting reels in fishless ponds. Why, after all, would he engineer an attack against the family he and his mother showered with generosity, from cash to clothes? Nothing happened to convert him from their benefactor to their oppressor. Where do you think he took his car to repair its front-end damage? Luis's shop!

Throughout the case, Howard's lawyers towed this line for him as masters of objection and deflectors of the embarrassing. When prosecutors dug into who enlisted those phony cops to harass Janice

Freeman, they squelched the DA's questions. They were tickled that Judge Wolf sided with them by ruling that it would've been prejudicial for jurors to hear about Howard's alleged clubbing and incineration of Tim Dwight. Marc Frenkel and Ronald Allen were less celebratory when it came to light that *they* personally returned to Howard his .45-caliber handgun after he was acquitted in San Bernardino.

As the trial wore on, Jonas and his peers noticed something else about their opposites. Their body language telegraphed worry about what their client might visit upon *them* if they failed to secure his exoneration again.

Dread of Howard's recall for such things was its own virus during the trial. Prosecutors effectively lost Jamie Jones as a witness who knew gobs about his ex-boss' homicidal lusts over it.

For their preliminary hearings, the Sheriff's Department transported Jamie and Howard on the same bus for the trip from county lockup to the courthouse. On the ride there, Howard warned his ex-employee about speaking against him. The DA earlier requested that they be separated to protect Jamie, but the sheriff's office forgot. Jamie, already mortified of the malevolent gleam in Howard's eye, refused to say a word after that bus trip. His abrupt flipflop compelled prosecutors to scotch Jamie's planned testimony, which they expected would buttress Johnny's account of events. Jonas was livid, terming it "unforgiveable for such a case to be endangered" by the sheriff's goof-up.

That bureaucratic fumble was soon followed by another: the quest to dupe tight-lipped Howard to talk now that he was behind bars with his dander up. For this, authorities wired one of the men who'd secretly agreed to testify against him, perhaps Johnny, in hopes a familiar face could spur him into divulging things the DA could use against him. The LAPD had no luck trying this with Jerry, and it didn't work here, either. The county put the kibosh on any clandestine recording of Howard, citing its policy against doing so in jailhouse settings.

For Paige, Richard's widow, the trial seeking justice for him was another loop in her ring of hell. Under oath, she admitted that Richard was sometimes physically abusive but maintained that her love for him was undiminished. She also recreated the dialogue of the anonymous call that claimed her estranged husband, the one with a bull's-eye on his back, should "start making nice" to acquaintances. Paige still had no idea who the messenger was until Susanne, who was roughly her age, introduced herself in the courthouse hallway. After matching a face with that voice, Paige fainted, as if she'd touched a hot stove.

For all the untangled knots, some skein of intrigue remained unsolved. Little or nothing, for instance, was made about the would-be kidnapper pursuing Richard and Paige's baby daughter. Had Howard commissioned Robert, during an unknown respite from jail, in an early show of force to induce Richard to repay him? Or did he recruit someone else, perhaps a goon he kept in reserve? More than four decades later, the identity of the intruder that Isabel, the Guatemalan housekeeper, rebuffed with a broomstick has remained a mystery.

Howard was several people in Judge Wolf's court. In front of the jury, he was a red-blooded blue collar being nailed to the cross for something he didn't do. Heck, he was a victim himself. But when he locked eyes with witnesses for the prosecution, that cool innocence was replaced by sly glowers and smirks that conveyed an icy message: though incarcerated, he wasn't the sort to absolve his enemies. Northridge, the Miracle Mile, Ann Arbor, San Francisco, Ontario; his spite contained no odometer.

Prosecutors, aware that his gamma-ray stare could dissuade witnesses from saying what they remembered, advised everyone testifying for them to skip looking at the defendant's table. They couldn't afford someone else deciding to clam up because a seated Howard got into their heads from across the room.

During Jerry's hours in the witness box—where he told a disjointed story of his life first as Richard's and Howard's colleague, then as their putty—he tried his best to avert his eyes from Howard's vulturous expression. The irony was pungent too. Here he was, one of a couple of dozen witnesses, sitting in the same chair as the backstabbing criminals who assassinated someone who didn't deserve it, plotted to maim his son, and fractured the company that proved he was a somebody, and yet the DA relegated him in the gear works of justice to a relatively puny role. The only person he knew from the other side of things was Howard's gofer, Michael Bailey.

Jerry was barred from the courtroom except when he was set to testify; as a formal prosecution witness, he was not supposed to be swayed by what anybody else said. His dad, Art, had no such restrictions, and he longed to assist his only boy. He was in the public gallery for many of the hearings that Jerry couldn't, next to the senior-citizen trial junkies that'd welcomed him into their opinionated little klatch. When he wasn't trading commentary with them, he occasionally tailed Howard's attorneys as they broke for lunch, sitting near them to eavesdrop. The Schneidermans loved their tape recorders because Art brought his. Sometimes he set it down, all secret-agent-like, near enough to capture defense-team chatter. Anything dicey it captured he passed along to the DA.

The Buonsantis themselves were there to help unmask the man they figured they knew, and it cost them sleep. In front of everyone, prosecutors made family members point for identification purposes where they least wanted to: at Howard as well as the two men they'd last seen aiming big guns in their living room—Johnny and Crazy Eddy. Luis's youngest boy, Maurice, now eleven, was about the only source of levity. Attorneys requested that he answer affirmatively to their questions with a simple yes, and not the "uh huh" that he had been. Asked if he understood the instruction, Maurice responded: "Uh-huh."

Near the end, the DA's Jonas realized that he had Howard tap dancing on a defense constructed on a buckling floor. Howard's baleful offer to describe to Jerry the precise caliber of the bullet that produced that spider-web-like crack in Richard's window tripped him up on his own conceit, even as Howard denied ever saying it. Jonas also had him reeling over inconsistent dates and shaky alibis, hostile testimony and flagrant motives. Then he dared him to disprove Robert's assassin-recruitment story, plus Johnny's garish, murder-night narrative in a double-team smackdown of his former toadies. If he were blameless, Jonas inquired, why did he snip out and preserve the newspaper articles about Richard's slaying and the Buonsanti robbery? Howard lamely tried to brush it off, saying he'd intended to mail the Buonsanti article to his mother, conscientious son that he was.

To all these shoddy explanations, the jury had a uniform response: We don't believe you!

On October 30, 1980, the day before Halloween, the panel convicted him of engineering Richard's murder in the first degree and related counts. The sentence was kneecapping, especially for someone smug about being able to get away with anything. It would be life in prison *without* the possibility of parole.

If Jonas and his colleagues were disappointed, it was that the jury did not convict him on the special circumstances charges that might have bedded him down on Death Row. The jury, in another downer that made fists clench, acquitted him of plotting against the Buonsantis.

Listening to an otherwise lead-ton verdict, Howard was defiant, fuming behind his poker face, convinced his incarceration would be temporary. His tenacity, coupled with the DA's errors, would free him on appeal before anyone knew it. Then watch out.

At his second trial in April 1981, where he challenged the guilty verdict in his first one, Howard's same lawyers emphasized three arguments. They claimed the evidence presented against him earlier failed to match the DA's assertions; that a superficial hallway conversation—when a juror asked LAPD Detective Jamieson how old he was—created bias; and that a hearing postponement so jurors could watch a World Series game "reduced and denigrated [the] trial to a farce and a sham."

Unsurprisingly, his appeal was denied, and Howard tumbled into the penitentiary system one angry middle-aged felon. Jonas, for this reason, requested that if Howard was sent to San Quentin State Prison off the San Francisco Bay, Johnny be placed in another prison. If not, Jonas wrote, Johnny's life would be in peril, given how "devastating his testimony was." Howard, as it were, didn't go to San Quentin. He was bused to Folsom State Prison northeast of Sacramento while Johnny went to Corcoran State Prison about three hundred miles to the southeast.

Should Howard be freed, prosecutors believed, some of those who told the truth about him would "be as good as dead."

CHAPTER TWENTY-ONE
BLUE-TINTED PHANTOMS

OUT IN NORTHRIDGE, THE lawn was trimmed, the newspaper deliveries long resumed. Jerry's Mercedes-Benz and Tammy's Seville were parked in the driveway again without anybody being jittery about a bomb under a car hood. Jerry was back in fine suits, having returned his denim Caterpillar Construction getup to Ari.

You never would have guessed that this was a household still knocked off its foundations.

They'd hoped the renaissance of their old routine would bind everyone's psychic gashes. By Jerry returning full-time to Space Matters and Tammy to motherhood in California, they hoped to warehouse everything that traced from March 27, 1979, to the fogbanks of distant memory. The Schneidermans just wanted their humdrum old bliss back.

It seemed attainable after Tammy delivered a healthy son whose existence had been debated, and Jude grew into a marvelous tyke with both ears attached. From the exterior of that largest home on their suburban block, the family seemed to be flourishing. But how would one really know through the drawn curtains and blinds?

It wasn't just Howard's trials they had to endure or his deadly stare that they pined to forget. There was the money. Bills from Jerry's lawyers and private detectives needed to be paid, and Space Matters gasped for new business to make up for lost opportunities.

Tammy, try as she did to be sunny, was a different woman by March 1980. Some days she was phobic, others survival-minded.

Predictability became her security blanket. She had asked an LAPD detective at the courthouse how long they would have if California's revolving-door justice system disgorged Howard from Folsom State Prison. Long enough, he told her, to collect their bags, race to LAX, and make themselves invisible in a fresh city. As much as she focused on her little ones and Jerry, not what might be hiding behind a shrub, that evacuation scenario whirled in the fear centers of her mind.

She now disliked anything defying snap identification. She scribbled down the license plates of unrecognizable cars by their home. She wanted Jerry home every night by five. One evening, alarm trebled through her when she overheard two men speaking on her porch; Jerry, without telling her, had extended a last-minute dinner invitation to a friend. She was furious over it, her tolerance for surprises worn to a nub.

"If you're going to keep this up," she said later, "I'm going to leave you."

She voiced and rephrased this, just as she did with her earlier incantation: "I hate California, hate this crazy life. This doesn't happen to normal people."

After hearing Tammy say she might pick up and go until he could no longer tolerate it, Jerry finally told her that she needed to make a decision. She could live with him in readapted happiness, coexist with him dolefully, or flat walk out the door on him. He favored choice number one, but Tammy refused to make any. This wasn't "Let's Make a Deal." She did speak authoritatively in one area. She wanted out of LA.

But to which Jerry was she negotiating? If it was the caring, imaginative cutie-pie who used to doodle cartoons of woodland critters for her, that Jerry was bleaching away. The colossal relief that danced through him after Howard's incarceration gave way to a reflexive assumption that every new person he met could be camouflaging wickedness. Running a scheme. Howard had ruined his predilection to trust, Richard his willingness to accept facts at face value.

Scouring the morning newspaper only revived what Johnny contended at trial about killers lurking under all sorts of rocks too. Assassins were snuffing trial witnesses. A Japanese importer commissioned someone to off his wife for insurance proceeds. A Native American tribal leader and two others were murdered near Palm Springs in a case tied to casino-skimming mobsters. A local designer like Richard was discovered brutalized in the hills. For every airhead caricature of California life, someone was hosing blood off the sidewalk.

Or calling for antivenom.

As the Schneidermans tried to recover, legal dominoes continued falling after the bizarre October 1978 attack that typified LA's payback culture. One afternoon that month, just as the opening pitch in the Dodgers-Yankees World Series was slated to be thrown, a young lawyer in sun-kissed Pacific Palisades stuck his hand into his mail slot. What Paul Morantz fished out, though, weren't letters or a package. It was an ornery, nearly five-foot-long Diamondback rattlesnake. A snake reared in a dark hole to harness its aggression; a snake whose warning rattles were intentionally lopped off. Two henchmen, calling themselves "Imperial Marines" from Synanon's Central Valley headquarters, had hidden the creature in there to silence the man in an attempted homicide by reptile. This was Morantz's thanks for crusading against the drug rehab/alternative society, which had started off idealistically in the sixties before succumbing to ambition, greed, and insularity that warped it into a xenophobic seventies cult.

The lawyer, who resembled Olympic swimming champion Mark Spitz, survived the spectacularly publicized crime, which whipped around the globe in a pre-Twitter flash. Synanon, unable to live down the infamy, was eventually sent into organizational death throes. Interestingly, it executed its last act despite the LAPD, state, local neighborhood, and even Morantz, who slept with a shotgun in his bedroom, on alert for an incursion. It was as if the sinking of those fangs into his wrist was preordained, not unlike Johnny's bullet.

Nineteen seventy-nine might've seemed a steppingstone to a better decade, a time to ponder buying a high-mileage Toyota, or donating old Birkenstocks to the Salvation Army, or loving to hate the Stetson-wearing J. R. Ewing of *Dallas*. But the universe said not so fast in its body counts and its inversions. This was the year when snowflakes dusted the Sahara, a swamp rabbit paddled toward Jimmy Carter's canoe, and Iran, America's old ally, took US embassy workers hostage. As a closer, an outwardly detente-minded Kremlin invaded Afghanistan, where Great Powers go to die.

An upside-down Jerry tried flying level. After Howard's arrest, he copied what Luis Buonsanti did to safeguard his family: he bought a gun for protection—a Walther PPKS, similar to the pistol James Bond wielded. He carried the firearm in his waistband to work, home, the car. He took it on a business trip to Denver without setting off the airport screening machine.

The pistol, however, carried no agency with his post-ordeal demons. They trapped him in a muddle of smoldering, unreconciled emotions that kept their own schedule. During all his weeks in hiding, he never could've imagined that once out he would be this lost. He just wanted back to where he was on March 26, 1979, not yoyoing with mood swings, tenseness, paranoia, and disassociation. One day on the freeway with Tammy, he began crying for no apparent cause.

"I just got to get it out," he told her, whimpering. "My system can't take it."

By the time he wept himself dry, it was three days later.

Tammy eventually persuaded him to attend therapy with her to regain equilibrium. It didn't go well. Jerry was either noncommunicative or combative, so the sessions crystallized around addressing Tammy's anguish instead of them as a couple. She craved resumption of the simple life. He wanted to stand on concrete that didn't crack, unwilling to allow treatment to rectify him.

Soon he was back in the Waring Blender of post-Richard Space Matters. His workweek upped to sixty hours, much of that detached from sketching and design, warding off legal claims. Reengaging clientele. Assessing a dazed staff. Some victory lap: out of the Hyatt and onto the hamster wheel.

Richard's shady remodels were a particular bugbear to wrestle. Three homeowners with unfinished renovations demanded refunds, cavalier as could be in the aftermath of murder. Others filed lawsuits or insisted on project completion. Jerry wore holes through his stomach lining trying to resolve them. Only one action brought satisfaction: suing a few homeowners who knowingly received stolen building materials, Mikey Krakow the most flagrant of them all.

And yet the financial landscape was still mostly rubble. Jerry and his companies owed hundreds of thousands of dollars in settlements, taxes, lawyer fees, and other expenses that dwarfed revenues. Even the $150,000 in life insurance proceeds on Richard, once the object of Howard's gluttony, did little to staunch the bleeding. After the IRS demanded its cut of CM-2's income, Jerry made an agonizing choice. He opted not to contest it by asserting the extraordinary conditions in which it was paid out, letting the federal government take the money. Nobody else got a cent. Not him. Not Paige. Not Richard's mother. Definitely not his former construction chief.

Another colossal change occurred as the one-year anniversary of the murder approached. Jerry ordered Space Matters sawed in half.

While too attached to sell the building where so much happened, he was too damaged by the serrated memories there to continue working at its address. So, under an engineer's watch, the structure was carefully segmented into two. Then it was levered onto massive, multi-wheeled trucks and rolled out of Hancock Park. It was quite the sight as the vehicles with that Spanish Revival on them lumbered across major streets and intersections, blocking traffic, and generating finger-pointing en route. Three miles to the north, the halves were lowered onto their new site near the corner of Beverly Boulevard and Rossmoor Avenue. The company was now close to the edge of the Wilshire Country Club and, fittingly, not all that far from Richard's and Jerry's maiden office on Pico Boulevard. Putting a wrap on everything, Jerry sold the land where the mansion resided for about seven hundred thousand.

Remarkably, the company and its associated units rebounded some in 1981, garnering work in major high-rises and elsewhere. Millions of dollars in revenue flowed across the transom, with dozens of people on payroll if you counted subcontractors. Jerry hired Paige, a talented interior designer in her own right, to give her income and attract new clients, even though she still bore her suspicions. One piece of cleanup was obvious. Done with luxury-home remodels, Jerry disbanded CM-2 as swiftly as Richard hatched it.

As if that was the end to falling rubble.

Paul Fegen's extraordinary success leasing buildings across the country once had him lording over a twenty-five-state portfolio estimated at seven million square feet. The conditions that enriched him in the 1970s proved thorny in the next decade, however. As the US lapsed into recession, this one during the Reagan administration, office buildings once crammed with "Fegen suites" hemorrhaged tenants. Las Vegas, one of Fegen's hotbeds, was now vacancy land; Texas, where Fegen also performed so well, was double-whammied by the listless economy and an oil slump. The rise of the personal computer itself was inhospitable. The bulky computers beginning to digitize everything once on paper meant endangered species status for the old-fashioned secretarial pool. Sole-proprietor lawyers that Fegen routinely leased six-hundred-square-feet offices to could retrench to half of that. Banks eyeing Fegen's shrinking income severed credit to him and battled to claw their money back.

Jerry, privy to the details, was among the first to decipher Fegen's unorthodox accounting practices. Now, he saw, those ledgers were splashed in red ink.

Two years after Howard's murder trial, the landlord of a Las Vegas property that Fegen rented flew out to LA to meet with the leasing king's bravura space planner. Having played that role for so long, Jerry believed he knew what to expect. For years, he watched how Bald Jesus's eccentricities dumbfounded some of his button-down financiers when they finally met him. A Kansas City banker nearly flipped backward in his chair when Jerry handed him a photograph of Fegen, sequins glued on his face.

But the Las Vegas property owner had no time for any frivolity. If Fegen defaulted on his debts, he told Jerry that he was going to "have Paul killed" to collect on his $2 million life insurance policy. Asked whether he heard that right, the executive apologized to Jerry for his crude hyperbole. Still, it illustrated that a Pandora's box was cracked. Other financiers, Jerry soon learned, had also taken out insurance contracts on Fegen, naming themselves beneficiaries. Appreciating that he might be worth more dead than alive, Fegen tightened security, remaking his penthouse office into a light fortress.

Who was Jerry to disabuse him that contract murders only happened in *Godfather* movies?

In the annals of Jerry, November 1982 stunk. As Fegen's business took on water, Jerry agreed to lend him $250,000 so he could make payroll and sidestep bankruptcy. Jerry did it for Space Matters's top client, as well as out of loyalty to someone who believed in him. What Jerry never envisioned was how Fegen's lawyers would pervert it. That they would pivot on their tasseled loafers to file a *quarter-billion-dollar* lawsuit against him, accusing him of profiteering. Their real motive? They needed an enemy to litigate against.

Jerry would've screamed into his pillow that life was dogpiling onto him, or how meritless the suit was, especially when Fegen owed his company $12 million. Yet who would've listened? The only strategy that made sense was allowing his enemies to overreach like he did with schoolyard bullies. He hired a swanky lawyer with a taste for Expressionist art to handle the complex case, conceding nothing. He underwent depositions and, thinking ahead, shrewdly bought legal malpractice insurance, knowing his attorney would probably trip up in the fine print. To make a tortuous story short, the attorney committed those mistakes, and the insurer paid Jerry a million bucks.

Triumphant there, his home turf was less rewarding. He and Tammy were not sure how much they liked each other's post-Howard personalities. Where again was that downy-soft, second chapter? The couple did greet another son, their third, but Jerry's workaholic binges worsened with his self-compact to never be defrauded again.

Tammy, dejected that he prioritized self-reliance over family rejuvenation, grappled with her own issues. Worry continued to pincushion her. The minute that Jerry was late arriving home from work, and he was constantly, was the minute she was alarmed. She wasn't beyond phoning the California Highway Patrol to check if its officers interacted with him. When there was no peep from Jerry after he was scheduled to be back from an out-of-town trip, she dialed the tower at LAX to ask the air traffic controllers if his jet landed. After she called them enough, they recognized her voice.

Nothing was as it had been.

She believed what they needed was a do-over in the Heartland, where people didn't slink around shooting each other in the skull over business squabbles; where there were fewer irascible people—serial killers, gang enforcers, vengeful drivers, surly parolees—than the cutthroat town at odds with its laidback, beachy image. Again, she broached the idea of them relocating to Ann Arbor. She had already discussed with her father the notion of Jerry working for his auto-junking business. It was the largest in four surrounding states, fed by contracts with the big automakers and insurance companies, and offered an added perk: getting to drive experimental cars. The West Coast held no monopoly on the future. To make the transition seamless, she would grant Jerry a year to wind down and sell Space Matters.

He delivered his answer about a fresh start the same month that Fegen's lawyers clobbered him with their giant lawsuit. It was no— an emphatic no! His life was here, even his survival scars. If Tammy for her own sanity needed to resuscitate herself elsewhere, Jerry told her, by all means go. She would just be doing so without him. What kind of man would he be if he abandoned his own hometown to haul jalopies through the snow?

Tammy grasped the implication: their marriage was over. It was a love, as the Beatles once sang, that should've lasted years, but the heartbreak of 1979 stole their mojo, replacing it with nail-biting and mistrust. Jerry was jaded at twenty-nine. She was preoccupied by strange license plates.

No more. Tammy and their three boys moved to a place in Ann Arbor near her parents. The supersized Northridge tract home, a McMansion of its seventies era, was rented out. It'd been two and a half years since those men hunted for Richard.

•••

JERRY, THE SPACE PLANNER, suddenly had no space to live. For a month, he was back in a hotel, this time a Sheraton near Century City. For something more permanent, he leased a Santa Monica condo that belonged to an associate who left to run for Congress in Utah.

Just when he prepared himself for some lonely years, there was a surprise. It was a good one for once: a secret admirer was waiting in the wings. Daphne was his personal assistant, and before that, one of Fegen's best secretaries. On their first date, she escorted Jerry to a beach house where she treated him to a scrumptious meal and then carnal desserts on silk sheets. She'd always hoped he would come back on the market.

What market? Jerry asked himself. He was overjoyed that anyone would fall for broken him, never mind someone as exotic and gorgeous as her. And yet early in their romance, his metabolism had its say about how he would live from hereon in.

During his time in hiding from Howard, his stomach had pretzeled itself into pink knots. Now, he was constantly parched and peeing every other hour. He downed 7-Eleven Slurpee's for his dry throat, but then his chest throbbed with blowtorch indigestion. When his doctor examined him, he discovered Jerry's breath shockingly acidic. Blood tests confirmed what that suggested: his patient was suffering with Type One diabetes. At diagnosis, his astronomic blood sugar brimmed above the level that caused others to fall into comas.

He was immediately sent to Cedars-Sinai Medical Center, in what is now West Hollywood, for treatment. As he was informed about his condition, he appreciated it was a manageable, if lifelong disease requiring lifelong attention. He was only thirty-two. He wanted to travel, explore, indulge his mischievous streak, eat as he wished. A glucose meter and syringe became shackles.

More than that, he felt cursed. Stalked. Condemned with the exact affliction as the man who obliterated everything. Two things spelled the end of his pancreas' insulin-making factory: the gene for the disease and 1979's roller coaster. Howard *had* struck again,

Not long after his diagnosis, at the Hollywood Bowl for a philharmonic with his sister, Jerry was clubbed by this symmetry. She packed a picnic that culminated with sugary chocolate cake, which someone cautioned Jerry that he should abstain from because of his new medical condition. He lashed out in an uncharacteristic fit, that cake his metaphor.

"I'll die if I don't eat this!" he said, injecting himself with a massive insulin shot to compensate. "I will."

He and Daphne wed in 1984, the year LA hosted a successful Olympic Games devoid of whiskey-brown air pollution and snarled traffic. The other milestone was a funeral worth hooting about: Howard was dead, dead from diabetes-related complications that his brooding, resentful nature aggravated. Tammy's whoop of joy about it reverberated from Michigan. Every year since his sentencing, she phoned his prison to ensure there were still high walls and barbed wire separating him from society. No more animal tracking anymore.

In the ensuing years, Jerry and his second wife purchased a house in Malibu and conceived two daughters. Destiny seemed to be recalibrating. Jerry would put the chaos behind him and relearn to trust. As with so much about him, the unanticipated interrupted the expected. It was Daphne being dragged back into a damaged past.

She had been born in South Korea to a US serviceman of African American descent and a local prostitute. Unprepared for a baby, the couple left her with an orphanage, believing she'd be adopted. It was wishful thinking because mixed-race children were often shunned in the nation. Unclaimed, Daphne was bundled off to US and right into the homes of cruel, abusive people. Now that she was a grown woman, that hurtful childhood socked her with crippling depression. She enrolled in psychotherapy for catharsis, and Jerry attended sessions for spouses. But he disliked it, just as he did therapy with Tammy, and tried instigating a mutiny. Nevertheless, Jerry lived with a newly enlightened person while he remained stuck inside himself.

The new Daphne kept busy. She converted to vegetarianism, headed her church, and explored scream therapy. Inspired by a feminist mentor, she enrolled in graduate school to become a therapist herself. Where she once concentrated on restoring Jerry, she threw herself into comforting the dying. That led to a job at a hospice treating AIDS-infected mothers. Jerry didn't fight her. Another divorce lurked.

He accepted that this was how things would be: that the dizzying, black ordeal of '79 was spreading low-grade infections among survivors, just when recovery flirted with them. So many entwined in the slow-motion jackknife of Richard's final year caught that bug.

Howard's trial had dissected the machinery of homicide without cracking the code of its quarry. Why did someone who promised to reform himself lie, steal, and cheat his way into isolation, and then that funeral home? Was he worried his fetching young wife would desert him if he didn't silken her life? Was it manic-depression-powered narcissism blinding him? Self-loathing that he failed to live up to West-LA expectations?

From his own thousand hours of retrospection, Jerry knew Richard shouldn't have required a hitman with a late-blooming conscience to try to thwart the killers from the east. As others, he couldn't fathom why he stayed within the firing zone. The only logical explanation was that Richard gave up. Capitulated. Threw in the towel. It's why he parked his car at his targeted home after his wife alerted him there was a murder contract on him, and why he plead with Jerry to look out for his family if something happened to him—nine hours before it did.

No opposite test needed here: Richard committed suicide by Howard.

Meanwhile, the path of destruction the man with the El Camino carved out long outlived him. Paige's trench was arguably the deepest. Through various legal settlements, she was able to afford a small house in the Valley near the Sherman Oaks Galleria. But a house is not love. She married three more times, never finding anyone who made her feel like Richard did. Between those relationships, she dated a medley of famous Angelenos that included the owner of a local sports franchise, a household-name actor, and a television executive. Cumulatively, none of them did her right, even after she got ill. When she recovered from it all, it was on her own two feet.

Luis Buonsanti was less concerned about feet than hands—hands that dampened recalling those diminutive men who terrorized his family for cash that wasn't there. He viewed the house on Hillcrest as hexed or marked; his wife, Norma, similarly no longer found serenity there. Eventually, they put it on the market, decamping to an adjacent community that Howard was never known to frequent. Janice Freeman needed a realtor too, bidding farewell to the Ontario residence that Howard and Johnny preyed on. Her brother, Robert, upended things as well. Before he returned to jail on charges unrelated to Howard, he urged his wife, Elena, to divorce him. He had exposed her to enough criminal poison.

For others, the break from 1979 was harsher. They turned to self-medication, toxic relationships, seclusion, and spent thousands on psychiatrists and psychologists. The woman in bed with Richard when Johnny fired his generation-altering bullet required long-term therapy. It wasn't just Tammy vehement about drawing curtains across windows, regardless of sunlight, either. From Beverly Hills to the Bay Area, dark rooms pervaded.

Deep into the 1980s, many of Jerry's dreams circled in a holding pattern from 1979. Some were about Richard in a recurring shadow play. In them, Jerry would notice his ex-partner at a restaurant immaculately attired, happy as a clam, and confoundingly alive. Dreaming Jerry would ask him how he could possibly be there when he saw his coffin. Richard, however, was disinclined to speak of the macabre. He smiled brightly, reassuring Jerry that he faked his own murder on the path to becoming a "new man."

At least someone was. Despite five beautiful children, a nest egg, and that mathematical brain, the double-divorcé moved sideways as much as forward. This should have been his time. Southern California was no longer the seething Valhalla it was in the late-seventies, and the sun glistened through the fading smog. *LA Law* re-glamorized the town, making divorce and patent applications hip. Ronald Reagan's defense buildup rained billions on local aerospace companies developing stealth bombers and space-based missile defenses. Jerry's city embraced aerobics, crack cocaine, soy diets, the Magic Johnson-led Lakers, and recycling bins.

New skyscrapers rose. What a city, back to new seductions. Back to reinventing the future.

Just not for Jerry. The past had gutted too much of him to be anything but mostly miserable.

CHAPTER TWENTY-TWO
LA'S MERRY PRANKSTER

NINETEEN NINETY-FIVE: THE GRAND opening of Hollywood's newest homeless facility promised goodies straight from a sinful dream. "Free food, drink, condoms, syringes, and surprise packages to all homeless guests," announced leaflets distributed in August of that year.

Jackie Goldberg, the area's stridently progressive councilwoman, would provide the indulgences. Or so hinted the fliers stenciled with cutesy balloons.

As word of the unusual event spread downtown, it sparked a fervor among a small group of street people determined not to miss out. Some of them hoofed it miles to the Gower Street location, pushing shopping carts to haul their expected swag home, others hopping a public bus. When the dozen or so would-be attendees showed up for the ribbon-cutting, their heart's ardor for bacchanalia was reflected in hands shoving so hard on the front of the building that a few of the occupants inside worried about a stampede and barricaded the door.

"Where are our freebies?" the indigents shrieked when the doors finally parted. "And what about those guaranteed good times?"

Goldberg's blindsided staff told them they were mystified by their presence. No celebration was underway because there was nothing to celebrate. Today's meeting was just to *discuss* whether to erect something here, at the Assistance League of Southern California, or at an alternative site. A decision was months away. Besides, did they really believe the city was in the business of distributing rubbers, needles, and alcohol to the public, particularly to a vulnerable population like them?

The spectacle of it—the orderly meeting waylaid by a rowdy intrusion, the vagrants' crestfallen expressions, the waved leaflets showing the party favors denied them—had the councilwoman's chief of staff flushed beet red. These bedraggled souls without five dollars to their names were lured under the false pretenses of a dirty trick. She contacted the LAPD to find whoever was responsible for organizing, in her charged rhetoric, such an "evil, horrendous deed."

Jerry 2.0 had everyone just where he wanted.

Now a pudgy estate developer and self-styled activist, he devised the bogus invitations as street theater to protest what he considered Goldberg's fiefdom tyranny. He had nothing morally against helping the downtrodden, in this instance by providing them job counseling, healthcare, and other services in a city cleaved by socioeconomic divide. He was just against doing it by ramming a center down the throats of a community afforded little input in the matter. To Jerry, this was egghead liberalism sure to depress local property values, including the five small buildings he owned in Goldberg's district, by fostering a seedy, crime-infested atmosphere. It's why he and his aides printed the pamphlets and slyly distributed them the prior Sunday.

He would readily admit his involvement, too, should the police question him about the kooky stunt. Then he would tell powerbrokers and the media to investigate why he instigated it. Should the facility open, Goldberg planned to bus in homeless daily from surrounding areas without making sufficient provisions about how to return them. If she succeeded, Jerry foresaw new liquor stores, flophouses, and petty crimes. Already-decaying Hollywood would further disintegrate, giving potential rise to a second Skid Row beyond downtown's Main Street. Somebody needed to stand up for longtime residents who would have to live next to what Goldberg beckoned in.

Jerry, with financial skin in the game and a sense of injustice in his veins, had anointed himself a civic pain in the ass. And he did it as a local, having moved inland from the coastal suburbs into one of his own Hollywood properties.

The politician whom Jerry humiliated, nonetheless, was no timid leader apt to cower in her office. Goldberg was one who normally made enemies shake. A rotund woman with apple cheeks and a blustery tone—one of California's first openly lesbian lawmakers—her legacy of dueling with entrenched interests for liberal causes earned her the nickname "Hurricane Jackie." Her baptism came in the 1960s Free Speech movement, and later on at the hidebound Los Angeles Unified School District, where she witnessed her allotment of political high jinks. Her negotiating prowess even stymied an orange-pompadoured celebrity developer (with an army of lawyers and lobbyists) from commandeering the grounds of the old Ambassador Hotel to construct America's tallest building, instead of converting it into a desperately needed high school.

But vanquishing Manhattan's Donald Trump gave Hurricane Jackie little insight into dealing with someone as original—or indecipherable—as Jerry. In addition to the apocryphal invites, he also wrote directly to the Assistance League's building owner on behalf of area businesses and residents, threatening to sue if he leased it for the homeless. Goldberg, who would later win a California Assembly seat, knew when she was beat. Shortly after that motley bunch whacked on the door, she abandoned the Gower Street locale as a potential candidate. Prolonging a skirmish with a crusader who'd resort to such left-field tactics on principle was toying with fire.

She should've known that was from her last rodeo with Jerry. The year before, in 1994, Goldberg threw her considerable heft behind a controversial Hollywood needle-exchange program managed by a nonprofit organization. Giving addicts turning in dirty needles a set of clean, unused ones, as well as distilled water and bleach, was lauded by experts as a practical way to temper AIDS-infection rates while coaxing junkies into treatment. Every Wednesday evening for six months, volunteers parked their Ford Bronco in front of Selma Elementary

School and did their work, and every time it made Jerry's blood boil. Again, he had no high-horse objection with the premise. He was just opposed to bringing the hard-drug world so close to a grade school without neighborhood input. In a *Los Angeles Times* article about the exchange, he lambasted it as "the height of stupidity."

Goldberg's people, bristling at his insinuation, tried to discredit him as the lone dissenter. Jerry knew that was poppycock and decided, this being the movie capital, to publicize the absurdity of the situation with cinematic flair. How? He armed old ladies and local Scientologists also perturbed about the exchange with video recorders and cameras to film what they saw. The nonprofit responded by camouflage, draping white sheets around the addicts entering and exiting the Bronco to block their faces from prying lenses. Jerry's activist auteurs got their shots anyway, and he shared the footage with area VIPs. Soon, the needle-swapping was shuffled off to a new street.

A common refrain arose: Who was this Jerry person?

Someone whose gothic past most couldn't comprehend. Someone out of obscurity, having the time of his life as a pinstriped do-gooder ascended from the tatters of the old him.

After jousting with Goldberg, Jerry was ready for a bigger stage, so he redirected his attention underground—to construction of Hollywood's stubby, $2 billion subway project. It was here he'd try to make his bones as a property-rights Robin Hood swinging his rapier for the trampled underfoot—without neglecting his own cut.

His Nottinghamshire were the dozens of office buildings and storefronts along Hollywood Boulevard destabilized by Metro Rail's gargantuan tunnel-boring machines. The subterranean shaking from them rippled upward like regular earthquakes, causing floors to sink, load-bearing walls to sag, sidewalks to crack, and landlords to binge Rolaids. The structural carnage there piggybacked on another Metro Rail debacle on the eastern edge of the boulevard, where a chunky sinkhole had recently split open.

As Jerry saw it, a public works projects costing taxpayers $300 million a mile shouldn't be riddled by contractors' incompetence and governmental indifference. To tally the wreckage, he walked the legendary street eyeballing everything from the splintered wooden floors at the kitschy Snow White Coffee Shop to the crumbling brass and terrazzo stars on the Hollywood Walk of Fame. Hearing reports about the damage, the agency in charge, the county's Metropolitan Transportation Authority (MTA), harrumphed that it was being inflated, first by sensationalizing journalists and then folks like Jerry, whom it belittled as a grandstanding "operator" fishing for deep pockets.

They would pay for that underestimation. Jerry, a businessman with little political experience, interviewed ten lawyers to represent Metro Rail victims for what would be a torrid fight against a formidable bureaucracy. The firm spearheaded by Thomas V. Girardi, which recently won a judgment for tens of millions of dollars in the California groundwater-poisoning case that made onetime paralegal Erin Brockovich an environmental rock star, was tapped. No longer, this pairing said, would the MTA dangle claimants lowball, take-it-or-leave-it settlements. They weren't kidding. Over the next few years, Jerry, the Girardi firm, and their associates hemmed together roughly three thousand affected property owners and merchants into a $2 billion class-action-like lawsuit that percolated into national news.

In September 1996, as subway work choked off more small businesses unable to entice customers into the dusty construction zone, Jerry outdid himself again. Many proprietors felt the MTA was still giving them the cold shoulder, only doling out funds to the well connected. Reading the situation, Jerry hatched something Mahatma Gandhi might have. He took a blind talent agent forced to vacate his drooping building on five minutes' notice and spotlighted his mistreatment where the political pooh-bahs could not ignore it. Tim Shumaker and his guide dog were positioned in front of then-Mayor Richard Riordan's city hall office for a two-day hunger strike.

The media lapped it up because, let's admit it, no one roots for Goliath. The MTA, under pressure from stagecraft depicting it as callous, released $2 million to assist entrepreneurs like Shumaker make their mortgage payments. Jerry's urban legend grew from there. When he strolled the boulevard afterward, shop owners, many of them foreigners and unshaven coots, bear-hugged him, then plied him with store trinkets. Some cooed he was their hero.

"You saved us!" they said.

Jerry, with his tailored suits and Rolls-Royce, was a different species than the rabble-rousers they'd encountered before. Typically, activists were a rumpled bunch that drove old Hondas, piled newspapers into apartments they struggled to afford, and wore mismatched plaid. Even fellow developers, one of them reputedly tied to the Russian mob, were bewildered why somebody who didn't have to willingly risked his neck raising Cain.

Executives for Metro Rail, a nascent, multibillion-dollar effort to pull commuters in the land of freeways out of their automobiles and into subway cars, would've preferred that Jerry remained mute. When he wouldn't, they tried to cow him into silence. After crossing legal swords once, the MTA's general counsel warned him that if he went through with his lawsuit, he would slink away from it "bankrupted." An employee for a contractor whose cut-rate practices Jerry publicized told him that he should "be afraid to walk the streets alone"—and that a remote ignition starter for his vehicle would be a wise purchase.

Decades earlier, Howard would have said something similarly disturbing. This time Jerry was better armed. He had stopped carrying a handgun for protection because he rediscovered self-confidence as his Kevlar.

•••

"THERE'S A NORTH HOLLYWOOD nightclub about to collapse," the stranger whispered over the phone that day in 1995. "Subway tunneling did it."

The tip rang at my desk at *The Los Angeles Daily News*, the only paper to write about the Chandler Boulevard execution sixteen years earlier. Another anti-MTA activist named John Walsh, a foul-mouthed, seersucker-wearing iconoclast with a talent for catching graft in phone-book-sized public documents, referred him to me. Intrigued by what the stranger said, I placed a few calls to confirm it. He was right.

During the next few years, Jerry became one of my best sources, feeding me scoops that led to front-page exposés on the subway. A boondoggle museum. Corporate welfare. Landmark neglect. I'd never met anyone as prolific, nor anyone whose network of government moles and community pot-stirrers leaked enough slimy deals to occupy a pod of FBI agents.

When not facilitating that, Jerry gleefully needled the Establishment.

His memory of disguising himself as a Levi's-clad construction grunt to throw Howard Garrett off his trail must've inspired him to lampoon his favorite political target. Around the time he started calling me, Jerry crashed a Democratic Party dinner by impersonating Goldberg in outlandish relief. To do it, he donned a plus-size tuxedo, floral vest, Beatles wig, and Rush Limbaugh mask, adding a sleeping bag and balloons under his clothes to imitate her girth. Cocktails in hands, guests there were unsure whether they were seeing a puffy Goldberg or a rubbery-faced imposter. One old crank believed it *was* her, yelling that the councilwoman should be embarrassed by "her" policies as Jerry giggled under his mask.

His real face was spreading around a town still licking its wounds from the 1992 Rodney King riots, the Northridge earthquake, O. J. Simpson's double-murder trial, and the collapse of the post-Cold War aerospace industry. Nobody could ruffle the feathers of officialdom like Jerry. He mailed the politicians whom he knew despised him, including Mayor Riordan, a modified dartboard with a grinning photo of himself in the middle and a reminder of the millions his crusading cost their bureaucracies. Back in his old digs, he advised residents contesting a North Hollywood urban renewal plan, which he deemed a "piggy bank" for insiders, on how to strangle it. His exhortation for property owners to seek reassessments weakened LA's Community Redevelopment Agency, deflating its budget to the tune of $300,000.

"It was an evolutionary time," Jerry told me when I pondered why he was moonlighting as an agitator. "I'd lost belief in society and could see evil in contractors willing to destroy communities. I also realized *I* could be a powerful guy. That I didn't have to be afraid anymore."

By then, he was no longer the babyface whom some Space Matters clients asked where his boss was or to bring them coffee. He had packed a doughy fifty pounds around his midsection and added a patchy beard and mustache. Those thick, brown curls of his twenties were now thinning, salt-and-pepper strands crowning a large, oval head. Edging Jerry's marble-green eyes were fine wrinkles shaped like miniature paw prints; puffy bags sat below. Before he divulged his past, I used to be struck how in a moment of reflection, an uncanny shadow swept across his cheeks.

Other than his clever antics and high batting average for being right with his tips, I knew precious little about him, though. Over two years, he breathed not a word about how he transformed himself from a picked-on Jewish kid from a throwaway section of LA into a successful developer/public advocate with an infectious cackle. Never once did he mention that he was the weak tip in a murder triangle. I guess he just fancied being a cipher.

•••

BY 1997, AFTER I RESIGNED from *The Daily News* to pen my first book and freelance stories, Jerry had flowered into a bonafide community star. Local reporters slotted him in as a turnkey source for quotes about LA's soft corruption. They sought him out for commentary about how absurd it was that Hollywood Boulevard remained a cesspool for sad people—panhandlers, runaways, hookers, drug addicts, conmen—rather than a buzzworthy investment overdue for a makeover. *Forbes* plastered his picture in an article about the sidewalk squalor and the ceaseless infighting over how to replace it with glamor.

"Garbage, garbage, and more garbage," Jerry told an *LA Times* reporter doing a ride-along with him in his Jaguar as he denounced rows of tacky souvenir shops, wig stores, and tattoo parlors. "You tell me, is this street ready for a Gap?"

The boulevard's slide disgusted him. Its future mesmerized him. Sometimes he prowled the blocks in a trench coat, listening for the crackle of subway workers' walkie-talkies or excoriating the suits who managed the Hollywood sign and the Walk of Fame. He attended raucous MTA meetings where John Walsh ripped board members with *ad hominin* attacks that'd make sailors blush, even as political aides moseyed up to me to anxiously ask what Jerry was probing next.

Wouldn't they like to know?

He soon formed Hollywood Damage Control and Recovery, which you might call a public-interest organization with private benefits. He staffed it with motivated people—former transit-agency bureaucrats, unemployed engineers, claims adjusters, gadflies with encyclopedic memories—full of specific expertise. Jerry's band of guerillas monitored Metro Rail and other public projects in FBI-style windbreakers and canary-yellow construction hardhats. He equipped them with seismographs, radar guns, sound meters, and gas-testing devices. Where data collection failed, the outfit practiced asymmetrical warfare. They slapped fake red tags from the "Metropolitan Terrorist Authority" on subway-compromised buildings. They paid street kids to chitchat with tunnel workers to discover if there were troubles brewing underground. In Jerry's most outrageous ploy to get the MTA chasing its tail, his people spread rumors of a vapory, superhero-like figure that scaled high walls to snap incriminating pictures of Metro Rail safety violations. "Tunnel Ninja" was its name.

Jerry and Girardi's multi-plaintiff lawsuit against the agency was no joke. While it was settled for far less than the $2 billion originally sought, the legal actions and embarrassing disclosures about the project that Jerry and others helped reveal slowed the money-eating subway to a crawl, lopping federal support for Metro Rail by ninety percent.

We'd gab for hours, Jerry and I, in the tumbledown tower where he kept an office. Our topics were always the same: real-estate-obsessed LA and the silly hypocrisies of elected officials. One day, he mentioned he'd heard about something fishy on a subject outside his wheelhouse, something about an East LA housing complex new to me too. Neither of us realized what we had.

Before long, I was working on an investigative piece for the *LA Weekly* about the Wyvernwood Garden Apartments, a labyrinth of two-story structures in a park-like setting of grassy commons and serpentine trails. With a capacity for ten thousand people, the funny-named compound was the largest privately owned housing compound west of Chicago. And below the surface of buildings in this urban bucolic was quiet danger.

Flaking, lead-based paint had sickened four children there and perhaps dozens more. Lead, associated with learning disabilities in children and other maladies, was the place's dirty secret, primed to spill into the open. Working-class Hispanics who constituted the bulk of Wyvernwood's renters were unable to persuade their landlord, Samuel Mevorach, to eliminate the sneaky toxin. He also disregarded their requests to plaster holes, fix their crummy heating, and exterminate cockroaches. Gangbangers who tagged walls with graffiti and tormented residents went un-rousted too.

Everybody knew that with LA's paucity of affordable housing, Wyvernwood was too valuable to mothball. Yet nobody realized how much backroom intrigue was aswirl allowing it to rot. Not until, that is, an anti-lead activist named Linda Kite heard about Jerry's muckraking reputation. She confided everything to him, who passed it along to yours truly.

Mevorach, facing citations and public-health inquiries, relied on Richard Alatorre, the longtime councilman representing the Boyle

Heights neighborhood where Wyvernwood was, to carry his water. He repeatedly intervened with the DA's office to keep it from filing criminal charges against Mevorach, who lived in Arcadia and had a fondness for racehorses. After Alatorre assisted then-DA Gilbert Garcetti, father of LA's current mayor, in winning reelection, Garcetti's office retreated from prosecuting Mevorach. The rationale: to give him time to literally get the lead out and sell the property to a reputable owner.

When my story tying Alatorre and the slumlord appeared, I had little idea of the kerosene I squirted. Months later, the LA Times picked up where I left off, reporting that Mevorach furtively—and illegally—handed Alatorre tens of thousands of dollars and arranged a sham lease for a condo. Alatorre, a swarthy, knuckle-brawling pol with a gravelly voice, was in quicksand. He sunk deeper into it after revelations of his alleged cocaine habit hit the press and the US Justice Department came calling about his finances. The next year, Alatorre disappointed his supporters by announcing he would not seek reelection. In doing so, the 2005 mayoral race lost its odds-on favorite to win. Antonio Villaraigosa, a slick-talking councilman with his own skeletons, got the job. And Jerry had tugged the thread making it possible.

Even after he delivered one of the prime stories of my career, I still couldn't tell you much about Jerry besides his contradictions. Like the fact that he parked his Jaguar and Rolls-Royce under a dingy skyscraper at the tourist-mobbed corner of Sunset Boulevard and Vine Street; that he kept a rathole office in the back when he claimed involvement in $200 million in real estate deals. I doubted that number. He just dodged the past. When I cajoled him to open up about it, he steered the conversation back to whatever agency he was plotting against at that moment. He'd erected a containment dome over himself.

For all that walling off, it was hard to dislike him, and dishonest to suggest he wasn't as original a character as LA's former eminence of exhibitionism himself, Paul Fegen. Jerry the public figure was a spinning carousel of personality, offering you enameled flashes of compassion and self-interest, dizzying you with whether he was an antihero or opportunistic prankster.

•••

ONE SUMMER DAY IN 1998, just before the Bill Clinton–Monica Lewinsky scandal exploded, Jerry finally unlatched the deadbolt on who he was. I'll never forget it. We were walking down Hollywood Boulevard on our way to lunch, weaving past a menagerie of fast-stepping people with no place to go. A ruddy vagabond gripping a half-strung banjo just passed us when Jerry said, ever so matter-of-factly, "Did you know that a double murderer chased me and my family?"

"Huh?" I responded, thinking he was testing if I was paying attention.

"Yeah, I had a partner killed. After that, I was in the crosshairs."

"Sure, you were, Jerry."

"No, I was. Really. My ex thinks it wrecked the old me. Turned me mistrustful."

"Are you saying this to make me think you're cool?"

"No, I'm saying it because it's true."

Jerry halted on the sidewalk, cocking his head. He said the ordeal unleashed the diabetes he wore an insulin pump to offset and sent his dreams skittering. Then he continued walking.

Braggadocio, I still figured. A pitiful bid for attention concocted from his lively imagination.

A little later, over greasy roast duck at a cheap Thai restaurant, Jerry ladled out more of his supposed backstory. My puckered grin communicated my doubt. I thought we were meeting for him to pass along another humdinger tip.

"Why don't you go to the courthouse and pull the trial records?" he said, tempting me.

"No thanks," I said. "This is weird."

"You have no idea. What do you have to lose checking the facts? If I'm wrong, you'll know I'm a patent liar."

I took a few bites of that disgusting food, feeling him stare.

"Fine," I finally said. "If it'll get you off my back, I'll waste a day in the archives."

"You'll see," he replied. "I had a partner murdered."

"Yeah, sure. Very funny."

Even in the restaurant's dim lighting, I spotted instigation in Jerry's eyes and detected, for the first time, almost a squiggle inside his irises. He knew exactly what I would uncover.

Before I grasped it all, a playful contest developed between us. I would dare Jerry to tell me something more bizarre about 1979, and then I would try to nail it down at the Hall of Records or in interviews. After months of this dare and check, my recourse was obvious. I needed to apologize to him for writing him off as another fabulist in a city of loudmouths.

"Don't beat yourself up," he said. "I wouldn't have believed it myself if I didn't live through it. Not that I wished I did."

Had Jerry known his mind games would tantalize me to write a book, or did he merely want me to admire him? Who knew with him? Time passed; I drifted onto other subjects; Jerry continued being Jerry.

In December 2001, all twenty floors of that wretched Hollywood high-rise where he rented his office plunged into darkness. A blown electrical transformer near the garage had conked out the power, spurring the city Fire Department to evacuate the building and red-tag it. Nobody was allowed to reenter it to grab their files, computers, and other belongings from the quarantined structure. Months later, tenants worried that they would lose their businesses, and with no income, maybe their homes. Stories appeared questioning the city's klutzy handling of the situation. One of the building's foreign owners, a scowling man named Roy, unsuccessfully tried to unload the property. Squatters then broke in and vandalized the suites. Besieged officials finally relented to let folks grab some of their stuff if they took the stairs, not the scariest elevator you'd ever rode on in the best of times. The landlord blamed the outage on a fried transformer on the public grid. Tenants disagreed, contending an illegal rooftop air conditioner triggered the short circuit.

Everything lined up for Jerry's intervention, understanding as he did the fatal ramifications of unheeded warnings. Months before the building went dark, he had written to the city expressing detailed concerns about the property's safety. Particularly alarming to him was what would happen if a fire that started in the elevator shaft fluted up to the penthouse nightclub. Dozens could burn in a deathtrap above Sunset Boulevard. Jerry vowed to take his warning public and hold officials accountable should disaster strike.

LA's fire chief ignored Jerry's threat. He adapted as only he could.

He banded renters together into a creditor's association that effectively tossed the building's owners into bankruptcy. Because of that, they paid settlements enabling tenants to extricate themselves from their leases. Everyone received a check except for muckraking Jerry. But he received something better: his wider protests about fire-prone high-rises led to inspections and a renewed focus on them citywide. His past had taught him how to knock adversaries off-balance.

CHAPTER TWENTY-THREE
JERRY'S KINGDOM OF SAND

FROM THAT BLACKED-OUT SKYSCRAPER, Jerry left Hollywood for good, relocating into a post-modern castle. His new office on Lacy Street was just off the Harbor Freeway in a drab industrial sector beneath the hill on which Dodger Stadium is perched. The facade was industrial aesthetic expressed in corrugated metal and bubble glass belying the large square footage inside. It appeared bulletproof.

Visitors entered an interior sparseness of large, black airducts overhead and smoothed concrete floors. This stark minimalism shouted money being made hand over fist, like a billionaire so rich he doesn't carry credit cards, and Jerry was.

He began accumulating his fortune as he transitioned away from creating blueprints for other people's benefit and into property acquisition and real-estate management for himself. Painful as it was, he pulled the plug on Space Matters, after it's twenty-plus-year life, and founded Creative Environments with a partner whose background he thoroughly vetted. What timing, too. Jerry jumped into the lucrative, urban-loft market just as planners were devising ways to encourage more city living and less corrosive suburban sprawl.

His lofts, like ice cream, came in assorted flavors—multilevel, one-floor retail, gallery setups, art studios. They could be decorated in "industrial chic" or "contemporary rustic." They were adaptable to filmmaking, live theater, or design work. It was a splash of vertical New York in horizontal Southern California. Some of these units were housed in onetime movie studios in zip codes that most of today's stars wouldn't be caught dead in without security.

Jerry, though, was enchanted by underutilized, overlooked properties, seeing gems where others saw quick tear-downs. Creative Environments did something right, filling a trophy case with medals for design, community citizenship, and historic preservation. One citation was presented by the institution that Jerry had regularly flummoxed: LA city hall.

His own office was ensconced in the middle of the building the way a nucleus is situated in a cell. His desk was solid granite, assuming you could see it under his paper tsunami, his furniture bright red Italian leather. Wall-to-ceiling glass dominated one set of walls, with three glass doors wrapping around. Know Jerry's story and you'd know that wasn't by accident. He wanted to observe what was happening. And a ton was.

He was still perpetually late, and when he did waddle in, his secretary and underlings trailed behind their shambling monarch. Throughout the day, they barged in to pick his brain to solve a development hurdle or share a victory anecdote. Jerry rarely grew mad at their interruptions, unless it was for show.

Despite his newfound riches and success, he was neither fully healed nor totally rebooted. Now that I'd rope-lined down into his history, I understood why his hands never stilled, why his eyes never settled. His signature cackle coexisted with a spirit that never fully recovered from 1979. Indeed, some of the qualities of the men who redirected his trajectory from its appointed destination leached into him. From Richard, Jerry practiced optics to razzle-dazzle those he needed to awe. From Howard, he absorbed the benefits of three-steps-ahead thinking—and the imperative to conduct business only with those who valued human life as little more than Styrofoam.

Whenever Jerry saw "Big," the devastatingly handsome and chronically flighty character on the HBO series *Sex and the City*, he told me that he instantly thought of Richard. That he remained enamored with his old partner, and was guilt-ridden he had been unable to rescue

Richard from himself. Jerry amused others with his gallows-humor double entendre—"you know, I had a partner killed"—but you got the impression it was levity reflecting his need to bring salvation to someone else for his *own* moral reclamation.

One beneficiary was a person from a world apart fom his: a former hardcore gang member who'd heard community folklore about Jerry's triumphs over the mighty MTA. Now out of prison, the ex-street soldier fantasized about opening a confection shop on Hollywood Boulevard, yet lacked the nitty-gritty knowledge of how to prosper. Jerry, admiring the man's grit to remake himself into something honorable, gave him a crash course in filing his first tax return, applying for a bank loan, and guarding profits. And, thanks partly to Jerry, profits there were.

Not everyone who approached him for assistance met his criteria for granting it. When one investor approached him, Jerry snooped into his background, concluding that he was a "scary guy without a conscience," and showed him the door. The stimulating thing about these days is that you never knew who would walk through it next.

A wealthy, pint-sized Chinese woman, delighted with how Jerry sold a piece of disputed land for her, afterward gave him money to invest. Her friends followed, eventually allowing Jerry to hoard the cash to acquire a succession of older buildings in or near downtown, Hollywood, East LA, Eagle Rock, even his old stomping grounds in the Miracle Mile.

His Chinese investor connected Jerry to something else too besides a fat payday. She gave him perspective. In the 1970s, she had netted big sums selling frozen egg rolls that she'd perfected deep frying and packaging to the US food conglomerates. Mobsters who decided they'd steal her business decided to incentivize her with icicles. They locked her in a commercial freezer unless she signed away her company. She wouldn't. Years after that incident, the egg roll queen refused to let it poison her resourceful, generous impulses, believing the good-hearted of LA outnumbered its barbarians. Jerry thanked her for the lesson.

One barbarian from Jerry's past was Howard's hitman, Johnny Williams, by then a long timer at Corcoran State Prison. Unsurprisingly, he coveted his last years outside its walls. And predictably, the parole board denied it at various hearings after state psychologists classified him as antisocial, depressed, and a moderate threat to society. He died in 2004—without ever receiving the sealed letter requesting an interview that I'd long wavered about sending him. Another roughneck, the bulldozer-steering, ex-Israeli commando who aided Jerry through the spring of '79, departed too. Ari Allon died in a suspicious fire.

Not only had Jerry outlived the characters of March '79, he transformed from being a local real-estate entrepreneur into a global businessman no longer much interested in entertaining activism or urban revitalization. (At least Hollywood got its foothold development with construction of a honking, five-story shopping center, valued in the hundreds of millions of dollars, decorated in a Babylonian theme.) The cash now rolled in at a breathtaking pace, and it bored him.

"Making money," he would say, "is a lot like sex. It's more fun when you do it with someone else."

He adopted his own creed in transactions around the world. In Japan, for example, he paired with the former chief of Sumitomo Corporation's US operations on a hotel, nightclub, and aquarium near Disneyland Tokyo. He invested in generating electricity in Ghana, a dirt-poor, war-ravaged country on Africa's west coast, through a solar-power farm ringed with modular housing. If you added up everything before the Great Recession wiped out so much, Jerry was involved in close to $2 *billion* worth of deals and property. Just don't expect to know where that money resided.

"You won't find my name listed prominently in the records," he once told me, "because I've been threatened with financial annihilation by the politicians and developers I ve gone after. But if they want to come after me, they can. I have had nastier people than them chasing me."

Under Jerry's rules, all deliveries were sent to his office and associates were not permitted to visit his comfortable Valley house.

His staff interacted with construction subcontractors as Jerry never forgot about being burned by one in particular.

•••

A MEANDER THROUGH HIS Lacy Street mothership was a tour through an eventful past. Lawrence, the same easygoing assistant with him when he declared war on the MTA, never left. Bert, the loyal draftsman that Howard tried ingratiating himself with, was down the hall. For a spell, the "kid" at the place was equally recognizable: Jerry's oldest son, Jude, the one marked for kidnapping. His other grown children excelled as Jude did before he transitioned into insurance, with jobs on Wall Street, in law firms, and in other professions. Once in a while, Richard Alatorre, the politician whose mayoral aspirations Jerry helped end over the Wyvernwood scandal, dropped by for consulting work. Jerry believed he needed some human rehabbing.

Deep into the aughts, the rarely dull life of sixty-year-old Jerry Schneiderman pulsated with contentment, workaholic hours, and personal bounties. He was now married to a third wife, a short-haired, younger woman (his former real estate litigator) with whom he had an adorable toddler son. Group dinners were fun and boisterous, reality-television caliber. Besides his kids' families, often attending were his two ex-wives, including Tammy, who long ago returned to LA from Michigan, and their spouses. Strangers whom he took under his flabby wing like Richard's widow, Paige, sometimes made appearances. He was living his own adaptation of the film *Big Fish*.

There was but one shred of unfinished business, in my unsolicited view, for him to bury. It was about character. About blood and consequences. While this book steamed toward completion, I pestered Jerry to hop into his car to confront the man who unlocked the cage of the reptile whose ghost continued stalking him. That phantom, I at last understood, was *the* source of the faint, if clingy vibration that still beat under his skin like a rhythmic inflammation stymieing his inner peace. Keeping him from leisure. Jerry needed to whack on Vic Platte's door, banging it off its hinges if he must. The purpose: telling him that he knew the putrid truth.

Before joining Space Matters in 1978, Howard had generated many of his paystubs from freelancing construction at Smythe & Hargill. One of his jobs, though, was of a private nature, off-book—a face-lift at Platte's West LA residence. It was bound to end badly. Howard, conscious that Platte controlled what future assignments went his way, supervised the installation of new windows and hinged doors, and personally did carpentry work and supplemental painting there. He billed the work "at cost," which meant no windfall for him.

His sweat, in effect, was a down payment on goodwill.

It's just that Platte wasn't satisfied with the quality, raising objections to someone only months removed from torching a person in the Yucaipa desert. The two argued about the remodel in a squabble that may have concluded with Howard threatening his sometimes-boss. Days later, Platte noticed smoke corkscrewing above his garage. The contactor at odds with him, it seems, had decided to play arsonist as an acrid reminder never to contest him again.

Platte wouldn't, never uttering a word about this to Richard when he phoned for a recommendation about the foreman. Had he possessed a fragment of spine, Platte would've warned Richard to steer a million miles clear of him—an act that might've spared Richard from having gunmen crouching on his sun deck and dozens of others from tumbling into the chasm it opened. By saying nothing except that Howard was solid, Platte's expedient amnesia saved only one person: himself.

In 1980, between the time of Howard's arrest and his trial, Platte delicately approached Jerry at a social event, confessing everything in case the detectives who'd interviewed him didn't tell Jerry. They did.

"Please!" he said in a plaintive whimper. "Don't mention my name on the stand. Howard could hear you, and he *never* forgets."

Disgusted, furious at the symmetry of the request, Jerry wasn't certain what he would do. Platte wanted insulation from the sequence that he set in motion. Jerry let him perspire for a moment, saying nothing before walking away and then never repeating anything about the jerk.

The court docket does not appear to have any record of the executive speaking at trial.

I tried whipping Jerry into a tizzy that the moment was right to accost the man who passed an apex predator down the line like a hot potato. After everything, he'd earned the right to verbally reduce him to bone and gelatin. Who was more responsible for this ocean of despair: an emotionally tortured underachiever like Richard, or a mentally sound coward like Platte? Jerry had always beaten himself up for not mouthing "don't shoot" to get SWAT sharpshooters to take out Howard near the La Brea Tar Pits. But he needn't have regretted forgetting to say something that he never should've needed to.

"Let's go," I said. "I'll drive. You unload."

Jerry contemplated it for a minute, vibration and all.

"I can't," he told me with a wistful laugh. "That's not me. Besides, it'd probably backfire on both of us. What if we went to jail? Wouldn't that be rich?"

The former gadfly that I'd first met as a journalist in the mid-1990s was showing his critics who he was. We both agreed that Platte would creep toward his judgment day with a spotted conscience.

How could Jerry embrace this position? Because, I guess, he knew better than the average person that space matters—as in the space to reclaim what goodness you have after life invariably saws you in half. That evil's worst side effect is the innocence it filches without permission. Jerry, while a grateful survivor, must've accepted that he'd never be whole.

•••

LIKE 1979, 2011 WAS turning out to be a bitch of a year for him. Many of his business opportunities, be they in real estate or foreign properties, were either slipping away or gone.

"Bad times," he'd sigh, eyebrows collapsing. "Lots of complications."

He was more dejected than I'd seen him in some time. Asked about the state of his company, or supposed deals in the hopper—for sugar, diamonds, land, you never knew—he practiced the art of deflection, as Howard's defense attorneys mastered. Either that, or he pivoted to what we both knew were pie-in-the-sky plans to partner with the Chinese government in California's solar-panel market. When he tried smirking that he would make it happen, a frown followed.

By winter of the year that saw Apple's Steve Jobs die and the killing of Osama bin Laden, Jerry's haphazard efforts to protect the assets that he divvied up into corporate trusts was eclipsed by something more urgent.

His health was spiraling downward faster than his net worth. Some months earlier, he suffered a minor stroke while driving. He now required his secretary to drive him and a cane to steady a faltering gait. He cracked wry about his concessions to a new reality because it was easier to joke than to commit himself to radical lifestyle changes.

For years, loved ones had implored, sobbed, and upbraided him to take better care of himself. But this now was a fail-safe point. If he intended to live into his seventies and beyond, he needed to improve his diet, blood-sugar maintenance, lack of exercise—and stop cavorting with sketchy, hard-partying associates he told himself contained potential. Failure to adapt, either by perpetuating his self-destructive habits, or acting blasé at his prospect of personal reformation, would signal mortal exhaustion, if not surrender at the hand life dealt him.

I too nagged Jerry with choir-boy bromides about all he had to live for, especially Teddy, the little boy that was his mini-me. Hearing this, he would mutter, often with a fatalistic grin, that it was too late for course corrections. I deluded myself that he'd recover, for he'd made a routine of evolving himself.

His inability—or refusal—to get himself well through perseverance exacted its toll. That fall, he underwent emergency surgery at a Glendale hospital to drain fluid from a swollen brain. He must've believed he would be okay because when he awoke from the operation, he faked being paralyzed for the momentarily horrified relatives ringing his bed. When I visited him three days later, he looked nothing like the merry prankster I knew, grunting and straining just to hoist himself up in bed. I assured him he would be back in the office saddle in no time. He waved me off, waddling toward the bathroom like he was a thousand years old.

The next time I saw Jerry, on December 4, 2011, he was too frail to remove the small palm tree that toppled across his front door after a howling windstorm. We sat in his house as he told me how much he hoped I'd benefit from retelling his story, and I wished him likewise. Though his pallor was egg white, his mind was lucid, and a picaresque light, thankfully, jitterbugged again through his eyes.

In his driveway, we shook hands. Jerry's affection could be sneaky, for he often saw the originality in people before they licensed themselves.

"Thanks for coming out," he said.

Yeah, he would rebound. He franchised the concept.

Seventy-two hours later, I learned the inevitable on Facebook while buying lunch.

Jerry was found dead at home on December 7—Pearl Harbor day. It felt like a tire iron to the back of my neck. I slumped against the restaurant wall. I could still hear his cackle.

•••

HIS MEMORIAL WAS CONDUCTED at Mount Sinai Memorial Park near Forest Lawn the next Sunday. If the measure of a man is the size of his funeral, Jerry measured up superbly. Hundreds attended in a crowd so large that dozens spilled out into the auxiliary chamber.

Jerry's widow and two ex-spouses paid pithy tributes to him, leavening the glum mood with anecdotes about his quirky habits and practical jokes. When one of them lofted the dartboard with his photo on it that he sent to LA politicians, laughter undulated through the pews. His sons and nephew then spoke glowingly about his principled shenanigans. Creative, maddening, rascally, unpredictable: that was him. Nostalgia and grief, however, were not the sole emotions. Many there with briny tears and grim mouths were irate that Jerry blasted off unnecessarily before his time. Before others who loved him were ready to let him go. I was one of them.

Everyone's world was suddenly less interesting.

At his gravesite, I tried picking out faces under the windless, chilly skies that mirrored the collective mood. I wondered if any old Hollywood Boulevard crazies or Space Matters' alumni snuck in. Maybe a politico there to bid a grudging farewell to a worthy adversary? If not them, perhaps one of his Dragnet duo PIs, or Paul Fegen, who gave up real estate to practice magic (sometimes with his reluctant cat). At least no one had to fret about any graybeard killer showing up.

One person I did recognize was the gang-chief-turned-cookie-shop merchant. He stood near Jerry's coffin speaking in sullen tones, as if his own magnetic north was contained inside that box. Another longtime associate, he of the polyester-pants/dyed-hair cadre, fidgeted. While the rabbi recited a final prayer, he loudly whispered a sweet memory of Jerry to me. When he turned away, I noticed his features smushed in on themselves like a toothless hillbilly. Shock glazed other colleagues, who, after all, had lost not only an incomparable rascal but also the IQ connected to it that'd feathered their nests.

Once the dirt was shoveled on his casket and other Jewish rituals observed, mourners dispersed with heads tucked down, car keys jangling in the heavy air. Jerry's widow kindly invited me to the shiva; I couldn't bring myself to attend, though, remembering Jerry's account of attending the wake after Richard's murder. Somehow, the sequence here felt just as annihilating.

Numb, I plopped into my car and wound out of the cemetery. At the Ventura Freeway onramp, I debated cruising over to the house on

Chandler Boulevard. Give it one last glimpse to curse the bullet that first soared through Richard's sliding glass window, then continued streaking through the lives of scores of the people entwined with him. Damn thing might as well have been a rocket-propelled grenade. I couldn't do it.

Instead, I drove home, shucked my dark suit, and wept like a child in the knowledge that none of this needed to be.

Howard, you animal, look what *you* did!

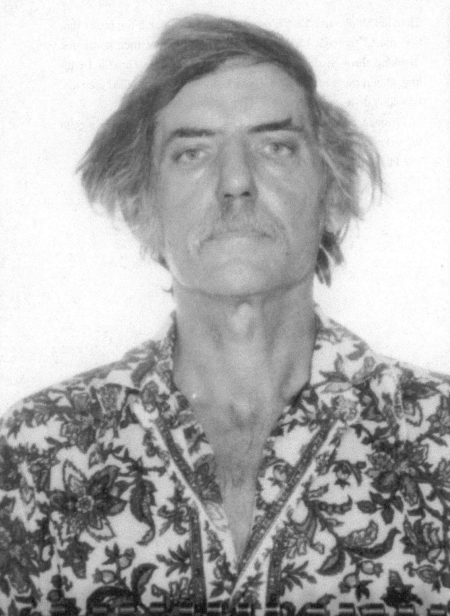

BK 5 2 4 3 7 9 9 05 11 7

Howard Garrett

LOS ANGELES POLICE VNY

Johnny Williams

K5252301   05-18-79

⚞S ANGELES POLICE⚟   VNY-M

	J #		LA #	
CRIME REPOR. INFO	CRIM'S OCCUPATION, DESCENT, AGE			

ARRESTEE'S NAME (LAST, FIRST, MIDDLE) MT: YES
GARRETT, HOWARD LANDIS

ADDRESS 2445 E. DELMAR BLVD #207 PASADENA **CITY** **SEX** M

DESCENT	HAIR	EYES	HEIGHT	WEIGHT	BIRTHDATE	AGE
WHT	BRN	GRN	6-01	180	9-25-32	46

VEH. LIC. NO NONE **STATE** **R.D.** O/S **AKA/NICKNAME** "PAT"

BIRTHPLACE (CITY & STATE) MT VERNON, MO. **PROB INV UNIT** **JUV. DETAINED AT** ADULT **AD. CHG** NO

DR # → 79-500 014

AREA/TEAM OR DIV./DET. ARREST'G /VNYS DETS **DATE & TIME ARRESTED** 5-11-79 0720 **TIME BKD** 1110

LOCATION OF ARREST 2445 E. DELMAR BLVD #207 **BAIL, INC. PA** NO BAIL

TYPE | CHARGE (SECTION, CODE, DEFINITION) F | 187 PC (MURDER) FC WARR **WARRANT NO.**

LOCATION CRIME COMMITTED 13416 CHANDLER BLVD

SOCIAL SECURITY NO. 557-40-8870 **OBSERVABLE PHYSICAL ODDITIES** MUSTACHE PANTHER TT LEFT ARM SKULL TT RT ARM **OCCUPATION-GRADE** GENERAL CONT

EMPLOYER (FIRM OR PERSON'S NAME, CITY & PHONE / SCHOOL) SELF EMPLOYED GARRETT & ASSOCIATES (20 YRS) 20 YRS **SPECIAL MEDICAL PROBLEM** SEE MT

CLOTHING WORN MULTI SHT, BRN PNS, BRN SHS **EXACT LOCATION-DISPOSITION ARRESTEE'S VEHICLE** NONE

LIST CONNECTING RPTS BY TYPE & IDENTIFYING NOS. CRIME-DEATH-EVID SAME DR# **VEHICLE USED (YEAR, MAKE, MODEL, TYPE, COLORS, LIC. NO., ID MARKS)** NONE

COMPLAINTS-EVID. OF ILLNESS-INJ - BY WHOM TREATED DR GILCHRIST **DRIVING VEH. (DIRECTION & NAME OF STREET) AT OR BETWEEN STREETS**

CODE: V - VICTIM (FIRM NAME IF BUSINESS) W - WITNESS P/A - ARRESTING PRIVATE PERSON **ON JUVENILES ONLY:** P - BOTH PARENTS

NAME (INCL. DOB & AGE OF VICTIM OF CRIME VS. PERSON)		ADDRESS	CITY	PHONE
V	RICHARD	RES. / BUS. DECEASED		
		RES. / BUS.		
		RES. / BUS.		
		RES. / BUS.		

AT THE TIME THIS REPORT WAS COMPLETED WERE THERE: ORAL OR WRITTEN STATEMENTS? BY DEFT. Y N BY WITS Y N TAPE RECORDINGS? OF DEFT: Y N OF WITS: Y N PHOTOS? OF DEFT (EXCEPT BKG.): Y N OF VICT: Y N PHOTO

SUPERVISOR (signature) **SERIAL NO.** 1193 **REPORTING OFFICER(S)** TOHIESON, R.L. **SERIAL NO(S)** 14219 **AREA/TEAM OR DIV./DETAIL** VNY SLS

DATE/TIME REPRODUCED 5-11-79 **DIV./CLERK** HUMPHRY, W.E. 14640

USE CONT. SHEET FOR NARRATIVE - AS PER INSTRUCTIONS ON BACK OF THIS PAGE BELOW SECTION TO BE COMPLETED BY INV

COMMENTS OF INVESTIGATOR - IF REFERRED, INCLUDE NAME OF AGENCY AND PERSON ACCEPTING REFERRAL

11 ☐ C&R	12 ☐ REL. INSUF. EVID	03 ☐ PROBATION	10 ☐ DEPT. MENTAL HEALTH	**INVESTIGATING OFFICER**
11 ☐ ACTION SUSP	03 ☐ COMMUNITY SERVICE	05 ☐ OTH. LAW ENF. AG'Y.	16 ☐ DPSS	
14 ☐ PROVED ADULT	15 ☐ PTI	18 ☐ JUV. TRF - MISD	☐ OTHER.	**SUPERVISOR APPROVING**

COUNTY OF LOS ANGELES
OFFICE OF THE DISTRICT ATTORNEY
BUREAU OF BRANCH AND AREA OPERATIONS
150 WEST COMMONWEALTH AVENUE
ALHAMBRA, CALIFORNIA 91801
(213) 570-1160

JN K. VAN DE KAMP, DISTRICT ATTORNEY
EPHEN SPANGLER TROTT, CHIEF DEPUTY DISTRICT ATTORNEY
HNNIE L COCHRAN, JR., ASSISTANT DISTRICT ATTORNEY

JACK D. CRAVENS, DIRECTOR

November 21, 1980

W. H. Damerell
Department of Corrections
Special Service Unit
3415 Fletcher Avenue
El Monte, CA 91731

To Whom It May Concern:

This letter is to indicate the Los Angeles County District Attorney's Office's concern regarding the incarceration at the same facility of John Harold Williams and Howard Landis Garrett.

John H. Williams presently is an inmate at San Quentin doing 25 - Life for first degree murder. I believe his hearing date is February 6, 1996.

Williams testified at the murder trial of Howard Landis Garrett, who is presently awaiting sentencing November 26, 1980, Department NWT, Judge Leonard Wolfe, on 1st. degree murder with two special circumstances; conspiracy to commit murder, solicitation of murder, and attempted extortion.

I would anticipate Garrett's sentence to be life without possibility of parole.

If Garrett is to be considered as an inmate of San Quentin, I would respectfully submit that Williams' safety would be in jeopardy and would recommend a facility such as CMC - East.

Williams' testimony in the case was devastating to Garrett.

Respectfully,

JOHN K. VAN DE KAMP
District Attorney

By
Jeffrey C. Jonas
Deputy-in-Charge
Alhambra Area Office

vlf

MEMORANDUM

TO: BILLY D. WEBB, Director
                Bureau, Branch and Area Operations

FROM: SHELDON H. BROWN, Assistant Director
                Bureau, Branch and Area Operations

SUBJECT: SPECIAL CIRCUMSTANCE PENALTY EVALUATION
                Peo. v. Howard Landis Garrett
                Case No. A 142639

DATE: AUGUST 23, 1979

I have reviewed the material forwarded by the Van Nuys Office in the Garrett matter and agree with their evaluation
that this is a proper case for the pleading of special circumstances and the imposition of the death penalty.

In the case at hand, the defendant apparently hired an assassin to eliminate the victim. Further, conduct on behalf
of this defendant indicates another apparent execution attempt that was thwarted by the arrival of the police. Ad-
ditionally, he was charged and tried for a murder in San
Bernardino County for which he was acquitted in 1978.

Since the acquittal on the 1978 murder charge, he has continued to engage in conduct that displays a callous disregard
for the sanctity of human life. It is highly unlikely that
he can be rehabilitated. The protection of society and de-
terrence to others would be served by seeking the death penalty in this matter.

lg

Att.

ACKNOWLEDGMENTS

REAL-LIFE HORROR STORIES HAVE a tendency of outliving their initial horror, and this tale was no different. It was shaped into a book only through the extraordinary willingness of people webbed into a *Kafkaesque* 1979 murder triangle to share their memories. I am honored that so many opened up to me, knowing that most of them spent years trying to forget the painful ordeal that I was pressing them to remember in detail. Jerry's family—the woman married to him throughout this bedlam, the now-widow who lived it vicariously, and the son who might have been butchered by it—couldn't have been more gracious. The victim's first wife—the lady who still sobs for him and carries his name forty-one years after losing him—bravely shared her recollections. It was her dream that in taking me back to that gruesome era Richard's daughters might better understand him. Except for a member of the Kasparovs who misrepresented himself as an attorney who intended to sue me—for telling demonstrable truths—not a single person shooed me away.

Members of the Argentinean family swept up as well by these events were equally welcoming, and their resilient spirit shines. Besides the Buonsanti family, my appreciation goes out to Armand Arabian; Mike Consol; Paul Fegen; Dave Ferris; David Honda; Kay Lang; Richard Lehman; Brie Levine; Bert Makabali; Rick Nathanson; Carol Rosenthal; Dominick Smacchia; Carlos Villalvazo; Ken Vorzimer; Marc Wax; Sharon White; Alex Young; and a woman named Arlene.

Former Los Angeles Police Department detectives Richard Jamieson and Howard Landgren provided crisp, helpful recollections. The lead prosecutor in the case, retired Los Angeles County Assistant District Attorney Jeffrey Jonas, was my shepherd in understanding the bigger picture of trauma and triumph. Tyson Cornell and the staff at Rare Bird Books never wavered in their hustle and their belief. And I could always count on my longtime friend Steve Eames of the *Los Angeles Times* for his wonderful copyediting. As always, my loving wife, Kate, and daughters, Samantha and Lauren, were there to catch me and prop me up during this book's winding journey to publication.

To all of them, and those I neglected to mention, you have my eternal thanks. May you always stand confidently in front of windows.

NOTE TO READERS

CHRONICLING A DATED MURDER and the human tapestry woven into it requires the donning of a lot of hats. The writer must be a storyteller, historian, truth seeker, and busybody searching for coherence where it doesn't always exist. As such, the tale presented here is not a formal journalistic rendition of what happened because who can say confidently what the absolute truth of any calamity is? I compiled this book by conducting thirty-plus interviews and combing through thousands of pages of court testimony, police documents, prosecutorial memos, business memos, personal correspondence, and photographs.

There are other things you should know. Almost all of the dialogue and the majority of background settings were approximated based on participants' recollections, witness testimony, and other knowable facts. When presented with conflicting accounts of the same event or a disputed timeline, I chose what I judged was the most probable scenario. Some of the written materials included were edited for brevity.

I also made promises to certain people that I'd provide them and their family with a measure of privacy. Because of this and other factors, I altered the names of about one quarter of the characters in these pages and modified one's physical description. None of the names changed are public figures, government officials, or anyone formally charged with a crime. The following names were modified in whole or part: Tammy, Jude, and Daphne Schneiderman; Richard, Paige, Rebecca, and Rachel Kasparov; Ari Allon; Mikey Krakow; Benjamin Wynn; Nicholas Torrini; Victor Platte; and the company referenced as Smythe & Hargill. Again, these are names that I invented exclusively for this book and any resemblance to real individuals in any way is inadvertent. Dollar values represented here are from their respective periods except where indicated.

While I am not including a bibliography, I want to acknowledge the publications from which I drew background material and a few specific quotes. These include *Bloomberg*; *The Daily News of Los Angeles*; the *Los Angeles Times*; *Los Angeles Magazine*; *Los Angeles CityBeat*; *LA Weekly*; *The Los Angeles Business Journal*; and *Forbes*. Two books by Kevin Roderick were also helpful: *The San Fernando Valley: America's Suburb* (Los Angeles Times Books, 2001) and *Wilshire Boulevard: Grand Concourse of Los Angeles* (Angel City Press, 2005).

PAUL & CHUCK

A Lonely Hero, A Secret Demagogue, and the Violent End of a California Dystopia

EVERYBODY, IT SEEMS, WAS watching the little white house on Bollinger Drive: pretty divorcées and kids on bikes, electronics whizzes and the LAPD. Everybody was keeping a lookout for sinister activity at the request of the owner, a feather-haired lawyer on edge after the creepy cult he helped expose promised to pay him a visit. Sure, it sounded melodramatic—killers skulking about a coastal town of rustic stores and quiet streets.

And still there was that lurking green Plymouth carrying two men up front and three associates in the trunk.

A real estate appraiser, who'd just stopped by a nearby corner market for a frosty drink, was the first to be alarmed by the otherwise drab sedan. The first to intuit there was something fishy. Here he was, idling behind it at a Pacific Palisades red light, unable after numerous attempts to decipher the seeming vanity license plate: 27 IVC. What, he asked himself, could those five characters possibly represent? *At twenty-seven I varoomed to California?* Something about Ventura County? His puzzle-solving brain worked the variations.

Then, by staring harder, Les Rahymer knew.

This wasn't cutesy, aluminum-engraved wordplay. It was flagrant deception. Lamely applied classic-blue tape—tape the same ubiquitous hue as the plate's background—concealed a "4" before the "27" and blurred the "G" into a "C." Snap!

The dark-haired thirty-something sat in his black Datsun 280Z prickled with goose bumps. After the suspicious vehicle motored nonchalantly away on Baylor Avenue, he wasn't sure what to do: tail it like a real-life Jim Rockford (whose TV series filmed blocks away)? No, he was supposed to glance into his rearview mirror, where, by sheer happenstance, a Los Angeles Police Department cruiser was whipping left onto Sunset Boulevard like him.

"Did you see that car with the tampered license plates?" Rahymer blurted after waving the patrol officer over. "Write down these numbers before I forget them."

Officer David Ybarro jotted as told and even sketched the passengers' likenesses from the good Samaritan's description. It was a wickedly hot October afternoon in 1978, a day before the World Series commenced at Dodger Stadium amid bunting and beer commercials.

Wait! Did he say an early seventies model Plymouth Executive? If so, Ybarro himself had noticed the car earlier while serving an unrelated subpoena. He'd assumed it was an undercover narcotics vehicle pursuing marijuana traffickers or coke dealers selling snow-white tans. When he called dispatch, it said the car was registered to the group Synanon at its Visalia outpost, a small farming town in the San Joaquin Valley.

Synanon? *Shazbot*, as any fan of *Mork & Mindy* would say: not good. Especially after the dude in the sleek Japanese import took off before Ybarro could record his contact information.

Ybarro, who walked a beat in this sun-glistened suburb a few minutes from Will Rogers State Beach, whistled for backup. Two LAPD colleagues arrived to hear him out, then departed, unconcerned. Out of precaution, another pair rolled past the lawyer's ranch-style home on Bollinger with bougainvillea out back, observing nothing abnormal. Ybarro, even so, couldn't shake the butterflies that diabolical events were in motion. A few minutes later, *he* was on Bollinger, counseling a boy on his bike to immediately call the LAPD if he spotted that Chrysler.

At shift's end, Ybarro wrote up his notes on a form. Only the next day would his report surface—in a department trash can, ignored.

•••

CHARLES DEDERICH, SYNANON'S BEARDED, pear-shaped leader, was about the last demagogue you wanted to rile in a Los Angeles ornery behind its Ray-Bans. A decade earlier, he'd been a kind of pied piper of clean living, transforming a dinghy Santa Monica club that sobered people up through acerbic group therapy into a multimillion-dollar alternative society legitimized by Hollywood and recognized by the courts.

"Today is the first day of the rest of your life," he told the desperate, pollinating gruff messiah with Hallmark cards pitchman.

But that "today" was metaphorical. In the here and now, Dederich was less America's visionary of abstinence than niche emperor—a one-man cult of personality pushed to the brink to consolidate his unraveling California fiefdom. One technique derived from the college dropout's appreciation of history: when internal cracks form among the troops, rally them by blaming—and demonizing—outsiders. Never a subtle man, the gravelly voiced Dederich did just that, heaping so much bombast at critics of his group's spiral into sexual deviancy, militancy, and other excesses that you'd expect FBI agents to have his photograph centered on a bulletin board.

Like a graying Shakespearean character, he had become what he once condemned about society *writ large*: power-hungry to maintain a status quo that'd enriched him.

And of all the dangers to his precarious reign, no one surpassed the swarthy do-gooder who lived on Bollinger. Not self-righteous journalists questioning his generous salary and shrinking membership. Not code inspectors investigating allegations of child abuse. Not defectors horrified at Synanon's bloodlust agenda. At an age when most men were retiring, the sixty-five-year-old Dederich ordered not a present for a grandchild but an exotic act of personal terrorism. To his thinking, a dissolute planet needed reminding: some New Age movements are best defended with Old Testament thunder.

•••

AT 3:15 P.M., THE gas-guzzling Plymouth with the bogus plates flashed by California Highway Patrolman Donald Growe, then en route to have the grime and smog grit washed off his car.

Ping. The sedan tripped his radar for things that shouldn't be.

Grove followed it up the California Incline, the steep, iconic access road connecting Pacific Coast Highway with Santa Monica, and toggled his siren.

Protocol next: wary approach, boots crunching asphalt, fingers twitching above revolver.

"You," he said. "Out of the car!"

The driver, twenty-year-old Lance Kenton, was lean and bluff, a choir-boy-type who did what Growe demanded. Joseph Musico, his older, surlier associate, wasn't as compliant, starting to climb out of the vehicle until the officer ordered him to freeze. The patrolman walked Kenton to the rear of car, making him pop the trunk. Nothing much was in there aside from a plain white canvas bag that went uninspected. Growe next radioed in the plate—the real one. He'd heard nothing about Synanon's pending attack on someone down there, which the LAPD itself had only recently been notified of through its network.

"Some people must have done this so we would be stopped" in a practical joke, Kenton volunteered about the tampered plate.

Without seeking permission, he bent down and began peeling the adhesive off one of the displays. Musico disembarked from his own seat, also without Growe's okay, to pick away at the tape on the other plate.

As little blue shreds fluttered in the Santa Ana winds, the lawman weighed his options. Although the Chrysler with the clumsily altered plates had an expired registration—both of which were illegal—neither passenger acted jumpy. Checking warrants and inquiring what the men were doing seemed overkill. As far as Growe was concerned, this could've been a juvenile prank—and pranks don't necessitate handcuffs.

So, he wrote nothing on his pad and freed them, an act he'd lament as "human failure."

•••

PAUL MORANTZ, WHO RESEMBLED Mark Spitz and wouldn't have minded playing Geraldo Rivera, was bored. On and off before that car stalked him, he'd led a perfectly normal life, perfectly uninspired. Could he have already plateaued? Legal crusading had twice thrust him into the spotlight, but those were receding glories in yellowing newspaper clippings and dimming memories. There had to be something more.

Another lifetime ago, he'd been a campus star at the University of Southern California, where he studied journalism and whooped it up one muckraking semester at a time. As sports editor of the *Daily Trojan* during the late sixties, Morantz had VIP access to John McKay— the wry, cigar-gnashing championship football coach—and prominent players alike. Nicknamed "The Wolf" after a sarcastic column (and his well-known skirt chasing), he welded ambition with gumption. He scooped professional sportswriters in nailing down the first local interview of transfer tailback O. J. Simpson, the future Heisman Trophy winner (and double-murder suspect). Then Morantz landed a McKay assistant in hot water for quoting him saying that the team would travel to the University of California, Berkeley, to "burn their barns and rape their women."

The *Los Angeles Times* took notice, offering the go-getter a staff job. But Morantz's girlfriend at the time, a graduate of the crosstown University of California, Los Angeles, thought law school was a better career alternative for him, as did his middle-class parents. That settled that. Three more years at USC delaying reality in a topsy-turvy America it was. Besides, everyone knew journalists earned chump change compared with attorneys' billable hours. Writing—his sacred passion—was something he could moonlight.

Bar exam passed, Morantz discovered the world was no longer the oyster it'd been in college. Sometimes he couldn't snatch the pearl before the shell snapped close. The Los Angeles County district attorney's office, where he hoped to be hired, rebuffed him, suggesting his tanned, blow-dried style was better suited for "defending the bad guys" than working in its more regimented, Brylcreemed setting. He heeded that advice to a T. A year before he lost his father, a compassionate, meatpacking executive he always looked up to, he joined the DA's opposite number at the public defender's office. He'd make those prosecutors sorry.

Or so he figured. Representing poor, mostly guilty clients didn't exactly stoke the romanticism conjured by Atticus Finch or Clarence Darrow.

Thankfully, Superior Court Judge Noel Cannon invigorated the wood-paneled workspace with her diva-esque eccentricities. As Morantz wrote in a profile for the *LA Times*, "She kept a live Chihuahua in her courtroom and a mechanical canary in her chambers. She decorated her office in pink to match her endless array of pink outfits and summoned select defendants for impromptu sermons there by her personal preacher, the good Reverend Blackstone."

But Cannon—the platinum-tinted showboat who periodically waved a Derringer pistol—wasn't just satisfied accenting everything in pink. When it came to procedure, she could be a black-robed tyrant who jailed any public defenders contesting her rulings, Morantz among them. What had been a decent relationship between the two devolved into entertaining squabbling, courthouse theater that regulars just about brought popcorn to watch.

One day, she took her arbitrary powers too far, imprisoning a client of Morantz's originally arrested for assault and battery, even *though* the victim later recanted and the DA's office dropped the charges. Morantz, the happy-go-lucky more interior-driven than he let on, could tolerate idiosyncrasy, not obvious misconduct. When not juggling his caseload, the rookie public defender took the initiative in the most delicate of terrain. He compiled evidence against the longtime jurist and bundled it off to authorities in Sacramento.

The initial response: a demoralizing chorus of crickets. Nobody seemed to care about fairness in the marble-lined halls constructed to seek it.

When his boss reprimanded him for freelancing without prior approval a magazine piece about the murder of a fellow public defender at a Sherman Oaks watering hole, Morantz had his ammunition to do what he wanted. And what he wanted was to quit. He tendered his resignation and joined his older brother, Lewis, at his private legal practice. During off hours away from it, he womanized like a playboy and wrote like a fiend. Hollywood interest in his article solidified his choice to leave his county job for this less confining life.

A year later, the California Supreme Court brought him further vindication when, aided by his evidence and testimony, it undertook the rare step of removing Cannon from the bench. Morantz, who idolized Frank Serpico, the principled New York cop, and explorer Davy Crockett, the "King of the Wild Frontier," was elated. Litigating garden-variety fender benders and business squabbles, he was finding, was an unchivalrous trade. He craved the adrenaline rush of being in the thick of public change like sweet tooths do a box of Godiva.

Back to his Remington typewriter he went, this time to tap out an article about a catering truck driver framed for robbery. Again, a movie producer optioned the rights. Then an even bigger signpost pointed toward a creative future. After *Rolling Stone* magazine published his feature about Jan and Dean, the progenitors of sixties surf rock, CBS announced that it would adapt it into a TV movie of the week. For someone drawn to launch pads, this was trajectory.

Out of nowhere, a cold-call tip from a liquor store owner brought him back closer to Earth. This one originated in downtown's Skid Row, where LA's homeless congregated—in their tattered clothes, gazing out from hollow eyes—like boxcars of forgotten people. According to the shopkeeper, a man named T. J. Renfroe, a sixty-ish alcoholic just released from county jail after a public intoxication charge, had recently been kidnapped and "sold" to a Burbank mental-health nursing center. Yes, sold.

Over the next weeks, acting on spec, Morantz anointed himself to investigate the mystery abduction. To smoke out the bigger picture, he leaned on his journalistic skills. He smuggled out documents. Posed as the relative of a patient for an inside view. Preserved incriminating records. In analyzing what he had, his suspicions about a human-trafficking syndicate deepened into a Woodward-and-Bernstein realization that it was *all* true. Sleazy nursing homes were paying $125 per person to middlemen who delivered them Skid Row alcoholics, by hook or crook, in a scam to bilk Medi-Cal, the state's insurance program for low-income residents. By billing government to treat these new "patients" for mental disorders they didn't actually possess, it was easy money. The *pièce de résistance?* Down-and-outers who resisted captivity were sedated with Thorazine, a potent anti-schizophrenia drug.

It was the scoop of a lifetime, and Morantz submitted reams of evidence to authorities. Using it, Los Angeles County's Board of Supervisors launched a massive investigation into the insurance grifting, later crediting the gumshoeing lawyer. Again, he could bask in a gratifying puff of fame. But puffs, as everyone knows, never last.

Two years later, in June 1977, living in a beachside home financed with his cut from the class-action lawsuit he filed in the Medi-Cal case, the attorney who wasn't sure he wanted to keep being one nine-to-five flirted with domesticity. It could all be his for the price of a diamond ring. Trudy reminded him of Cheryl Tiegs, the blonde supermodel, but it was how she made his heart loop-de-loop that telegraphed she was "the one." If they wed, he'd become the stepdad to her kids from a previous relationship, producing instant family for this committed bachelor. Goals-wise, little would change. Even in a crowded house, he could still play beach volleyball on the weekends and write when turgid litigation made him yawn.

Another unexpected phone call about a different type of abduction, though, was about to thrash everyone it touched.

•••

CHARLES DEDERICH WAS BORN to a planet where people he adored were always departing.

By his early childhood in Toledo, Ohio, he'd lost his father to a fatal car accident and a brother to influenza. Nothing was the same with his mother, either. Not after she wed a second husband that the bright, easily distracted boy reviled, and told him that he'd go to hell if he didn't attend Roman Catholic Mass. The more he read from the likes of H. G. Wells, the more he questioned where God was. From then on, the self-indoctrinated atheist put his trust in alcohol as liquid companion and painkiller.

His love of the bottle caused him to flunk out of the University of Notre Dame, USC's longtime gridiron archrival, and scuttled his first marriage. Sliding further, he contracted a near-lethal case of meningitis at twenty-nine. Even recovered, the disease had ravaged the right side of his face, making it droop and periodically quiver like a stroke patient. The disfigured wanderer headed west, sleeping on the streets of Santa Monica. Dederich briefly got off of them, marrying another woman and securing a job. Once more, however, liquor plowed him back into a hole too deep for his meaty hands to clamber out. The person who later discovered him passed-out drunk on his kitchen floor relayed the obvious: without treatment, he wasn't long for this world.

Dederich, bottomed out at forty-three, started attending roving Alcoholic Anonymous meetings nightly; soon, he was the most loquacious speaker there. Reading was his other antidote to stop drinking, and he gobbled up Ralph Waldo Emerson's *Self-Reliance*, then books by Skinner and Thoreau. In 1956, with little to lose, he agreed to ingest an experimental drug being tested by the federal government at UCLA. He emerged from his LSD trip spiritually baptized and clear-eyed.

"I became a different person, really and truly," he said. "Everything that has happened to me since...dates to that point."

He'd seized on his purpose, his *raison d'être*: he'd devote himself to sobering up alcoholics through cold turkey and determination, not psychiatry. He'd evangelize them about the enormity of human potential to conquer any demon. He'd lift up the marginalized, and the marginalized listened. Before long, drunkards from the shabbier portions of Santa Monica and surrounding areas shoehorned themselves into his tiny apartment to slurp free soup and hear Dederich's self-help sermons. He believed that they fraternized with Jim Beam and Jack Daniels because they underestimated their innate strength to resist them.

The annals of twentieth-century addiction treatment would be revolutionized by what he'd do next. With cash from his thirty-three-dollar unemployment check, he chartered an AA splinter group that'd operate from a Venice storefront. He fashioned his concept's name in an alliterative mash-up, a portmanteau of "symposium" and "seminar." Dederich predicted Synanon (pronounced sin-a-non) could wind up as influential as Coca-Cola.

In no time the group outgrew its storefront, decamping into the larger National Guard building in Santa Monica. There, Dederich pulled his first surprise. He'd throw open his detox to not only problem drinkers but also to "dope fiends"—heroin users, pill poppers— regardless of their vomiting and wall climbing. Roughly five dozen junkies took him up on it, and backlash flared among his original followers: the alcoholics he'd sworn to rescue.

Homeowners and apartment dwellers who resided nearby also seethed: out their windows were now cigarette-smoking rabble traipsing through what had been peaceful blocks. They complained about public nuisances to city hall, and police arrested the subversive from the Midwest and some associates only ten days after they'd moved in. The charges: counseling addicts without a license and running a hospital in a residential zone.

"Apparently," Dederich quipped, "we started saving lives on the wrong side of town."

Those handcuffs were worth their weight in gold. His incarceration transformed his image from sketchy, mouthy street activist into folk hero, a martyr persecuted by cavalier public officials at the expense of lost souls with no place else to go. Governor Edmund "Pat" Brown, the so-called "builder of modern California," heard about the uproar and wasted no time making himself the first major politician to hop on the Synanon bandwagon. The bureaucratic strings that Brown pulled would prove long-lasting. They granted Dederich's motley bunch wide-ranging code exemptions to treat the addicted.

Celebrities and trendsetters, in that wake, adopted the group as their pet cause, intrigued by the elixir that Dederich had concocted to get people right. They toured his building. They donated money. They met prestigious jazz musicians trying to kick heroin habits. Synanon had itself a mini red carpet of champions in performers Charlton Heston, Milton Berle, Jane Fonda, Natalie Wood, Robert Wagner, Leonard Nimoy, and Ben Gazzara. Also impressed were union-organizer Cesar Chavez, psychologist/writer Timothy Leary, and thinker Buckminster Fuller, originator of the "Spaceship Earth" term. Their involvement catapulted Synanon's name all the way to Washington, DC's corridor of power. So enamored was Thomas Dodd, the US senator from Connecticut, of Dederich's innovation that he exalted it as a "miracle by the beach" for addicts. Maybe, he said, it'd whip juvenile delinquents into shape.

The media lapped up the endorsements, not only repeating the praise but also regurgitating Synanon's contention that its unvalidated techniques had spared thousands from dying in the gutter. The *Los Angeles Times* and *Los Angeles Mirror* each published series about the sobriety movement. A fourteen-page *Life* magazine photo spread in 1962 about Synanon, especially known then for its exuberant, youth dance parties, equated to an unpaid infomercial.

Unlike AA, which revolved around the twelve-step philosophy, Synanon's hallmark therapy was the "Game." In it, group participants verbally unloaded on newly admitted "Synanites" by rubbing their faces in the destructive consequences of their compulsive behaviors. Other than forbidding physical violence during these taut sessions, all bets were off. Newbies berated for hours and deprived of sleep usually broke down, often on the floor, into sobbing, heaving messes racked with guilt and remorse. Once, in group parlance, their "dirty brains" were cleansed, they experienced clarity of thought, at least temporarily. Dederich explained that the goal of his hodgepodge psychotherapy, social ritual, and public shaming was "to get you loaded without acid."

A taxonomy sprouted around the attendant caste system. There were witches (robed ceremonial guides) and "headsuckers" (over-caring Synanon mothers), "squares" (non-addicts seeking enlightenment) and "splittees" (untrustworthy defectors). Dederich himself was surprised by how many he could proselytize as the E. F. Hutton of the chemically needy.

"When I sit down and start to talk," he gloated, "people start gathering."

What was so complicated? To him narcotics, crime, and deviant behavior boiled down to a common weakness that you'd never find listed in psychiatrists' bible, *The Diagnostical and Statistical Manual of Mental Disorders*, or Freud's writings: an "addiction to stupidity."

Synanon, richer by the day, hipper by the moment, was booming. It relocated to the Club Casa del Mar, a vintage, brick-winged beachfront structure just north of Santa Monica's artsy, boutique-filled Ocean Park area. It needed to primp for its own star turn. In 1965, a year after the Beatles appeared on *The Ed Sullivan Show* to an audience of screaming teeny-boppers, Columbia Pictures released a feature-length movie—*Synanon*—to the general public. The film, featuring Edmond O'Brien and Chuck Connors, was a stark, black-and-white depiction of the "Game." It flickered with the harsh, *noir*-ish aesthetic of a Sam Fuller production, even as it doubled as the organization's global brand-maker.

Dederich was one of the few privy to the bombshell at odds with his rocketing fame. Statistically, his methods remedied addiction at no *higher* percentage than licensed rehabs. But why ruin a parade when it's raining dollars? And it's not like parades can't alter their routes.

In 1967, nervous the truth of Synanon's cure rates would leak out, influenced by the era's flowering of group-living experimentations, he redrew his conception. "Big Daddy," as his disciples referred to him, declared his movement would phase into an alternative lifestyle commune free of society's distractions. The majority of Synanites would bolt Santa Monica for the freer spaces—and fewer community hassles—up north. At Tomales Bay north of San Francisco, Synanon could develop a giant swath of land. At a second locale in Tulare County, a rural expanse between Bakersfield and Fresno, they hatched plans to inhabit buildings, fly into an airstrip for private planes, and haul trash to their own garbage dump. The state was there as a partner in this expansion, donating an empty San Francisco warehouse for the group's benefit. Synanon parlayed that momentum by establishing affiliates outside California and as far as Malaysia.

By the early seventies, as Americans wrestled with the protracted war in Vietnam, civil strife, and economic doldrums, Dederich's so-called "People Business" was approaching its apex. America might've felt tapped out for resources, but Synanon's flush coffers were, funding mini cities over the 5,500 acres it controlled in California. On top of housing and mess halls there were libraries and offices, movie theaters and sewage plants, medical clinics and barbershops. Members had access to hundreds of cars, planes, and boats. At Tomales Bay, they could ride horses, swim, swat tennis balls, or relax in bathhouses. Jitneys zipped members between settlements. A one-legged DJ emceed a closed-circuit radio station, KSYN. Synanon's fire department collaborated with first responders during natural emergencies.

The pedigrees of some in the ranks further buttressed the idea of an alternative mainstream. Professionals in banking, architecture, and law had left their old ways behind, as had professors from Stanford and UCLA, even an *LA Times* alum. With them, Big Daddy could say that he wasn't running a gravy-train haven for the dregs of society. These were Americans seeking refuge from civilization's copious temptations—from overdosing, as it were, on excess freedom expressed through cocaine vials, rolling papers, vodka bottles, wanton sex, or abject materialism.

Dederich's talent for readapting what Synanon meant was rivaled only by his ability to channel rivers of money. By mid-decade, his organization had amassed $30 million (about $186 million today) in assets. Affluent believers such as Reliable Mortgage's Ed Siegel donated nearly a $1 million in stock; another deep pocket handed over the title to his accounting firm. Deeds for valuable real estate, from San Diego to San Francisco, Reno to Puerto Rico, were gifted. Synanon's trophy property: Santa Monica's beachside Club Casa Del Mar. Supplementing benefactors' largesse and member-paid room and board were three other cash streams: a line of promotional items like pens, key chains, and lighters; gas stations; and philanthropic-subsidy contracts with a large percentage of Fortune 500 companies.

Its pitch to sponsors was as catchy as any soap seller, and more poignant: "Buy from us and save a life."

The media continued embracing that theme despite the movement's one-eighty from its provenance as a cold turkey detox. Two well-known trade publications, *The Hollywood Reporter* and *Billboard* magazine, anteed up free ad space, as did others beyond the entertainment world. Why wouldn't they feel warm and fuzzy when top law enforcement officials advocated for Synanon in a high-crime / high-drug-use era?

"We spend so much on mace, helicopters, clubs, and other devices," remarked San Francisco Sheriff Richard Hongisto, "when money could be spent on programs like this."

"Like this" was sweet music to Big Daddy's ears. He grew so comfortable with his mutating kingdom that he sometimes satirized his reign, donning a Hawaiian shirt and "crown" glued from popsicle sticks for events. But he wasn't so secure in his convictions that he'd shrug off criticisms of himself as a pop psychology crackpot projecting his complexes—namely his terror of desertion—onto his subjects. Nowhere was that insecurity revealed more than in the 1972 takeout by the *San Francisco Examiner*, the first large media outlet to aggressively question Synanon's foundations. It, the *Examiner* reported, wasn't so much an alternative-lifestyle archetype as the "Racket of the Century." Instead of prodding Dederich to soul search, as he had before, the series appeared to push his buttons into inculcating an us-against-them mentality. Lawyers became the tips of his spear, filing a massive libel suit against the Hearst chain newspaper; they eventually won a $600,000 judgment and forced a page-one apology.

If only those *Examiner* journalists knew about how Synanon circled its wagons.

No longer were recovered addicts permitted to "graduate" to the outside world, which Dederich and his cronies scorned as evil and selfish. Families were combined in Marin County, and Synanite mothers in the "headsuckers" class were further limited in how often they could interact with *their* own newborns. These and other Draconian restrictions generated an ominous tread line: an off-the-grid utopia of good-hearted-if-brainwashed citizens under the thumb of an increasingly mercurial ruler. There was a Dear Leader quality to Big Daddy. When he quit his three-pack-a-day cigarette habit in 1970, his flock had to quit smoking, too. When his wife, Betty, dieted, it was *sayonara* to everyone's fatty foods. Followers once had their heads shaved to affirm their loyalty to the group in a hazing rite; a young filmmaker named George Lucas cast some of these baldies as extras in his futuristic movie, "THX 1138." As Dederich tightened his grip, that hairless 'do became mandatory for many.

L. Ron Hubbard, the science-fiction writer who'd chartered the Church of Scientology, once quipped that the "best way" for a man to make a million bucks is to "start his own religion." Dederich parlayed that same notion when Synanon reclassified itself as a tax-exempt "religion." The idea, the brainchild of Dan Garrett, Synanon's lawyer and Dederich's chief whisperer, was shrewd. Operating a religion perpetuated Synanon's waiver from state licensing regulations. It also stalled questions about which members could leave on their volition.

When Dederich sent down orders from the mountaintop now, it was as a secular god. But one decree had few falling to their knees in rapture. Instead, it fueled Synanon's demise. Every male there, except for him, was *required* to undergo a vasectomy; at least eighty men had it done. Similarly, all pregnant women were forced to abort their fetuses; one had the procedure in the baby's second trimester. In justifying his Orwellian command, Dederich harped on economics, explaining that children were a "very bad investment," just as he told the rank and file he was tired of them doing nothing but enjoying the group's wealth and status while he sweated the finances. Almost as many bailed over the sterilizations as received them. Dederich's own brother, William, was one of those who departed.

"I'll give you my life, Chuck," one member later wrote in his book, "but not my balls."

Any doubt that Dederich's commune was warping evaporated when his wife died of lung cancer in 1977. Betty, a former prostitute and junky who joined Synanon while going through withdrawals, had been the only person able to restrain his worst impulses. Grieving her loss, Big Daddy issued another commandment: all married couples needed to dissolve their unions every three years to pair with new partners. What slang referred to as "swinging," he termed "love matches." Some Synanite couples were connected through lecherous auctions. What did Dederich, sixty-four, care? He'd remarried a devotee thirty years his junior.

Since little of this spilled out, judges, parents, and others continued entrusting Synanon to rehabilitate wayward children. None of them were knew that a "punk squad" had been formed to dole out corporal punishment—beatings, being slammed into the sides of buildings—for kids who acted out or tried escaping. Outwardly, Dederich remained the "Great Hope," his followers patriotic humanitarians. And many were, redistributing food, clothing, and whatnot to charities in collaboration with different agencies. Los Angeles Mayor Tom Bradley remained a believer, naming a day to honor Betty Dederich on her passing.

Time magazine was about to yank the wool off everybody's eyes. A December 1977 feature portraying Synanon as a "kooky cult" hiding in the open was a haymaker to its reputation. In addition to publicizing Dederich's sexual preoccupations and compensation—a $100,000 annual salary, plus a $500,000 pre-retirement bonus—the article disclosed Synanon's plunging membership, down one-third to about twelve hundred people, and the Marin County grand jury probing child-abuse allegations. Dederich, photographed in a hat reading "I'M THE MEANEST S.O.B. IN THE VALLEY," had believed that he'd charmed *Time*'s journalists with folksy self-deprecation into writing puffery.

"A lot of guys," he told *Time*, "could do this from an old Ford roadster. They're holy men. I'm not. I need a…Cadillac."

TV viewers watching him growl about the magazine's "contemptible hatchet job" must've cringed with déjà vu about another messianic circus bubbling. In a January 1978 interview with CBS-LA's Connie Chung, a newscaster that Dederich admitted having a crush on, he vented unfettered warnings. Any journalist assailing Synanon's "religious freedoms," the group's majordomo snarled, should be "as nervous about the safety of their children and their grandchildren" as he was about his. Appearing on camera again, this time looking like a malevolent Burl Ives, he told Jess Marlow of LA's NBC affiliate that "Bombs could be thrown at…some of [*Time*'s] clowns." He then compared his misunderstood persona to Jesus Christ, who he claimed also "ran with a bunch of smugglers, drunks, and crooks." Not long after, Dederich's brutes showed their Jesus wasn't bluffing, harassing *Time* reporters in person in New York. To impress the point, a pair accosted the magazine's editor-in-chief, promising, "We are going to ruin your life."

These were the first salvos in the "Holy War" that Dederich was unleashing, much of it for internal consumption to staunch dissension and defections. After the California Department of Public Health announced it would visit Synanon's grounds, he promised his followers would "surround" any inspectors with guys "twice their size"—and also determine which of them practiced sodomy or bestiality. Not even Charles Manson had said that in his race-war baiting. Synanon's band of lawyers mirrored the truculence, filing $400 million ($1.6 billion today) in libel and slander suits against multiple defendants: *Time*, the health department (for likening Dederich's threats to Nazism), San Francisco's ABC affiliate (for a segment alleging Synanon guards "terrorized" neighbors), *Reader's Digest*, and others. Think of it as artillery blasts by docket.

Whatever his emphasis on confronting naysayers with lawyers, guns, and money, like the Warren Zevon song, Big Daddy still touted his own candidacy for a Nobel Prize. It all meant that time was nearing for him and a certain bold lawyer to tangle.

•••

IN JUNE 1977, A young homemaker struggling with mental illness went, on the advice of her husband, to a Venice health clinic for tranquilizers. All Frances Winn needed, her spouse, Ed, believed, were sedatives to tide her over until he could get her more comprehensive treatment. But rather than prescribing her Valium, the clinic referred her to Synanon's Santa Monica reception facility for counseling. Yes, the intake people there said: they could help her. Before they did, she had to formally request assistance under one of the few rules governing them. What ensued was never promoted in any brochures.

From the moment she completed the paperwork, Frances became a prisoner sucked down a rabbit hole about as un-calming as you could imagine. Her welcoming party mowed her hair with electric scissors. It subjected her to the Game and locked her in the basement. The next day, against her will, she was transported to Tomales Bay, where she was jettisoned into a tent.

Once he knew where she was, Ed Winn did everything he could to liberate her from the group's clutches. His wife's captors stonewalled him, telling him their marriage was over. That he should forget her. He wouldn't, and wrote to reporters, local politicians, even President Carter for assistance. None of them did anything of consequence. But an acquaintance of Ed's did. He mentioned that a former neighbor of his was the attorney who'd emancipated those Skid Row alcoholics some years back. Contacted by Frances's now-frantic mate, Paul Morantz barely hesitated. Of course he'd take the case.

Looking at his life like a film, he believed everything that had happened to him heretofore—the rogue judge, freeing T. J. Renfroe, his own encounters with cults—was culminating in a finale he was determined to prove he could ace. Him vs. Synanon. How, he wondered, could an entity as vast as Dederich's continue without anything even approximating oversight?

When he phoned Synanon about his client, nobody there chewed any fingernails. Over the years, it had rebuffed any number of nosy outsiders, often by citing Synanon's exemptions from licensing rules for drug rehabs and mental health providers. Morantz, unfamiliar with this gray-area turf, negotiated a compromise that touched none of that: allowing Frances and Ed to speak over the phone. On the line, she reasserted that she wanted to leave. As in today! Synanon, keen to ditch problem members in the aftermath of the *Time* story, demanded a waiver first. So, Morantz typed up a hollow agreement—a Trojan horse document providing scant lawsuit protection if Winn sued—that a Synanon rep rashly signed. After he got Frances released from captivity and back home, he returned to Santa Monica, flipping off her abductors in a "fuck you" that reverberated hundreds of miles north.

At a foothill ranch outside Visalia three months later, Big Daddy held court about encroaching perils. As his followers dined, their froggy, basso-voiced leader spoke into "The Wire," Synanon's internal broadcast system. Any of them, he lectured, afraid of the Holy War should leave; any of them confused that the "sound of cracking bones" was fundamental to their survival held no agency with him.

The message they should be spreading: "Don't mess with us. You can get killed. Physically dead...If we have a good thing here, then we are not going to permit people, like greedy lawyers, to destroy it."

And speaking of one, he said, "Who is this guy, Morantz?...Why doesn't somebody break his legs?"

How lucky Synanon had groomed bloodthirsty men to keep the peace. Interspersed through Synanon's population was now a private militia dubbed the "Imperial Marines," a roughly two-hundred-man force designed to repel invaders and execute commands. They weren't showpiece soldiers: they'd gone through their own version of basic training and survival maneuvers. They practiced with firearms and trenched holes for secret weapons. By the time of Morantz's heroics for Frances Winn, some of those Marines and their comrades had already illustrated what happens when strangers disrespect the People Business.

A pair of seventeen-year-old surfers who parked near Synanon's Santa Monica building, the one legendary for its black, rooftop sign, did something that warranted a response. They'd peed outdoors on or near the group's property. A gleeful mob of shitkickers in blue shirts and signature overalls set upon on the derelicts, assaulting them in a teeth-flying, body-dragging scrum that extended into a parking garage.

"This is not the type of place Synanon is," a female Synanite shouted, trying to halt the group thumping.

She was wrong. It was *exactly* that type of place if you were a sadist.

Around Thanksgiving, a redneck-type trucker from the Fresno area received his education after he got into a traffic miscue with a Synanon vehicle. Its occupants insisted on an apology; Ron Edison refused, believing he'd done nothing wrong. Following the incident, someone located his address and four goons brandishing sawed-off shotguns appeared at his house one evening. In front of Eidson's horrified wife and three children, the Synanites pounded and pistol-whipped him, leaving him bloodied and in a coma. Eidson, once he was on the mend, tried identifying his assailants at a police lineup. To confuse him into tripping up, the group sent in look-alikes to those who nearly killed him.

Meantime, certain Synanon alumni dropping by facilities where they'd shed their particular poisons—LSD, heroin, speed, weed, Scotch—were treated to homecomings you'd expect in a gulag, not a "sober paradise." They'd hoped to see old friends, express their dismay about recent trends, or reminisce about youthful experiences. Denied those chances, they were manhandled by security personnel. Then was pick-the-torture. They could berate the ex-members as "scumbag" defectors or kick them with steel-toed boots. They could snap their fingers, one by one, or chase them into ditches for their beatdowns. Don't breathe a word about what happened, they were warned, unless you want to see us pop up at your house.

Firearm dealers selling the Imperial Marines and their associates weapons nurtured a more positive relationship. The transactions enabled Synanon to stockpile roughly $300,000 worth of rifles, Colt .45 handguns, and automatic pistols, as well as pallets of ammunition, including armor-piercing bullets. The sole item in the munitions cache that Dederich's people couldn't acquire? A bazooka.

The US Bureau of Alcohol, Tobacco, Firearms, and Explosives, noting these bulk purchases, reached out with questions. Why, agents inquired, did a registered "religion" need to arm itself so prodigiously? Synanon's answer teemed with Second Amendment, don't-tread-on-me defiance. The guns, it said, were legal self-defense against trespassers and troublemakers incited to provoke conflict by the dishonest news media. Decades before Donald Trump called journalists the "Enemy of the People," Dederich's group beat him to it.

•••

BACK AT HIS SMALL Brentwood law office near Hamburger Hamlet, Paul Morantz was swamped with calls from exasperated parents anxious for him to spring their children from Synanon, just as he had Frances

Winn. When not charging ahead for them, he immersed himself into the Kool-Aid–tinged waters of mass-behavior psychology, reading Mao, Maslow, Skinner, and Werner Erhard, the father of "est."

He'd experienced his own brushes with cults before they spread like wildflowers in the seventies. At his 1963 high school graduation party in Santa Monica, he'd lurched away from the boozy, hormone-laced crowd and right under the bluff of Synanon's former headquarters at the National Guard Armory. Seeking a little breathing room, he got something else. From the building's illuminated windows, he could hear incoming Synanites shrieking as they were being harangued during the "Game." Horror movie soundtracks were less scary.

"It's a rehab place," a pal tried comforting him. "That's Synanon."

Years passed before his next interaction with someone about to be reprogrammed. During his college years at USC, Morantz had taken a part-time job selling women's hairpieces at Contessa Creations at Melrose and La Cienega. One of his coworkers there was a conservative, tie-wearing Texan new to big-city life. After their shifts, the native Angeleno delighted in escorting his Southern friend around to LA's bounteous supermarket of sex, drugs, and rock and roll. Then they went their own ways. Only later, amid the media blitz and sounds of "Helter Skelter," did he connect identities. The buddy he'd known as Charles Watson at the wig store had hardened into the stony-eyed killer the public knew as "Tex" Watson, a Manson lieutenant in the gruesome Tate-LaBianca murders, which ended perceptions of LA as the land of milk and honey.

Now, in his third encounter with cults, he marveled that the stars were trying to tell him something; that predetermination was unspooling itself. Not that he still couldn't have walked away from these degrees of separation and straight into the inviting arms of Trudy, who was uneasy about him provoking people who attacked anyone over trifles. His house on Bollinger—two bedrooms, red brick barbecue, bay windows—was teed up to be their Shangri-La if he merely engaged a more civil adversary. CBS demonstrated what could be in airing *Deadman's Curve*, the Jan and Dean TV-movie inspired by his *Rolling Stone* article. Trudy, proud of what he accomplished, hoping he'd duplicate it for their joint future, even hosted a celebratory dinner for the show's *premiere*. Legal work, safer causes, and a film deal or two could be a fulfilling career.

Except that was *her* notion of fulfillment. Where's the satisfaction for achieving a public good? The thrill of a fresh hunt? Some personalities stick on the trails; others need to muddy their boots on unpredictable hillsides. As if to prove that, Trudy's mustachioed, image-conscious, work-consumed boyfriend made the *LA Times* again through sheer initiative. This time, he helped persuade assistants to LAPD Chief Daryl Gates to end the department's growing embrace of est seminars for stressed-out officers, citing what he'd learned in his deep-dive research into Synanon: the sneaky methods by which brainwashers netted fresh recruits.

The couple was at a now-forgotten Washington Boulevard restaurant when Trudy dropped her bomb. Sorry, she said during a heart-to-heart. She couldn't marry someone more obsessed with digging up wrongdoing by hucksters and monsters than burrowing into family commitment. Love only got you to the altar. It didn't guarantee a common vision.

In the days after she dumped him, Morantz rarely felt bleaker. His snooping around into the Medi-Cal scam brought him a death threat. Trudy's departure was its own kind of death, even if he knew it was a death he had to swallow. Who, after all, would want a spouse telling his better half over pillow talk, "They're coming to kill me"? Because that's what he sensed was his destiny and repeated it to friends. If Synanon intended to do to him what it did to "splittee" Phil Ritter, he should be on the first plane to a remote village.

Ritter, a Greenpeace antinuclear activist, had never wanted a bitter goodbye with the society he joined as an antidote to the rat race. He had spent eight years at Synanon, some of them quite pleasantly as its transportation czar. It was Dederich's militarism, the coterie of toadies amplifying it, and the mass sterilizations that he suspected were illegal that forced his hand. Still, just because he was out didn't mean he stopped caring. Indeed, he encouraged authorities to step in—to effectively save Synanon from its unraveling self. Ritter had vested interests there as well, with a wife and child remaining behind, the latter of whom he petitioned to regain custody of through the courts.

Former cohorts, coded to associate the slightest resistance with the actions of a quisling, knew what to do. They waited until Ritter returned to his Berkeley home from the supermarket one evening and jumped him. Before he could defend himself, henchmen clubbed him in the head with wooden mallets in a wordless pasting. His fractured skull probably would've killed him had his screams not drawn neighbors to chase off the men who'd arrived in a Toyota. Ritter, miraculously, recovered. His attackers went un-apprehended.

Morantz, fast becoming *the* legal authority on Synanon's dark permutation, realized this was no aberration. Dozens of beatings meted out by Imperial Marine and others waging the Holy War had resulted in strikingly few punishments. The reasons were many: Synanon's Teflon credibility with sponsors; governmental budget cuts; rising general crime. Sticking out in that last category was a bumper crop of murders—by gangs, drug dealers, hitmen, and serial predators ("The Freeway Killer," "The Hillside Strangler," et al.)—overwhelming local police forces on a daily basis.

In this skein of yellow crime tape, scattered reports of violence by bald-headed, overall-wearing zealots were blips. Fights between Synanites and outsiders, this logic went, were a kind of cultural misunderstanding that spun out of control. When prosecutors did file felony charges against them, they often reduced them to misdemeanors or sentenced offenders to community service and probation. Synanon, with its feisty reputation for saving addicts and pop-psychology lifestyle, hadn't lost its trusted brand. Questioning whether it had changed its stripes was like doubting Monty Hall or Sears.

Hence, tilting one's sword against a formidable windmill, one whose outrages were either dismissed or tolerated, was not only perilous but also isolating. The young man from Pacific Palisades continued thrusting and parrying anyway. The battle that cost Morantz the love of his life could just be what he was born to fight. And it was about to crescendo.

Courtesy of him, Synanon was on the cusp of three consecutive defeats, each one more humiliating than the prior one. After learning from Morantz of a house in San Francisco where three adolescent Synanites were trapped, police encircled the property and freed the youths. Next, in a legal precedent, he secured a $300,000 judgment against the organization for what a judge dubbed Frances Winn's "unpardonable" treatment. Lastly, at the solicitation of two Marin County supervisors—up-and-comers (and future US senators) named Dianne Feinstein and Barbara Boxer—he lobbied against state legislation that would have perpetuated Synanon's golden ticket: its long-running waiver from licensing regulations. The bill failed by a single vote. If other counties copied Marin's lead, every secret, perversion, and deception that Synanon had gotten away with for years could tumble out into public as a prelude to organizational implosion.

Aware he'd just enshrined himself Public Enemy Number One, Morantz lived fidgety in the shadows. While LA radio blared Joe Walsh's tale of rock stardom in "Life's Been Good," he purchased a shotgun with the firepower to blister multiple assailants, propping it near his bed. As theatergoers howled at the college antics in *National Lampoon's Animal House*, he peered around and under his Volvo hatchback for telltale signs of a bomb before starting it. And what about his border collies, his beloved Tommy and Devon? Who'd safeguard them after the dog of Synanon's former president, a man on the outs with Dederich, was found hanged?

Every precaution—even paranoia—was justified.

"When is someone," Dederich ranted over the Wire, "going to be brave enough to get Morantz?"

His men explored that goading by communicating with a professional assassin. When he bid the job at $10,000, Big Daddy's chief advisers blanched with sticker shock. They knew they could do it cheaper—and more spectacularly—in-house. Decision made!

As they planned it, their target treated himself to well-deserved R&R in Hawaii, where he guessed Imperial Marines were unlikely to be quaffing Mai Tais. Stateside again, still missing Trudy, Morantz hyperventilated watching USC nip Alabama on the football field. October 5 was another day for palpitations. At a local recording studio, he met the world's Aussie sweetheart, star of the blockbuster musical *Grease*. He let slip, in an effort to impress Olivia Newton-John, that he wrote the article that propelled CBS's Jan and Dean TV movie. Unexpectedly, flirtatious embers smoldered between them. Then again, what celebrity goddess would want to date a marked man?

The following weekend, with a cluttered head that still needed clearing, he drove to San Diego to whack volleyballs back and forth across the net. At a bar later, a friend who heard about his offensive against Synanon said he'd be nervously scanning his rearview mirror too.

On Tuesday, October 10, Morantz awoke about 7:00 a.m. like any other ordinary day. He donned his typical work getup—button-down shirt, slacks, cowboy boots—gulped coffee, and took his Volvo to his Brentwood office. After lunch, he stopped focusing on law clients and concentrated on something more urgent. In his conference room, he sat across from three serious men: two officers from the LAPD's intelligence unit and a representative from the California Attorney General's criminal investigative branch. He recapped what he'd gleaned from sources knowledgeable about Dederich's thinking, then requested police protection.

Shouldn't be a problem, the men replied, once they conducted a formal threat analysis. Just standard procedure. Morantz, incongruously cocky and cautious, said fine, calculating Synanon's revenge in days, not hours. The mighty LAPD wasn't going to be cowed by some plump demagogue with a drop-down microphone.

LANCE KENTON AND JOSEPH MUSICO, who were circling his house just then, were the least compatible of killers. Young Kenton approached tasks with Eagle Scout verve, determined to excel in anything life at Synanon provided: academics, karate, outdoor activities. His father, admired jazz-swing composer Stan Kenton, had entrusted Dederich to keep his boy drug-free while he toured, never picturing what he'd become.

Musico was Kenton's polar opposite—a profane New Yorker and vet who arrived at Synanon less as a lifestyle choice and more as a trapdoor to stay out of prison. The Pentagon had dishonorably discharged him after a stint in Vietnam as a military policeman, though he didn't speak much about that. He bragged about fragging prick sergeants and stringing necklaces from "gook ears." Out of the armed forces, Musico's troubles deepened with a heroin addiction. His mother, hellbent he be spared incarceration, convinced the courts into shipping him to a California rehab. He actually fit in for a change too. Female Synanites were weak-kneed for his rugged good looks; men listened raptly to his colorful stories.

Dederich's Holy War, unfortunately, stunted whatever maturity Musico had gained by reawakening the part of him enchanted by violence. Quizzed how he'd prefer to execute Morantz, whom Big Daddy characterized as a hunched-over, Jewish ambulance chaser, he suggested ambushing him with a shotgun blast on an LA freeway. In the end, they pulled their instruments from an earthen pit.

The pair's dilemma was now whether to go through with the mission after their close call with that CHP officer, who sniffed out their camouflaged license plate a few hours earlier. The stop had deflated some of the air from Kenton's enthusiasm. Perhaps, he suggested, they should take a hint and pull the plug. Return to the Central Valley to regroup? Absolutely not, Musico answered. To him, this second-guessing was cowardice crystalizing in crunch time. He wouldn't have it! Different as could be, they reportedly exchanged punches about whether to turn tail or carry on. Musico prevailed, and they soldiered on with their associates in tow.

An eleven-year-old boy was outside pedaling his bike when the Plymouth looped Bollinger on half a dozen passes. Each time it reached Morantz's home, it slowed conspicuously. The strange car doing those strange things rang some bells. The child, whose brother Morantz sometimes paid to walk his dogs, scurried to his mother. Relax, she shushed him; it was probably an unmarked police car ensuring all was safe.

Edie Ditmars, remembering her neighbor's admonition to stay vigilant, was equally spooked. The attractive woman, fresh from a divorce and chummy with Morantz, beelined to her kitchen window after hearing his border collies barking. Gazing out, she saw an unfamiliar Chrysler had parked in his driveway, and next watched a clean-cut lad in a sports coat and tie march toward the front door with something in his hand. Ditmars hurried to her living room window to see more but the angle obstructed her sightline. When the mailbox lid, the one chiseled into Morantz's stucco front wall, slapped closed, she sighed in relief. Routine delivery: that's all.

A nine-year-old girl across the street was the last to be creeped out by the swooping green sedan. She crept toward a bush and ducked beneath it, feeling like a spy as she, too, recalled the heads-up for anything eerie. She tried making out the license plate but before she could the car blazed away, as if it had eyes in its taillights. She intended to mention it to her neighbor the first chance she had.

There was a lot of that going around.

The main attraction pulled up around 5:30 p.m., with Vin Scully's pregame catchphrase on the brain: "It's almost time for Dodger baseball!" The 1978 World Series pitted the opposing sides of America's two coasts: Tommy Lasorda and the Boys in Blue against the Reggie-Jackson-led Yankees, Sunny Lotusland versus the Gritty Big Apple. Morantz's border collies, per custom, gave him a friendly mauling after he cracked the door, and then loped outside onto the front lawn to do their business and frolic. As always, he surveyed the interior of the house before entering, though today he was surveying with imperfect vision. He wasn't wearing the eyeglasses he thought made him look dorky; the stylish pair he ordered hadn't yet materialized.

He plopped the Synanon evidence files he had toted from work on his green-tile kitchen counter. He needed a respite from Dederich's mind games. Reclining in his bedroom with a cold beer and the TV remote in time for the opening pitch of the Series would do the trick. All that lay between him and batter-up was a menial task. He had to retrieve the mail from his shoebox-sized chute a few feet away.

Peculiar. Blurry vision and all, he picked out an elongated object in the receptable. No worries. Must be a scarf that someone crammed in there, assuming it belonged to him or a girlfriend. As he'd done hundreds of times, his right hand popped the tin cover while his left hand dipped inside.

Surprise. What it clasped wasn't silk or a bulky letter. It was alive.

•••

THE FOUR-AND-A-HALF-FOOT-LONG WESTERN DIAMONDBACK rattlesnake in Morantz's left hand was displeased about its confinement and even angrier about being gripped. "Little Chuck," as the LAPD would nickname it, behaved as any caught reptile would. It lunged its V-shaped head forward, sinking fangs into the edge of his wrist just below his watch band. The strike took a blink of the eye.

Fuuuucck!

"Bastards!" Morantz said aloud, cursing himself for being so gullible. "They did it. They really did it."

In the seconds before venom coursed through his veins, he spun through the absurd unnecessity of this happening. The dog claw marks he now noticed on the mail chute, where his pets knew danger slithered; the agencies briefed about the price on his head; the block full of neighbors on high alert; warnings about an attack in the works from Dave Mitchell, editor of *The Point Reyes Light*, a small Tomales Bay weekly that would earn a Pulitzer Prize for its Synanon coverage; his vain refusal to wear nerdy glasses. He had a virtual watchtower on his side, and yet between his fingers wiggled a scaly monster capable of ending his life at thirty-three. Ending his life waiting for a threat analysis.

So, yeah, double fuck, one for each fang mark.

He dropped the checkered, grayish-brown animal with a skin pattern akin to oak-tree bark onto his hardwood floor. It coiled by his ankles, forked tongue curling, eyes glaring. The two shared a moment. The *Crotalus atrox* wasn't unlike him—terrified, enraged, confused—as it readied itself for another lunge to incapacitate its enemy. Morantz's boyhood fascination in herpetology washed back. He'd trapped and kept garter snakes as a kid; one escaped to climb up his mother's draperies. Still, they're not poisonous. He realized he needed ice on his wounds and his heart rate kept down to slow the neurotoxins.

But a simultaneous emergency required quick thinking. From the corner of his eye, through his opened front door, he could see Tommy and Devon galloping toward the house, where they'd heard their best friend yelp. In seconds, they'd be fighting with a poisonous serpent quicker than them. Then there could be three corpses near his mail slot, plus one live snake. Distraction was his only option.

Morantz juked his head the opposite direction of the door, the way USC tailback Anthony Davis once juked defenders trying to tackle him. When the creature swayed, he stretched his right arm diagonally over it to slam the door closed. He'd take his dogs roaming free on his lawn than suffering those fangs. Carefully, he edged away from the diamondback that hissed but never rattled.

Delayed shock clobbered him as he stumbled through his kitchen, pitching outside toward Edie Ditmar's house. He crashed his right shoulder into her door, smashing it off a hinge, then hollered for ice. Next he beseeched someone to call the police—and beckon an ambulance!

Neighbors darted toward the hullabaloo, thinking, "Oh, no." Among the first to reach him was Irv Moskowitz, a Caltech electronics supervisor home early from the school's Pasadena campus in observance of Yom Kippur. That very day, he'd completed a CPR course that included treating snakebites. He yanked the resistant victim to the ground and tore off his shirt to wrap Morantz's left hand in a makeshift tourniquet. As Moskowitz knotted it, someone else piled ice on the lawyer's wrist. A jacket was laid over him in the Indian summer swelter.

Inside the wailing ambulance, with a hand pinching like it was caught in an industrial vice, he worried he was a goner. He flashed to Newton-John's cherubic face to soothe himself. He attempted pain relief by self-actualization. He feared this was karma from his USC days, when he pranked a law professor by sending him a large alligator lizard in a registrar's envelope. None of that quelled his panic, or the excruciating compression around the teeth marks.

Two firemen soon stood in his entryway, eyeballing the biggest, most badass rattlesnake they'd ever seen; they knew they had to kill before it bit anyone else. One fireman diverted it while the other pinned its writhing, muscular body, as wide in spots as Steve Garvey's bat, with a shovel. Decapitating it through its carbon-fiber-like skin required numerous whacks. After they lopped off Little Chuck's head, they flushed it down Morantz's toilet, forgetting, or not realizing, it could be crucial evidence in a felony murder case. An LAPD officer who later saw the snake's carcass harkened to the squad-room briefings about Synanon.

Morantz "should've had protection," he muttered.

By the point he reached what is now UCLA Medical Center in Santa Monica, he was in near-blackout agony. Before he received any narcotic relief, things turned Kafkaesque. The older, hearing-impaired nurse who filled in his intake form needed his insurance information, but her cotton-mouthed patient with the swollen left side and tingling extremities could hardly speak—other than imploring her for goddamn drugs! Was he really sure, doctors then asked, it was a rattlesnake, not something else?

Word by now was spreading at pre-Twitter light speed. Morantz's friend Nicki, with whom he was supposed to have dinner that night, raced to the ER, where she had a nurse slide a magnet bracelet over his wrist for cosmic healing. At last, he was administered eleven vials of antivenom, then produced from horse antibodies, and the morphine-like Demerol. The drugs ferried his mind from watching the tail end of the World Series game, which the Dodgers won in an 11–5 romp, to a hallucinated shoreline.

After three hours there, he was transferred to USC County General hospital because of its expertise with snakebites. He was in serious condition and would have probably died of "severe envenomation" without the nimble work of the paramedics. The *LA Times's* Narda Zacchino, one of the few reporters brave enough to write about the true Synanon, evaded security. She pecked her source/friend on the cheek and told him to forget she'd been there, lest Synanon find out and manipulate it. Through the haze of that awful day, the best face over him wasn't a journalist, nurse, or relative. It was Trudy—his Trudy—whom he'd requested the LAPD to contact. When the doctor mandated everyone to leave, she refused, plunking herself into a bedside chair. The next morning, she was still there.

On October 11, 1978, the same day Angelenos learned their city would host the 1984 Summer Olympics, the globe learned about the weaponization of animals. Anchorman Walter Cronkite harrumphed on the *CBS Evening News* about the "bizarre event," even by cult standards. Comedian Chevy Chase, on *Saturday Night Live*'s Weekend Update, joked about Synanon selling rattlesnakes for Christmas. The movie "Jaws" had made millions of swimmers petrified of becoming dinner for great white sharks. What happened to the lawyer would make some waver before sticking their hands into a dark mailbox.

Dithering by law enforcement was over. A detective working the Hillside Strangler investigation was reassigned to the case, even if it wasn't much of a whodunit. Within a day of the attack, splittees phoned in tips ratting out Musico and Kenton, both of whom were arrested up north. CHP officer Donald Growe, guilt-ridden he hadn't checked the bag in the Plymouth's trunk, confirmed they were the two men he'd stopped. LAPD officer Ybarro contributed too. Both wanted redemption after that witchy car got through the perimeter.

Later that week, in a press conference rivaling John Lennon and Yoko Ono's 1969 "Bed-ins for Peace," Morantz was wheeled out of his hospital room for a jam-packed meeting with the media. Someone normally covetous of public adulation looked overwhelmed, less modern-day Sir Lancelot than goldfish-eyed center of attention. Reporters barraging him with questions were curious and sympathetic. From his tilted-up hospital bed, bare chest showing, Morantz told them what he'd emphasized earlier, largely to tin ears: dangerous cults were still around. Wasn't that evident now? When pressed, however, whether he was *certain* Synanon was responsible, he paused, knowing the group's "long ears" would hear his reply. Cautiously, he said he'd only been alterted he was on an "enemies list." Sharp move.

Synanon lawyer/spokesman Dan Garrett denied any connection, describing the group as "law-abiding" in its quest to solve societal problems and character disorders. Stories to the contrary, he added, were "inflammatory and irresponsible." Translation: watch your step.

Staffers at NBC *Nightly News* and *Time* already were. After NBC broadcast a critical series, two men from "SCRAM"—the acronym for the "Synanon Committee for a Responsible American Media"—frightened a producer at her New York residence. Not far away, *Time-Life*'s forty-eight-story skyscraper in Manhattan was evacuated after a phoned-in bomb threat. Unnerving things had also been happening to *Time*'s editor Hedley Donovan since that unflattering story on Dederich the year prior. He'd received hate mail predicting that a "sleeping giant" would chase him. Later, US Customs agents searched him on his return from Europe after receiving word that he was smuggling jewels and drugs.

Synanon's tentacles were now a suspect, too, in a strange break-in at Morantz's Brentwood law office while he was hospitalized. The intrusion fanned press speculation that the group or another cult he was dogging was searching for something. Even after the LAPD ruled it a "common burglary" that occurred at an uncommon time, how could anyone be positive?

•••

USC COUNTY GENERAL DISCHARGED him to a swarm of TV cameras capturing him in a plaid-blue bathrobe. The man described as LA's "reluctant crusader" returned home after six days with white bandaging entombing his injured arm. Greeting him in his doorway, feet from his now notorious mail chute, was Connie Chung, there for an exclusive interview. Local TV stations, partly motivated by the attack, were scrambling to produce series on cults now that they were hot again. Four years had elapsed since the LAPD's fiery shootout with the Symbionese Liberation Army.

Everyone who cared about Morantz could only pose questions with unknowable answers. How would he adapt as the victim of a crime that propelled global headlines? Would he discontinue investigating Synanon after it tried murdering him? Would he relocate? Request his own tranquilizers?

In his cross-streaming emotions, he wasn't sure. All at once, he was grateful for surviving Big Daddy's kill shot, newly sensitized to violence he caught on TV, while experiencing murky anxiety about anything crossing past his window. The rest of him bottled up the pressure inside. How surreal it was to read, as he nursed a numb left hand, a fangirl write that he was "undoubtedly" the most handsome man she'd ever seen. Her letter arrived through the mail. The woman whose words still mattered the most was Trudy. If there was one upside to his near-death encounter with what he fished through his postal receptacle, it was that it precipitated a reunion with his "it" girl.

Weeks later, after the Dodgers blew the series to the Yankees, another cult messiah flexed his muscle to decimate lives. This one was on an apocalyptic scale in Jonestown, Guyana, a sliver of a country on the northeastern tip of South America. More than nine hundred members of Reverend Jim Jones's People's Temple sprawled lifelessly in a macabre quilt after drinking cyanide-laced punch on his command in a mass suicide. Tracking the coverage, Morantz grimaced. Among those murdered by the reverend's gunmen there were two NBC journalists who had attended his hospital press conference. They'd flown with a California congressman to uncover the truth about what a magnetic xenophobe could do.

Because police appreciated what Dederich himself was capable of, Sheriff's Department deputies lived at his Pacific Palisades residence with him for months. Better late than never, he had protection. Despite that layer of defense—and multiple investigations into their alternative society—Imperial Marines harassed him with messages that they weren't done with him. They now phoned, asking about where he socialized and about his Volvo. They made sure he knew that they knew his mother's address. They ridiculed him with midnight calls about what they could see inside his house using binoculars. They giggled sadistically about his love of volleyball—and promised "another snake" was coming. And one might.

If his standard-size mail chute had been larger, Kenton and Musico would've deposited into it all *three* of the rattlesnakes they'd transported in their trunk. Their original intention was to unloose into his house fifteen feet of collective predator, a veritable hydra's worth of venom. In preparation for the mission, Dederich's Marines had collected diamondbacks, hoping to condition them just as they'd been conditioned. The snakes, penned together in a cool, shallow pit in California's Central Valley, coexisted docilely. But that same seclusion also bred aggressiveness around foreign heat sources. Such as a human hand. When Kenton, Synanon's All-American boy, was unable to squeeze two other snakes into the mail container, he and Musico released them into Pacific Palisades, their fates unknown. None of them had rattles because they'd been lopped off to prevent their target from hearing what hungrily awaited him.

Early December became the second full month of Paul Morantz's discombobulated life; a life in which he stashed a gun under the seat of his car; a life in which his punctured wrist healed and his fire in the belly to take the fight against cults reignited. He couldn't abandon the cause now. That epiphany, naturally, spelled the end of his brief reconciliation with Trudy. It was a love affair just not meant to translate into a life together.

Morantz limped back to Hawaii to grieve everything, and while there, the sledgehammer of justice finally slammed down on Synanon. A thirty-cop phalanx raided the organization's million-dollar hideaway in Lake Havasu, Arizona. Sitting inside, staring ahead in a stupor, was America's "reformed alcoholic," plastered after draining a bottle of Chivas Regal. Dederich would need two hospitalizations to recover before facing arraignment.

"Even though he's drinking now, we have to remember all the good things he's done," one follower rationalized.

Reports were that he'd begun tippling again on a visit to Italy that summer—the same European trip where Synanon opened secret bank accounts and Big Daddy sanctioned the hit on Morantz (though questions remain about whether he or a lieutenant personally drew up a kill list). At least he was apprehended before he could do to his followers what Reverend Jones did to his in Guyana.

Kenton and Musico stared daggers at Morantz during their preliminary court hearing. He had too much invested, including sacrificing two slivers of flesh, to be intimidated, especially in a case with a headless murder weapon. To bolster the prosecution's evidence, he did what he always did. He took the initiative, in this instance by placing a classified ad in the *LA Times*. Its purpose: seeking the identity of the 280Z driver that Ybarro testified about. Lo and behold, a gas station owner who saw the ad recognized the car. Les Rahymer, before long, spoke about crossing paths with the Plymouth whose license plates were a lie.

Now cornered, the Imperial Marines plead no contest to the charges, and again Morantz acted independently in their names.

Surprisingly, it was about saving *them*. He requested the judge show his assailants leniency as victims themselves of systematic brainwashing. His testimony seemed to cushion their punishments; both were sentenced to only a year in prison. Out of jail, the would-be assassins traveled different roads in their post-cult existences. Charlie Sheen, the actor known as much for his flamboyant affection for cocaine and buxom women as his performances, eventually hired Kenton as his right-hand man. Musico, unable to reinvent himself, was thrown from a roof to his death in a "pimp-dope" turf war.

Dederich, in tanking health by 1980, plead no contest, as well. After his lawyer argued he was too frail to survive in prison, he was given five years of probation, a $5,000 fine, and the stipulation he stay hands-off his former utopia. In short, he'd skated again.

Yet the ghost of Little Chuck had the final say about the group that Big Daddy erected from the ground up. Trying to erase the memory of what transpired on Bollinger Drive, Synanon's new leadership dropped its defamation suits and tried ingratiating itself in Washington, DC. It was pointless. In 1991, with the FBI deep into its affairs and the IRS's revocation of its nonprofit status, the organization was hamstrung from doing anything except shuddering operations. A reclusive Dederich died in 1997 of heart failure after years of living in a Visalia mobile home.

By then, Morantz was an inductee in a club he'd never leave, recognized as California's foremost expert in cult-brainwashing practices.

Through his activism, he filed groundbreaking suits against the Church of Scientology and the Moonies. He hounded the Center for Feeling Therapy, where doctors beat patients or had sex with them, and Bagwhan Rajneesh, whose followers poisoned the salad bars of ten Oregon restaurants. He swayed legislation, striving to be somebody not coasting on fumes in a humbler persona.

Away from the office, recovering cult members constituted his new friend circle. A failed marriage produced a wondrous son unfamiliar with the scope of what he endured in October 1978. Sometimes, the LA Memorial Coliseum during USC football season was his only sanctuary, noisy but comfortingly familiar.

As time wore on, he shrunk from hero to newsmaker to historical footnote—the answer to the pop-culture reference about the "snake in the mailbox." Buzz from autograph-seekers and journalists petered out. Showtime, ABC, and *Vanity Fair*, all at different times, cultivated feature projects that would've reacquainted the public with his stand against demagoguery. None were made; entertainment company lawyers remembering Synanon's legal aggressions remained jittery about being sued. After 9/11, Hollywood's focus shifted. It could leave one fatalistic.

At a New Year's Eve party in the dwindling hours of 1978, *before* he decided this would be his life, before he deposed a still-cagey Charles Dederich, Morantz shambled outside, a broken man. Trudy; literary stardom; the remotest definition of normalcy: he'd relinquished them all to embark on this lonely battle. Tears streamed down his cheeks and dread blanketed him like an X-ray vest.

That's when he heard the voice he never heard speak before, a voice louder than loony threats garbled over Synanon's PA system.

Stop crying, the voice said. *This is who you are.*

What was a wolf to do but oblige?

•••

SOURCES: FROM MIRACLE TO *Madness: The True Story of Charles Dederich and Synanon* by Paul Morantz (Cresta Publications—2015); *Gizmodo; Los Angeles Magazine; Los Angeles Times; Escape: My Lifelong War Against Cults* by Paul Morantz with Hal Lancaster (Cresta Publications—2013); *The New York Times;* paulmorantz.com; *Palisidian Post,* Paul Morantz interview September 2015, *People, Time, Washington Post*

A shorter version of this story appears in the Rare Bird Books anthology: *Los Angeles in the 1970s: Weird Scenes Inside the Goldmine* (November 2016).